# BOARDWALK
# EMPIRE

# BOARDWALK
# EMPIRE

## The Birth, High Times, and Corruption of **ATLANTIC CITY**

### Nelson Johnson

Foreword by
Terence Winter

EBURY
PRESS

3 5 7 9 10 8 6 4

Published in 2011 by Ebury Press, an imprint of Ebury Publishing
A Random House Group company
First published in the USA by Medford Press,
an imprint of Plexus Publishing, in 2002

The Random House Group Limited Reg. No. 954009

Addresses for companies within the Random House Group can be found at
www.randomhouse.co.uk

A CIP catalogue record for this book is available from the British Library

The Random House Group Limited supports The Forest Stewardship Council
(FSC), the leading international forest certification organisation. All our titles that
are printed on Greenpeace approved FSC certified paper carry the FSC logo. Our
paper procurement policy can be found at www.rbooks.co.uk/environment

**Mixed Sources**
Product group from well-managed
forests and other controlled sources
www.fsc.org Cert no. TT-COC-2139
© 1996 Forest Stewardship Council

Printed in the UK by CPI Mackays, Chatham, ME5 8TD

ISBN 9780091941246 (trade paperback)
ISBN 9780091941321 (hardback)

To buy books by your favourite authors and register for offers visit
www.rbooks.co.uk

In memory of an extraordinary person,
my mother, Jennie Johnson, from whom
I acquired my passion for the printed word.

*If the people who came to town had wanted Bible readings, we'd have given 'em that. But nobody ever asked for Bible readings. They wanted booze, broads, and gambling, so that's what we gave 'em.*

— Murray Fredericks

# CONTENTS

# FOREWORD

Shortly after sunrise on a cool August morning in 1987, my friend Chris and I walked along the beach in Atlantic City, its Boardwalk and hotel-casinos looming directly to our right. With our ties undone, bellies full, and pockets empty after a night of gambling, drinking, and general debauchery, we were completely exhausted and wiped out financially; we couldn't have been happier. As we trudged along, the waves crashing at our feet, I reached into my pocket and pulled out the last few coins I had. Twenty-three cents. I hurled them all into the Atlantic Ocean and turned to Chris. "Now we're *really* wiped out." After a good laugh, we headed up to the Boardwalk and started our long trek home, two hard-luck characters with another fun story to tell about our time in Atlantic City. What I didn't know then was that versions of this scenario had been playing out there for over 100 years.

Ever since the railroad made it accessible to the average working person, Absecon Island—or Atlantic City, as it came to be known—was "The World's Playground," a kingdom of dreams built on sand, a place where, for a reasonable sum of money, any man, woman, or child could be treated like visiting royalty. With luxury hotels, theaters, and restaurants lining its famous Boardwalk, there was nothing the city didn't offer—legal or illegal. Food, drink, and entertainment of all kinds, from highbrow to low. If you couldn't find it on the Boardwalk (or on one of its many side streets), it didn't exist.

When I was first approached by HBO to use Nelson Johnson's book as the basis for a TV series, my biggest challenge was choosing a time period in which to set it. From the Gilded Age of the Robber Barons, to the Roaring Twenties and the Prohibition Era, to the Glamorous 1950s of Skinny D'Amato, to the city's decline and subsequent resurgence with the advent of legalized gambling in the 1970s, Atlantic City and its people have been nothing if not compelling.

Ultimately I settled on the 1920s of Atlantic City's legendary Treasurer Nucky Johnson (fictionalized as Nucky Thompson in the HBO series), which was the era that most struck my creative fancy. Atlantic City at that time was a place of excess, glamour, and, most of all, opportunity. Loud, brash, colorful, full of hope and promise— it was a microcosm of America. A place of spectacle, shady politics, fast women, and backroom deals, but also a real community with real people, not only on its Boardwalk, but in its churches, schools, and neighborhoods. It was a place of real Americans, a melting pot of ideas and cultures.

On my last trip there, I walked the same streets as Nucky, stood in his hotel lobby, ate in one of his favorite restaurants. I strode the Boardwalk where he reigned as king, looking out at the vast ocean that he considered his own. I was taken back in time and imagined the place as it had been, and though I enjoyed it all immensely, I needn't have traveled so far to recreate the experience. Nelson Johnson had already taken me there in his wonderful book.

—Terence Winter
Emmy Award-winning writer of *The Sopranos*
and Executive Producer of *Boardwalk Empire*

# PROLOGUE

Luxury hotels weren't something she knew about firsthand. Until now, she had never been inside the Ritz Carlton. The closest she'd come to the grand hotel was when walking on the Boardwalk. But here she was in the anteroom of a large suite of rooms, seated in a chair that nearly swallowed her. She was frightened, but there was no turning back. She sat there trembling, folding and refolding her frayed scarf.

As a housewife and summertime laundress in a boardinghouse, she felt out of place and her nervousness showed. Flushed and perspiring, she noticed that her dress and sweater needed mending and she grew more self-conscious. It was all she could do to keep from panicking and running out. But she couldn't leave. Louis Kessel had told her Mr. Johnson would see her in a moment and she had to wait. To leave now would be embarrassing and, worse still, might offend Mr. Johnson. If it weren't winter, and if there weren't so many unpaid bills, she never would have worked up the courage to come in the first place. But she had no choice; her husband had been a fool and she was desperate for her family. Louis Kessel appeared a second time and motioned to her. She followed him, not knowing what to expect.

As she walked into Mr. Johnson's sitting room, he took her hand and greeted her warmly. It was several years since she met him at her father's wake, but Johnson remembered her and called her by her first name. He was dressed in a fancy robe and slippers and asked what was troubling her. In an instant her anxiety vanished.

In a rapid series of sentences she recounted how her husband lost his entire paycheck the night before at one of the local gambling rooms. He was a baker's helper, and during the winter months his $37 each week was the family's only income. She went on and on about all the bills and how the grocer wouldn't give her any more credit. Johnson listened intently and, when she was finished, reached into his pocket and handed her a $100 bill. Overwhelmed with joy, she thanked him repeatedly until he insisted she stop. Louis Kessel motioned, telling her there was a car waiting to drive her home. As she left, Johnson promised that her husband would be barred from every crap game and card room in town. He told her to come back any time she had a problem.

Enoch "Nucky" Johnson personifies pre-casino Atlantic City as no one else can. Understanding his reign provides the perspective needed to make sense of today's resort. Johnson's power reached its peak, as did his town's popularity, during Prohibition, from 1920 to 1933. When it came to illegal booze, there was probably no place in the country as wide open as Nucky's town. It was almost as if word of the Volstead Act never reached Atlantic City. During Prohibition, Nucky was both a power broker in the Republican Party and a force in organized crime. He rubbed elbows with presidents and Mafia thugs. But to Atlantic City's residents, Johnson was hardly a thug. He was their hero, epitomizing the qualities that had made his town successful.

Originally conceived as a beach village by a doctor hoping to develop a health resort for the wealthy, Atlantic City quickly became a glitzy, raucous vacation spot for the working class. It was a place where visitors came knowing the rules at home didn't apply. Atlantic City flourished because it gave its guests what they wanted—a naughty good time at an affordable price.

Popular recollections of the old Atlantic City, believed by many, is that it was an elegant seaside resort of the wealthy, comparable to Newport. Such a notion is fantasy. In its prime, Atlantic City was a resort for the blue-collar workers of Philadelphia's industrial economy. The resort was popular with people who could afford no more than a day or two stay. These working poor came to town each summer to escape the heat of the city and the boredom of their jobs. Atlantic City gave them a place to let loose.

There were four ingredients to the resort's success. Each was critical. Remove any one of them and Atlantic City would have been a very different place. The first ingredient was rail transportation. But for the railroad, the development of Absecon Island would have waited at least 50 years. The second was Philadelphia and New York real estate investors. They brought the money and expertise needed to build and manage dozens of hotels and hundreds of boardinghouses on an island of sand. The third was a large volume of cheap labor to run things. There was only one labor source: freed slaves and their children. The final ingredient was a local population willing to ignore the law in order to please vacationers. From the turn of the 20th century and for the next 70 years, the resort was ruled by a partnership comprised of local politicians and racketeers. This alliance was a product of the relationship between the economy and politics of the city.

From its inception, Atlantic City has been a town dedicated to the fast buck. Its character as a city is uncommon because it never had any other role to perform than that of a resort. It has always had a singular purpose for its existence—to provide leisure time activities for tourists. Atlantic City's economy was totally dependent on money spent by out-of-towners. Visitors had to leave happy. If they didn't, they wouldn't return.

The key was to cater to patrons' tastes in pleasure, whether those desires were lawful or not. Resort merchants pandered to the visitor's desire to do the forbidden, and business owners cultivated the institution of the spree. Within a short time after its founding, Atlantic City was renowned as the place to go for a freewheeling good time. It grew into a national resort by promoting vice as a major part of the local tourist trade. However, maintenance of the vice industry required Atlantic City's government to make special accommodations. It was inevitable that the principals of the vice industry would make an alliance with the local political leaders. Without some type of understanding between these two spheres of power, Atlantic City's major tourist attraction would have had a tenuous existence.

The resort's guests couldn't be harassed while enjoying themselves. It would be bad for business. That gambling, prostitution, and Sunday sales of liquor violated state law and conventional morality didn't matter. Nothing could interfere with the visitors' fun or they might stop coming. Atlantic City's leaders ignored the law and permitted the local vice trade to operate in a wide-open fashion as if it were legitimate.

The resort's singular purpose demanded a single mentality to manage its affairs. This need, combined with the dominance of the Republican Party in southern New Jersey for several generations after the Civil War, produced a mind-set that didn't permit traditional politics. Reformers and critics were a luxury that couldn't be tolerated. Success of the local economy was the only political ideology. There was not to be a "loyal opposition" nor a bona fide Democratic Party. You went along with the system or you were crushed. By the beginning of the 20th century a political juggernaut bearing a

Republican label, and funded with money from the rackets, was firmly entrenched.

The first "boss" of Atlantic City politics was Louis "The Commodore" Kuehnle, who ruled from approximately 1890 to 1910. The Commodore recognized the potential of the local vice industry as a reliable source of income for his political organization. It was Kuehnle who established the procedure for assessing and collecting extortion payments from the racketeers who provided unlawful entertainment. Under the Commodore, gambling parlors, speak-easies, and brothels operated as if they were legal. The only time the local police clamped down on anyone was if they were late with their payment. Money from extortion, together with bribes and kickbacks paid by government contractors and vendors, formed the financial basis of Kuehnle's machine. After banging heads with Woodrow Wilson in the gubernatorial election of 1910, Kuehnle went to jail for election fraud.

Kuehnle's successor, Nucky Johnson, was the absolute master of Atlantic City politics for the next 30 years. Johnson understood people and power and knew how to handle both. There was not an elected official or city or county employee who did not owe his job to Nucky. He shared in the profits of every municipal contract and gambling operation in town. Prior to going to jail, Kuehnle tapped Johnson as his successor because he had the support of both the politicians and racketeers. By this time, the people of Atlantic City were conditioned to political bossism, and they accepted Nucky as the resort's new boss. Atlantic City's residents expected, and wanted, the type of government from Johnson they had known under the Commodore. They weren't disappointed.

By means of guile, finesse, and the shrewd use of money obtained through various types of extortion, Nucky Johnson established himself as a force in two different worlds. He was both the most powerful Republican in New Jersey, who could influence the destinies of governors and senators, and a racketeer, respected and trusted by organized crime.

Nucky Johnson gave Atlantic City the brand of leadership it needed. The political and economic power structure that had evolved was thoroughly corrupt. If Johnson had refused to work with the racketeers he would have been replaced. However, Nucky took one giant step beyond what the Commodore had achieved in terms of his alliance with the vice industry. Johnson included the key racketeers as members of the Republican organization, making him head of both the political machine and the rackets. Under Nucky, the two rings of power became one.

The repeal of Prohibition in 1934 marked the beginning of the end for Atlantic City's days of glory. Two years later, at the prompting of William Randolph Hearst, President Franklin Roosevelt sent the FBI to town and it didn't leave until it had a conviction against Johnson for income tax evasion. It took five years, thousands of investigative man-hours, dozens of indictments of Johnson's associates, scores of witnesses who perjured themselves, and several incidents of jury tampering, but Nucky was finally dethroned. In 1941 Johnson went to jail and served four years.

The power structure Nucky left behind was far more complex than the one he inherited from the Commodore. Atlantic City's next boss had to be someone who could command the respect of the local politicians and racketeers alike. Johnson's successor, Frank "Hap" Farley, was the Irish American lawyer/politician par excellence. His career and method of operation have striking similarities with the fictional character Frank Skeffington, created by Edwin O'Connor in *The Last Hurrah*. Prior to Johnson's troubles with the FBI he hand-picked Farley to run for the state assembly in 1937. During the next several years Hap Farley ingratiated himself with two of Johnson's most influential lieutenants—Jimmy Boyd, clerk of the board of freeholders and Johnson's political right hand, and Herman "Stumpy" Orman, a streetwise real estate salesman who had done well for himself during Prohibition and was well-connected with the national crime syndicates.

Farley, Boyd, and Orman—it was the perfect relationship. Farley was the leader who went off to Trenton and dealt with the public at large. Boyd was the hatchet man, the political enforcer who kept the troops in line. Orman controlled the rackets and collected the protection money used to finance the organization. Boyd and Orman were Farley's buffer and insulated him from anything that might send him to jail. Hap inherited Jimmy and Stumpy. He couldn't have replaced them if he wanted to.

Farley's relationship with Boyd and Orman gave him the opportunity to be a full-time legislator and public servant. Hap immersed himself in the problems of his town and never hesitated to use his power to promote Atlantic City's interests. He was out in front on every issue affecting the resort's economy. During the 30 years he served as state senator from Atlantic County, Hap Farley established a record of accomplishment that made him a legend in Trenton. His seniority, combined with his mastery of the legislative process, made him, for more than 25 years, an insurmountable reality with whom every governor had to contend when creating an agenda. Farley dominated the senate so thoroughly that it was political suicide to oppose him. The governors either dealt with Hap or saw their programs frustrated. To his disappointment, much of Farley's effort as a legislator was directed at delaying the deterioration of his town. It was like trying to stop the tide. Atlantic City was a victim of post-war modernization and as its fortunes declined, so did Hap's. Farley clung to power as long as he could and was ousted by a Democrat in 1971.

The several years following Farley's departure were a desperate scramble to revive Atlantic City through casino gaming. The adoption of the Constitutional referendum in 1976 legalizing gambling in Atlantic City is a tribute to the resort's long-time knack at promoting itself beyond its true worth. Gambling and the money it brought to the resort has breathed new life into a sorry town, and the climb back to national stature has begun. Regardless of how this experiment in urban renewal ultimately plays out, Atlantic City will remain a creature of the values that made it great the first time around.

# 1

# Jonathan Pitney's Beach Village

Medicine wasn't enough. He needed to be something more than a country doctor. Jonathan Pitney had been caring for the sick and injured for more than 30 years, and he was growing weary. A medical practice in 19th-century America wasn't yet a path to wealth and prestige, and Pitney hungered for both. He knew he'd find neither caring for his patients.

Jonathan Pitney looked like a character out of a Dickens novel. Tall and lean, nearly always draped in a long black cape, Pitney's piercing blue eyes and long thin hands were the first thing others noticed. His pale craggy skin, together with his large hooknose and high forehead crowned by flowing gray locks, made him a striking figure. Jonathan, the son of Shubal and Jane Pitney, was born in Mendham, New Jersey, on October 29, 1797. The Pitney family had arrived in this country circa 1700. As told to a biographer, Pitney's great-grandfather and his brother had come from England to "enjoy civil and religious liberty, of which they were deprived at home." They eventually settled in Morris County, New Jersey. After graduating from medical school at Columbia College in New York, Jonathan left his parents' home in Mendham and headed south to the bayside Village of Absecon. He was 23 when he arrived in southern New Jersey, and he remained there the rest of his life.

There wasn't much to New Jersey south of Trenton in 1820. During the two generations following the American Revolution, things had changed little. With the exception of the city of Camden along the Delaware River and the summer resort village of Cape May at the southern tip of the state, southern New Jersey was a vast pine forest. This pine wilderness was interrupted by narrow, sandy stagecoach roads that followed the footpaths of earlier residents, the Lenni Lenape. Sprinkled throughout this green expanse from the Delaware River and Bay to the Atlantic Ocean were tiny villages whose residents descended from the British Isles and Northern Europe. Their lives were centered on farming, fishing, and the manufacture of glass, bog iron, and charcoal. In time, these pioneers became known as "Pineys." Absecon Village was part of that world and the place Jonathan Pitney chose to begin his medical practice.

Pitney was dedicated to his profession and worked tirelessly. He made rounds by horseback up and down the South Jersey coast to places a doctor had never been. Eleven years after his arrival, on April 21, 1831, Jonathan Pitney married Caroline Fowler, daughter of Rebecca Fowler, owner of the Sailor Boy Inn in Elwood, 15 miles west of Absecon and one of the many villages Jonathan Pitney visited. For years, Pitney was the only doctor many families knew and it was common for him to be called away from dinner or awakened in the middle of the night. Delivering babies, comforting the dying, stitching wounds, and setting broken bones from farming and fishing accidents made him well known throughout the region and loved by his patients. But his income was meager. Oftentimes he had no choice but to barter, and some say he relied upon his mother-in-law to get by. As the years piled up Pitney's enthusiasm shrank, and he became as weather-beaten as his doctor's bag.

Pitney wasn't satisfied just being a doctor, and about 15 years into his medical career he took to politics. A Democrat in a region overwhelmingly Republican, Pitney had his own agenda and bucked the status quo. In 1837 he led the successful fight to have a new county, "Atlantic," carved out of what was at the time Gloucester County. On the strength of that victory, Pitney was elected the first chairman of the new county government. He was also chosen Atlantic County's representative to the State Constitutional Convention in 1844. In 1848 he ran for the U.S. House of Representatives. South Jersey wasn't ready for a Democratic Congressman and Pitney lost, bringing his political career to a dead-end.

Political power beyond his grasp, Jonathan Pitney decided to reinvent himself—this time as an entrepreneur. His hopes lay with a sandy little island off the South Jersey coast.

Early in his career, Pitney crossed Absecon Bay in a rowboat to treat a patient at a site known as "Further Island." Created by the tides and storms, this barrier island was a wild place dominated by sand dunes, marshes, and waterfowl. The Lenni Lenape had called this island "Absegami," meaning "Little Sea Water." Before the American colonists arrived, Absegami was a campground for the Native Americans who came to avoid the summer heat. Further

Island was a desolate place with a handful of residents all from the same family, living in seven cottages scattered about the island. Aside from these solitary cabins, there were only "shanties for oystermen and fishermen, and a rude hostelry that served the purposes of the jolly fellows from Philadelphia, who came down in wagons to fish and shoot or to rough it." Early Americans enjoyed Further Island much the same way as the Lenni Lenape.

The Lenni Lenape gave up their rights to all of South Jersey in exchange for finished goods such as woolen cloth, iron kettles, knives, hoes, and axes. The first record owner of the land comprising Further Island was Thomas Budd. He bought 15,000 acres on the north and south sides of the Great Egg Harbor River in 1678 from William Penn and a group of trustees of the Quakers. The Quakers had become owners of the land—together with the rest of South Jersey—in payment of a debt owed to them. Budd sold off his holdings to other settlers for sale prices of 4 cents per acre on Further Island and 40 cents-plus per acre for mainland property.

When Pitney arrived the only people living on the island were all descendants of a Revolutionary War veteran, Jeremiah Leeds. Several years after the war, Leeds built a cedar log cabin on Further Island and settled there with his wife, Judith. (The Leeds' homestead was the site of what was later to become Columbus Park and after that the "Corridor" at the foot of the Atlantic City Expressway.) Leeds and those who followed him called their home "Absecon Island."

Jeremiah Leeds was a bear of a man, standing six-foot-tall and weighing 250 pounds. With the help of his 10 children, he cleared the fields around his home and raised crops of corn and rye. The crops he grew and sold, plus his catches from fishing and hunting, allowed the Leeds family to want for little. Leeds enjoyed the solitude of the island. The thrifty farmer bought land every chance he could but never sold any. At the time of his death, Jeremiah Leeds owned nearly 1,200 acres on Absecon Island, having title to everything except a single tract of 131 acres.

Pitney was charmed by the serenity and unspoiled beauty of Absecon Island. He returned often and grew convinced that this was where he would make his mark. Pitney believed that Absecon Island had potential as a vacation retreat for the wealthy. As a doctor, Pitney felt the island could be promoted as a health resort. He wasn't going to get rich from his medical practice, nor would he ever have any real clout in politics, but as the founder of a resort he might gain both money and power.

Pitney's dream was to build a "city by the sea." He tried selling his idea by touting the healing powers of salt water and sea air, recommending a stay at the beach for every ailment. The problem was getting people to South Jersey and then to the island.

Rail transportation was the answer. During the second half of the 19th century, railroads opened vast tracts of land, otherwise inaccessible, to development. In Pitney's time the railroad locomotive became a symbol for progress and opportunity. Pitney knew it was his best and only hope to exploit Absecon Island.

Pitney began his campaign by writing letters to any newspaper that would print them, concentrating on the Philadelphia dailies. He recognized the potential for a link between Philadelphia and Absecon Island. If his plans were to become a reality he needed to position his health resort within the orbit of a major population center. Philadelphia was his only choice. In his letters, from "Doctor Pitney," he expounded upon the health benefits of Absecon Island. In all his letters he stressed that the only thing necessary to make this health-giving island available to everyone was a railroad from Philadelphia to the seashore. Pitney's letter campaign continued for years without success. The only people excited about his idea were the descendants of Jeremiah Leeds. Some of them had no desire to farm and hoped to sell their land.

But even the Leeds family had trouble believing Pitney could ever make anything of Absecon Island. The island that existed in 1850, as Pitney wrote in his letters, consisted "almost exclusively of fine white sand, piled in hills like snowdrifts." There were "several ridges found on these old beaches separated by long, narrow valleys in which were found coarse grasses, rushes, low bushes, and vines in addition to oak, cedar, and holly timber." The summit of one of these sand dunes was more than 50 feet high. The island was covered with a growth of trees: "wild fruits, beach plums, fox grapes, and huckleberries were found abundantly in some places."

Less appealing than the holly trees and wild fruits were the insects. Between the months of June and September, the mosquitoes and greenhead flies ruled the island. During the summer, whenever the ocean breeze subsided, the greenhead flies were everywhere.

They were so large they cast a shadow as they swarmed about their victims. These flies were nasty creatures and the pain of their bites lingered for days. Cider vinegar was the only lotion that helped ease the sting. Absecon Island may have been a pristine wilderness, but it wasn't a vacationer's paradise or a place one would think of as a health resort. No one reading Pitney's letters who was familiar with South Jersey's barrier islands could have taken him seriously.

With no success from his letter campaign, Pitney decided to pursue a railroad charter by presenting his idea to the state legislature. The right to construct a rail line would give him credibility with investors. In 1851 he made several trips to Trenton to meet with political leaders and lobby for his railroad. The trips by horseback were long and lonely, and the reception wasn't friendly.

The legislators labeled his idea "Pitney's folly." They rejected it with almost no debate and ridiculed it as the "Railroad to Nowhere." The consensus of the legislature was that it wasn't possible for a new seacoast resort to compete with Cape May, which was America's first seashore resort. Wealthy businessmen from Philadelphia and Baltimore, as well as plantation owners and tobacco brokers from Maryland and Virginia, had been vacationing in Cape May since the 1790s and there was no reason to believe that would change.

Cape May had evolved from a sportsman's fishing village where the upper class went to "rough it." Staying overnight in cedar log beach houses and tents, these early vacationers spent their days fishing and hunting waterfowl. With the help of slaves, visitors prepared their own meals and passed the evenings gathered around campfires. Over the next several decades, businessmen from Philadelphia and Delaware constructed hotels and boardinghouses, extending the pleasures of a summer vacation at Cape May's beach to the less hardy.

One visitor to Cape May in the summer of 1850 wrote to her readers at home describing the "parti-colored scene" created by the new sport of "seabathing." She reported that thousands of people, "men, women and children, in red, blue, and yellow pantaloons and yellow straw hats adorned with bright red ribbon, go out into the sea in crowds, and leap up and down in the heaving waves amid great laughter and merriment." The reporter, Swedish novelist and travel writer Frederika Bremer (1801–1865), reporting on the scene at Cape May's beach continued, "White and black people, horses and carriages, and dogs—all are there, one among another, and just before them great fishes, porpoises, lift up their heads, and sometime take a huge leap, very likely because they are so amused at seeing human beings leaping about in their own element."

In pre-Civil War days, Cape May was renowned as a "Southern resort" and was a mecca for the cream of Southern society. Southern planters and the elite of the North brought their gleaming horse-drawn carriages and paraded in the sun along the water's edge. Nationally celebrated bands performed for the ladies in the fine hotels, while the men passed their time gambling. The most popular gambling house was *The Blue Pig*—for "gentlemen" only.

By 1850, no resort in America could compare to the Jersey Cape in terms of attracting the rich and famous. More national figures made Cape May their summer retreat than any other place. Saratoga made claims to the contrary, but only Cape May could boast of frequent visits from presidents; several made it their summertime headquarters. The only resort that rivaled Cape May in the quest to be the Summer White House was Long Branch, New Jersey, more than 100 miles north. There was no need for a third resort, especially one in the southern part of the state.

A majority of Cape May's visitors made the trip by sailing sloop and steamship, though some arrived by stagecoach. Regardless of how one traveled, the trip was expensive and time-consuming. But Cape May's vacationers were loyal and their resort prospered. It was popular with Trenton's leaders and most of the legislators believed that if there were to be a railroad to the Jersey Shore, it should be to Cape May.

Another obstacle facing Pitney was the monopoly of the Camden-Amboy Railroad. In 1832 the legislature gave this North Jersey-based railroad an exclusive right-of-way across the state. While the Camden-Amboy had no plans to construct a railroad in South Jersey, the legislators were not about to permit someone like Pitney to get into the railroad business. Having neither financial resources nor the right political contacts, Pitney's idea for linking Philadelphia to an obscure, undeveloped island was nonsense. In rejecting his idea, the legislators asked, "Whoever heard of a railroad with only one end?"

Pitney's humiliation before the state legislature forced a change in his strategy. He quit trying for popular support and set about selling his idea to the rich and powerful. In the mid-19th century, the elite of South Jersey were the bog iron and glass barons. A dozen or so families, these barons controlled most of the wealth, owned nearly all of the undeveloped land, and employed almost anyone who wasn't a farmer or fisherman. Pitney cited the need of iron and glass factories for better transportation and argued that their goods could be shipped more cheaply by the iron horse. Things began to happen for Jonathan Pitney when he won the support of Samuel Richards.

The name "Richards" cast a spell. From the American Colonial era to the Civil War, the Richards family was the most influential in southern New Jersey. Centered in villages of Hammonton and Batsto, the Richards' empire included iron works, glass furnaces, cotton mills, paper factories, brickyards, and farms. As a family, the Richards were among the largest landholders in the Eastern United States for several generations. At their peak the Richards' family holdings collectively totaled more than one-quarter million acres.

Samuel Richards, as one biographer noted, "looked like a bank president and worked like a horse. For all his handsome appearance and meticulous dress, no task was too small, no problem too intricate for him to tackle personally." Richards was a buccaneer-type entrepreneur who lived the high life. He owned a beautiful mansion with sprawling grounds and servants in South Jersey, as well as a palatial Victorian home in Philadelphia. He was part of the aristocracy. Vital to Pitney's dreams, Samuel Richards understood the importance of a rail line between Philadelphia and Absecon Island. He saw the economic potential of Pitney's railroad and realized it could make his family even wealthier.

Railroading was high adventure for entrepreneurs in the 19th century, and Samuel Richards was anxious to become an investor. More than anything else, it was the rise of the railroad that transformed the American economy in the 1840s and '50s. The development of railroads throughout the country had an enormous effect on the economy as a whole. While the demand for iron rails was first met mainly by importation from England, the railroads, in time, spurred development of America's iron industry. Because railroads required a huge outlay of capital, their promoters pioneered new methods for financing business. At a time when most manufacturing and commercial concerns were still owned by families or private partnerships, the railroads formed corporations and sold stock to the general public.

This type of financing set the pattern for investment, which led to the creation of the modern corporation. Railroads were a catalyst to economic growth the likes of which the country had never known.

Richards knew that a rail line linking his landholdings to Philadelphia would increase their value and make it possible for him to turn some of his vast acreage into cash. Even if a land boom didn't materialize, Richards and his fellow businessmen would still benefit from reduced costs of transporting their glass and iron. At the time, goods manufactured in South Jersey were shipped to Philadelphia by horse and wagon over sandy trails, which were often impassable in bad weather.

Samuel Richards latched onto Pitney's idea and all but made it his own. Richards took charge of the lobbying effort for the railroad charter. At the time he was approached by Pitney, Samuel Richards had just turned 30 years old. But his family's name alone was enough to get the attention of the state legislature. Richards made a sales pitch that his Republican friends in Trenton understood well. He convinced them that the railroad was necessary for the local glass and iron industries to remain competitive. As for Pitney's plans to build a railroad to a sand patch of only seven cabins, and the expense of laying rail all the way to Absecon Island, that would be the risk of the investors.

There were no objections from the Camden-Amboy Railroad, which probably didn't take any of it seriously. In the end, the legislators yielded to the force of Richards' personality and the common belief that nothing would ever come of Pitney's schemes. Thus, what had been the Railroad to Nowhere in 1851 became the newly chartered Camden-Atlantic Railroad the following year.

With the granting of a railroad charter Pitney's dream took one giant step forward. Richards and Pitney then proceeded to secure investors; nearly all were in the iron and glass industries or large landowners. Pitney could dream the big dream, but he wasn't much help in raising money. Of the initial 1,477 shares of stock issued, Pitney purchased 20 and made a sale of 100 shares to his friend Enoch Doughty of Absecon. Samuel Richards secured the remainder of the investors, with a majority of the stock controlled by his family. For most of the investors, the success of Pitney's beach village was irrelevant. Their factories and landholdings were in Camden and western Atlantic Counties, 30 to 50 miles from the seashore. As long as the railroad reached their properties, they cared little whether the train made it to the seacoast and even less what became of Absecon Island.

Samuel Richards later admitted that he first saw Absecon Island in June 1852, only a week before the organization of the railroad, and three full months after the legislature had granted the charter. "We drove down in a carriage to Absecon Village, then went over in a boat to the beach. We landed on the usual landing place on the thoroughfare, not very far from the Leeds' farm."

Richards was overwhelmed by all of the sand. Years later he confessed, "In my mind ... it was the most horrible place to make the termination of a railroad I had ever seen." Several other investors made the visit with Richards and they nearly scuttled the project. "The island appeared uninviting to their eyes, and its sterile sand heaps, naked in their desolation, gave it a weird, wild look, a veritable desert. ..."

The investors were skeptical that this place could ever be turned into a health resort and felt that "to build a railroad to such a wild spot would be a reckless piece of adventure." Richards' friends doubted that a rail line could be installed across the meadows leading to the bay side of the island. Richards reminded them that the main reason for the railroad was to link their factories and land to the growing population centers of Camden and Philadelphia and assured them that Pitney's health resort was secondary.

The money raised by the new Camden-Atlantic Railroad was used for more than acquiring a right-of-way and laying track. Richards and Pitney set about purchasing all the land they could on Absecon Island. Only 10 miles in length and little more than a mile at its widest, the island offered tempting possibilities for monopolization. For the small sums involved, Richards couldn't resist speculating that real estate values on Absecon Island might increase after the rail line was completed. Because Jonathan Pitney had the trust of the locals, title to the property was taken in his name and later transferred to the railroad company.

The Camden-Atlantic Railroad gobbled up real estate so aggressively that the state legislature adopted a law prohibiting it from buying any more land, but that didn't stop Richards and Pitney. They promptly formed the Camden-Atlantic Land Company and continued to purchase property. With Jeremiah Leeds gone and his heirs no longer interested in farming, Richards and Pitney were able to acquire most of Absecon Island. All the real estate needed to satisfy the investors was acquired in less than two years, with the Leeds family selling the bulk of their holdings by 1854. Together, the Railroad and Land Companies bought nearly 1,000 acres at prices between $5 and $10 per acre.

While Pitney negotiated land purchases, Richards saw to the construction of the railroad. The original choice as contractor was Peter O'Reilly. Ground was broken in September 1852 but after several months of floundering, it was obvious O'Reilly wasn't up to the task. Richards decided O'Reilly had to go. He was replaced by Richard Osborne, who had previously managed the Richmond and Danville Railroad. British born and educated, Osborne was a civil engineer trained in Chicago, the boomtown of the 19th century. Osborne was formidable looking, distinguished by his sideburns and mustache, both of which grew down below his chin. He was working in Philadelphia when approached by Samuel Richards to serve as consulting engineer to the Railroad and Land Companies in the development of their bathing village. Osborne knew an opportunity when he saw one and was excited at being on the ground floor of Richards' venture. He hoped that the raw landscape of Pitney's island might allow him to carve out a fortune.

Richard Osborne's first task was to select a right-of-way for the construction of the rail line. It was an uncomplicated matter. He set the course for the tracks in a straight line from Cooper's Ferry in Camden to the middle of Absecon Island. Osborne and his survey crew mapped the train route directly through the heart of South Jersey's pine forest. Stagecoach roads and existing rights-of-way used by wagons or horsemen were ignored. The tracks would go around nothing.

Construction of the railroad under Osborne's direction began in earnest in August 1853. Starting from Camden, trees were cut, hills leveled, and swamps filled as the Camden-Atlantic Railroad chopped its way through the forest. There were no curves in Osborne's steel ribbons. The only thing that broke the woodlands was the railroad itself. The single most difficult portion in constructing the railroad was over the marshes between the mainland and the island.

The weather that winter had been favorable to work on the railroad, "but in February a storm tide made a clean sweep of the roadbed which had been graded on the meadows." Osborne's crew worked for two months to restore the rail line when again in April "a terrible Northeast storm prevailed for a week, flooding the meadows, sweeping away miles of the graded roadbed which was ready for the track and scattering the ties and wheelbarrows for miles along the coast." Finally, the weather relented and the rail line was extended to the bay across from Absecon Island in July 1854.

At the same time work was progressing on the rail line, the Camden-Atlantic Land Company had Osborne prepare a street plan for Pitney's beach village. Having acquired nearly all of Absecon Island, the investors were eager to create lots for resale. As he had in drawing the right-of-way for the rail line, Osborne's map for this new village paid no regard to the virgin landscape. Any physical obstacle in the way of the street lines, such as sand dunes running the length of the island, fresh water ponds, and nesting areas for waterfowl, had to go. Under Osborne's direction, Absecon Island was cut into neat little squares and rectangles, creating lots ideal for maximizing profits from land sales.

When Richard Osborne unveiled his map of this new seashore town, the words "Atlantic City" appeared across the top on a background of breaking waves. According to Osborne, the investors accepted his suggestion for the name immediately. Hoping to appeal to visitors beyond Philadelphia, the street map assigned each state in the nation its own avenue. Richard Osborne believed that it was this new resort's "manifest destiny" to become "the first, most popular, most health giving and most inviting watering place" in the country. While he knew Philadelphia would provide the bulk of the visitors, Osborne dreamt that Atlantic City would become a national resort with patrons from around the country.

Opening day for the Camden-Atlantic Railroad was July 1, 1854. The first train, an "official special," consisted of nine passenger cars and left from the Cooper's Ferry terminal in Camden. Ferryboats from Philadelphia brought a stream of guests, each with a printed invitation, and hundreds of curiosity seekers who came to see the first iron horse leave for the seashore. "Finally, a bit after 9 A.M., the engine whistle sounded, the iron horse belched a great cloud of black smoke, there was a grinding and creaking—and the train got under way."

The 600 passengers on board were chosen carefully by Samuel Richards and Jonathan Pitney. They were newspapermen, politicians, and wealthy notables of the day—all having been invited to help in promoting the resort. There were several stops along the way to permit the major shareholders to make speeches and show off their investment to their friends and employees. One of the riders wasn't terribly impressed with the trip, describing the ride as a "desolate succession of pine trees and cedar swamps," adding, "No towns or cities were found along the way; only here a woodcutter's or charcoal burner's hut and there a rickety saw mill."

Two and a half hours after leaving Camden the train ride ended at the mainland, and the passengers were taken across the bay in rowboats to Atlantic City. A bridge linking the mainland to the island would be completed several months later. After arriving in Atlantic City, a second train brought the visitors to the door of the resort's first public lodging, the United States Hotel. The hotel was owned by the railroad. It was a sprawling four-story structure built to house 2,000 guests. It opened while it was still under construction, with only one wing standing and even that wasn't completed. But by year's end, when it was fully constructed, the United States Hotel was not only the first hotel in Atlantic City but also the largest in the nation. Its rooms totaled more than 600, and its grounds covered some 14 acres.

Upon their arrival, the resort's first visitors were treated to an extravagant meal followed by speeches and music. After dinner many of the guests strolled on the beach where they entertained themselves exploring the remains of shipwrecks. Following this private debut, the Camden-Atlantic Railroad was opened to the public on July 4, 1854. For the remainder of the summer, nearly every train that left Camden was sold out.

It was a proud time for Jonathan Pitney. While his profits didn't begin to measure up to those of Samuel Richards, Pitney had saved himself from obscurity. The railroad made it possible for the populations of Philadelphia and Camden to visit the seashore in a single day without the need or expense of a long vacation. It also fulfilled Samuel Richards and the other investors' hope of generating a land boom along its route. In less than three years, 15 train stations sprang upon between Camden and Atlantic City. The Richards family sold much of their land and reaped a huge windfall. Land values on Absecon Island skyrocketed. Sand dunes and meadowlands purchased for as little as $5 per acre were resold several years later at prices of up to $300 per acre. Jonathan Pitney never made this kind of money practicing medicine.

Success at real estate speculation came quicker than the development of a full-fledged resort. Pitney was pleased with his beach village, but it was a long way from being a serious resort. He knew that a permanent community had to be established, which would take time and a great deal of money. The obstacles to be overcome were many. First, there was the trainride itself—at best, it was an adventure. The early trains had no windows, only canvas curtains, and it was common for visitors to arrive covered with soot, their clothes and skin pocked by flying cinders from the coal-fired locomotive. A linen duster with hat and goggles were important accessories to the traveler's wardrobe.

One of the early conductors of the Camden-Atlantic Railroad recalled his experience: "Atlantic City in 1854–55 was reached through sand hills and forests of pine and scrub oaks. Most of our cars were open coaches. My, how the dust did fly!" The early trains weren't equipped with signals of any kind and, "When I wanted to stop the train to let off passengers, I went through the train and attracted the engineer's attention by striking him with a splinter of wood and by holding up my fore finger told him a passenger was to get off at the next station."

The adventure didn't end with the train ride. When travelers arrived, they found a much bigger dose of nature than the resort's promotions had led them to believe. The island was dotted with hundreds of wet places where insects could breed, and early guests were greeted by swarms of greenhead flies and mosquitoes.

Summer 1858 saw a plague of insects that nearly closed the resort down. Greenhead flies, gnats, and mosquitoes tormented the visitors all summer long. By mid-August most guests had stopped coming to town. One vacationer wrote home, "In my last letter I said mosquitoes were numerous here. They have since become a plague and there is no peace in this place." The resort's inability to deal with the problem was painfully obvious to its guests. "Last week the place was crowded with visitors; now they are escaping the scourge as rapidly as possible. This house is now surrounded with bonfires, in the hope that the smoke therefrom will drive off the enemy. The horses attached to carriages containing guests from the United States Hotel became so maddened from the attack of greenhead flies that they ran away demolishing the carriage, and broke the arm of one of the ladies."

It was a nightmare that summer. According to reports from the time, horses covered with blood laid down in the streets, and cattle waded out into the ocean to escape the torture of the insects. Men, women, and children scratched and screamed and day visitors begged the conductors to start home ahead of schedule. For the next 10 to 15 years, the problem with the mosquitoes and greenhead flies was dealt with by pouring coal oil on the water of the ponds and wet spots that dotted the islands. The pests were eventually eliminated when the dunes were graded and the ponds filled with sand.

During these early years, the only refuge from insects for the visitor who went down to the beach was to either go into the water or hide in a bathhouse. The bathhouses were crude wooden structures that were carried down to the water's edge in the spring and dragged back to the dunes in the fall. Another difficulty was the lack of something to separate the developed portion of the island from the beach. Sand was everywhere and it was common for the streets to flood at high tide.

Though seawater was everywhere, it wasn't drinkable. For the first 30 years of Atlantic City's existence, residents and visitors alike had to rely upon rainwater collected in cisterns as the sole source of water. True to its beginnings as a farm island, the cattle of local farmers were allowed to run free during the first decade of the resort. "Prior to 1864, the cattle, swine, and goats were permitted to run at large in the city. Up until that time every permanent resident of the place owned one or more cows." Atlantic City's main thoroughfare, Atlantic Avenue, was originally a cow path for cattle driven by farmers in the inlet area to the lower end of the island. As late as the 1880s one could see herds of cows being taken from one end of the town to the other and returned at night through the center of the village on Atlantic Avenue.

Finding the money for the improvements needed to establish a permanent community on Absecon Island was a lot more difficult than securing investors for the railroad. The original investors had gotten what they wanted and cared little about Pitney's dream of a city by the sea. The Camden-Atlantic Railroad and the Land Company would finance only so much to help build Pitney's resort. Plans for cutting through streets, leveling the dunes, filling ditches, and beginning the infrastructure needed for a city simply had to wait. The result was that for the first 20 years of its existence, Pitney's beach village limped along, remaining a wilderness island.

As predicted by some of Pitney's critics, Cape May remained a popular resort and posed stiff competition. Pitney had envisioned his resort as an exclusive area for the rich. The wealthy were slow to change their habits and while a few of them visited the fledgling resort, Cape May held a strong attraction. Anyone with enough money for an overnight stay generally preferred to visit Cape May. As for the working class, whose numbers in Philadelphia and Camden were growing steadily, the cost of vacationing remained beyond their reach. The blue-collar masses couldn't afford the price of both a train ticket and the cost of lodging. The few who visited arrived in the morning and returned home at night.

At first, the Camden-Atlantic Railroad was barely able to break even financially. As an early observer noted, "Unpropitious times, flooding and washing away of tracks, and depression of bonds threatened to overwhelm the enterprise at its beginning. For 16 years it was one continuous struggle against these difficulties." The railroad was forced into bankruptcy during the Panic of 1857, and if not for cash from the Land Company, the train would have gone under. The financial uncertainty produced by the Civil War denied the new resort badly needed investors and retarded the town's growth. By 1872 things began to look up. The quality of the ride had improved and the passenger cars were clean and comfortable; there was even glass in the windows. The railroad was carrying more than 400,000 passengers annually to the resort and was able to pay a dividend to its stockholders. The volume of passengers continued to grow, and by 1874 nearly 500,000 passengers were brought into Atlantic City by rail.

After 20 years, Atlantic City had finally gained a foothold. Pitney finished out his years living quietly in Absecon Village and passed away in 1869. But for the younger Samuel Richards, Atlantic City was still a long way from its potential. There remained hundreds of undeveloped acres and no new investors to inject sorely needed capital. The businesses that survived the first two decades were only marginally successful. Their owners returned to Philadelphia each fall, leaving the resort a ghost town. Samuel Richards realized that mass-oriented facilities had to be developed before Atlantic City could become a major resort and a permanent community. From Richards' perspective, more working-class visitors from Philadelphia were needed to spur growth. These visitors would only come if railroad fares cost less.

For several years Samuel Richards tried, without success, to sell his ideas to the other shareholders of the Camden-Atlantic Railroad. He believed that greater profits could be made by reducing fares, which would increase the volume of patrons. A majority of the board of directors disagreed. Finally in 1875, Richards lost patience with his fellow directors. Together with three allies, Richards resigned from the board of directors of the Camden-Atlantic Railroad and formed a second railway company of his own. Richards' railroad was to be an efficient and cheaper narrow gauge line. The roadbed for the narrow gauge was easier to build than that of the first railroad. It had a 3½-foot gauge instead of the standard 4 feet 8½ inches, so labor and material would cost less.

The prospect of a second railroad into Atlantic City divided the town. Jonathan Pitney had died six years earlier, but his dream of an exclusive watering hole persisted. Many didn't want to see the type of development that Samuel Richards was encouraging, nor did they want to rub elbows with the working class of Philadelphia. A heated debate raged for months. Most of the residents were content with their island remaining a sleepy little beach village and wanted nothing to do with Philadelphia's blue-collar tourists. But their opinions were irrelevant to Samuel Richards. As he had done 24 years earlier, Richards went to the state legislature and obtained another railroad charter.

The Philadelphia-Atlantic City Railway Company was chartered in March 1876. The directors of the Camden-Atlantic were bitter at the loss of their monopoly and put every possible obstacle in Richards' path. When he began construction in April 1877—simultaneously from both ends—the Camden-Atlantic directors refused to allow the construction machinery to be transported over its tracks or its cars to be used for shipment of supplies. The Baldwin Locomotive Works was forced to send its construction engine by water, around Cape May and up the seacoast; railroad ties were brought in by ships from Baltimore.

Richards permitted nothing to stand in his way. He was determined to have his train running that summer. Construction was at a fever pitch, with crews of laborers working double shifts seven days a week. Fifty-four miles of railroad were completed in just 90 days. With the exception of rail lines built during a war, there had never been a railroad constructed at such speed.

The first train of the Philadelphia-Atlantic City Railway Company arrived in the resort on July 7, 1877. Prior to Richards' railroad, round-trip tickets on the Camden-Atlantic were $3, and one-way fares were $2. The train fares for the narrow gauge railroad were $1.50 and $1. The device, which packed Richards' trains, was the "excursion." Richards understood that the majority of the people visiting Atlantic City could only afford a day trip. His railroad exploited that reality and related businesses provided attractions for people of modest means who were only able to visit for the day. The development of a resort where people would stay overnight in hotels would come later.

Richards geared his new railroad to a class of customers who cared little that the cars they rode in were the dregs of the train yards. They didn't mind that there were no windows, which meant they'd be a sooty mess by the time they reached the shore. Nor did they mind riding on seats made of wooden planks with cushions. The train may have jerked and creaked the entire trip over the iron rails, but that didn't matter either. Excursion rates were $1 round trip, and to a majority of Richards' customers the price was all that mattered. Richards' new railroad was eventually sold to the Philadelphia and Reading Railroad Company in 1883 and converted to a standard gauge railroad line.

Despite its short life, the impact of the Philadelphia-Atlantic City Railway was enormous. It spurred development in a new part of the island and brought in hundreds of thousands of first-time visitors. Richards had unleashed Atlantic City's potential as a resort for the masses. In time, new hotels went up, investment capital was attracted, and Atlantic City launched upon a growth period spanning more than 50 years. Business in every town with a railroad station was stimulated, particularly in lumber, glass, and agricultural products. New development sprang up along the train route and real estate speculation was rampant, with fortunes being made overnight.

More than a generation after its founding, Jonathan Pitney's beach village was finally on its way to becoming a major resort.

# 2

# The Grand Illusion

Thud! The huge net hit the floor of the pier and the crowd squealed with joy. Salt water splashed everywhere as hundreds of fish squirmed about. Presiding over it all was John Young, grinning from ear to ear, while the people crowded around him gaped in amazement. These landlubbers had never seen such creatures of the deep, and Young played his role as "The Captain" for all it was worth.

John Lake Young was the owner of Atlantic City's largest amusement pier, "Young's Million Dollar Pier," and his twice-daily, deep-sea net hauls were famous, attracting thousands of wide-eyed tourists. Wearing knickers, an old sweater and cap, he was a wiry and weathered, red-faced man with sparkling blue eyes, reminiscent of a leprechaun. As he lowered the net to the floor of the pier, Young went into his routine of identifying the sea animals he had caught. It was an animated performance that mesmerized his customers. He was able to name as many as 48 species and bluffed on the ones he couldn't. With a little luck, there might be a shark or a horseshoe crab, which always excited the crowd. They went away thrilled, likely to return on their next visit to Atlantic City.

Young was the resort's answer to P.T. Barnum. He had his finger on the pulse of his times. The Captain knew his customers and gave them what they wanted. The people who came to town on the cut-rate excursions had simple tastes. They wanted a high time at a bargain price—something to tell the folks about when they got home.

Samuel Richards' second train to Atlantic City ignited a war for the visitors' dollars and local businessmen learned quickly that working-class tourists had money to spend, too. What they lacked in sophistication they made up for in numbers. Shortly after Richards' narrow gauge railroad, a third train, the West Jersey and Atlantic Railroad, was organized purposely to transport "the medium and poorer classes." The fare was "the astonishing sum of $.50 each—less than hack fare from Market Street, Philadelphia, to the Park."

Travel to Atlantic City, especially on the weekends, increased dramatically. Competition among the railroads for the excursion ticket buyer guaranteed a large volume of working-class patrons, most of whom came only for the day. While there were families and single people who came to town for week-long vacations, the weekends were vital to a profitable season. Success, and oftentimes survival, of many resort businesses hinged on 12 to 13 weekends, with Sunday being the day everyone anticipated. The six-day workweek of most visitors forced them to squeeze every bit of pleasure they could into their one day off. The result was that "the crowds in the city were so large at times, especially over Sunday, as to nearly exhaust the supply of meat, milk, bread, and provisions in stock."

In the early years following the second railroad, weekend tourists were entertained in excursion houses. These large open-air structures were built at the end of the railroad tracks entering the city. They were more than a reception point. Excursion houses generally included an entertainment pavilion with vaudeville acts, a dining hall, which sold food and provided space for visitors who brought their own, and an amusement park for the children. The West Jersey Railroad excursion house was known for its affordable all-you-can-eat meals, including fish, chicken, roast meats, vegetables, pies, pudding, ice cream, tea, and coffee. It also provided free music and dancing in its ballroom, a bar, a bowling alley, and a poolroom. Bathing suits and lockers were available, too, at a daily rental of 25 cents. Most excursion houses admitted customers at 5 or 10 cents apiece, aiming at high-turnover, low-cost entertainment. At the end of each season, most excursion houses offered their lowest priced outings for what were known as "Colored Excursion Days." It was all made possible by affordable train fare.

After the narrow gauge railroad there was no turning back. Within a few short years Atlantic City was a boomtown. Pitney's sleepy little beach village had awakened. Each summer found dozens of new hotels and boardinghouses, appearing like mushrooms, popping up from nothing at sites that had been beach sand the year before. Year after year, late winter through spring, Atlantic City was a beehive of activity swarming with construction workers sleeping on cots, living in tents, eating in temporary cafeterias and working seven days per week. Workers signed on for the season, knowing they would work every day until the weather became too nasty. For nearly three decades, from the latter part of the 19th century into the second decade of the 20th century, a "Tent City" rose up from the sand every spring, pitched at a different location, following the growth of the resort. The residents of Tent City were mostly itinerant laborers and tradesmen, sometimes with their families, usually not. These crews of workers were brought to town by Philadelphia contractors and established businesses looking to get in on the action at the shore. They worked at a fever pitch from sunrise to sunset and made the city hum.

The air was filled with the sounds of shovels, hammers, saws, and masonry tools. A walk down any street would bring sounds of men working: from bricklayers shouting at their helpers, "brick, block, mud" as they worked to complete a foundation, to carpenters calling down from a roof for more shingles and nails. Going from one job site to another were women and young children hawking sandwiches and beverages. At the end of each day, make-shift beer gardens were packed with thirsty workers. There was never enough beer, nor women, to go around, and late evening brawls were common. During peak building periods the local police had their hands full. Except for the most serious crimes, arrest and jail weren't the answer. Local authorities relied upon employers to keep their laborers under control. For them it was back to Tent City, where the offender could sleep it off and return to work the next day.

The resort quickly became a blue-collar town. Thousands of building tradesmen and laborers came to Atlantic City looking for work and many remained to make it their home. For nearly two generations after the second railroad, the resort was a place where strong hands could always find work. While things slowed down with the coming of fall, a laborer's wages, along with odd jobs in the off-season, were usually enough to see a family through to spring. Between the years 1875 and 1900, the resort's year-round population increased from less than 2,000 to nearly 30,000. Pitney's beach village had become a city. By the turn of the 20th century, there were several neighborhoods taking shape. First- and second-generation Irish, Italians, and Jews, most by way of Philadelphia, came to town and brought their citified ways.

The Irish were part of the work gangs that built the original railroads and laid out the city's streets. They formed construction companies and established taverns and boardinghouses. Italian craftsmen followed the Irish and worked with them in building hotels, boardinghouses, and homes. The Italians started local firms involving all the building trades and opened restaurants, food markets, and bakeries. Jewish merchants arrived at the turn of the century establishing retail businesses and playing a vital role in commercial development. Many were involved in banking, finance, the law, and accounting. Within a single generation after Samuel Richards' second rail line, Absecon Island was transformed from a quiet beach village that shut down at the end of each summer to a bustling city based solely upon tourism.

Nationally, tourism and the hotel and recreation industry were in their infancy. There were only a handful of vacation spots and they were reserved for the wealthy. Outside of cities, the hotels that existed were generally large guesthouses and no one viewed the working class as potential patrons. But Atlantic City did and tourism became the only game in town. Scores of Philadelphia and New York businessmen saw the opportunity to profit from the hotel and recreation business and came to town in a frenzy. They brought the capital—in amounts Pitney and Richards could have only dreamt of—needed to build a city. In no time there was a fourth railroad providing direct rail service to New York City.

The speed in constructing new rail lines was matched only by the swiftness in constructing new hotels. The seven-story, 166-room, and 80-bath Garden Hotel, constructed in the 1880s, was erected in 72 working days. The five-story Hotel Rudolph, with a dance floor to accommodate 500, was constructed in 100 days. The 10-story landmark Chalfonte Hotel was erected in six months, breaking ground on December 9, 1903, and opening for guests on July 2, 1904, the 50th anniversary of the coming of the train. Year after year, construction on dozens of small hotels and boardinghouses began in the early spring and was completed in time for the summer season.

Boardinghouses lodged the bulk of Atlantic City's visitors; by 1900, there were approximately 400 of them. Though lacking the glamour of most hotels, boardinghouses made it possible for blue-collar workers and their families to have an extended stay at the seashore. The accommodations were simple to the point of monotony but they were clean and comfortable, which was more than what most of the visitors had come from. It was common for strangers to double-up in a single room, and there were no private baths nor room service. Regardless, patron loyalty was strong and many guests returned to the same boardinghouse summer after summer. During the peak season, one could usually find a room in the large first-class hotels, but the low-end, smaller hotels and boardinghouses were always crammed to capacity.

Boardinghouse owners and their patrons were a critical cornerstone of the resort's tourist economy. The visitor who came to town by an excursion couldn't afford a stay in any of the larger hotels. If blue-collar workers and their families were to vacation for an entire week they needed a place within their means. Despite today's notions of Atlantic City as a vacation spot for the wealthy, the resort could never have survived by catering to the upper class. It was the lower-middle and lower classes that were the lifeblood of Atlantic City. They comprised the great mass of visitors to the resort and the rates of most rooms were structured for them. That wasn't true of the large hotels along the ocean, which charged rates ranging from $3 to $5 per day. Generally, the larger the hotel, the more expensive the rates and the more limited the clientele.

Rooms in the low-end smaller hotels could be rented for only $1.50 to $2, and that included food. Weekly rates of $8 to $12 were common. While there are no records of the rates charged by boardinghouses, it's known their rooms were less than the cheapest hotels. As for a precise number of boardinghouses in the resort during its heyday, one can only speculate. There was no obligation for an owner to call his lodging a "boardinghouse" or "hotel." Many small guesthouses of four to six rooms included "hotel" in their name. To make things more confusing, many establishments used the term "cottage."

One historian has estimated that boardinghouses accounted for about 60 percent of all businesses renting rooms to tourists. With annual real wages of $1,000 or less for positions such as office clerks, government workers, postal employees, ministers, teachers, and factory workers, boardinghouse rates brought a week at the shore within the means of most visitors. Even the lower classes could afford a week at the shore if they planned ahead and saved for their vacation. Thousands of families did just that, setting aside small sums throughout the year for a week-long fling at the shore. With Atlantic City the only vacation spot to which there was direct rail service in the Northeast, hoteliers who treated their guests well could count on repeat business. And the railroads and resort merchants worked together to keep their working-class patrons coming.

One of the gimmicks used to lure visitors was to continue touting the resort as a health spa, with Pitney's original promotional efforts evolving into pamphlets distributed by the railroads. Exaggerated claims of the health benefits of Absecon Island's environment were an important part of selling Atlantic City to both Philadelphia and the nation. After Pitney died, the railroads hired other "distinguished men of medicine" who continued the tradition. These doctors were paid to make written endorsements and to prescribe a stay at the beach as the cure for every ailment. The railroads supplied the doctors with complimentary passes, which were passed on to those patients who had yet to visit the resort. Handouts published at the expense of the railroad distributed this medical advice to the general public and invariably described the resort's air as "hostile to physical debility."

There were no limits to the hype. "Next to being an inhabitant of Atlantic City, it must be one's highest privilege to find rest, health and pleasure at the City by the Sea." A favorite subject of the railroads' doctors was ozone, "the stimulating, vitalizing principal of the atmosphere," which was in large supply only at the seashore, especially Atlantic City. According to the railroads' pamphlets, "Ozone has a tonic, healing, purifying power, that increases as the air is taken into the lungs. It strengthens the respiratory organs, and in stimulating them, helps the whole system." But that wasn't all. By breathing Atlantic City's air, "It follows naturally that the blood is cleansed and revived, tone is given to the stomach, the liver is excited to healthful action and the whole body feels the benefit. Perfect health is the inevitable result."

In addition to the pamphlets cranked out by the railroads, there were a series of travelers' handbooks published from 1887 to 1908 by Alfred M. Heston, a self-appointed cheerleader for the resort. Heston was well-educated and had worked for several newspapers prior to making Atlantic City his home. An owlish, scrawny little man, Heston's appearance was marked by pince-nez eyeglasses and a closely groomed mustache. Somewhat eccentric, he was drawn to the study of ancient civilizations and progressive Republican politics. Heston was the editor of a local newspaper, the *Atlantic City Review,* and served as city comptroller from 1895 to 1912. His annual handbooks described a life of enchantment waiting for all who came to Atlantic City. They were filled with sketches of charming scenes of vacationers, hotel listings, recommended merchants and restaurants, activities for the family, and romantic little tales all intended to present Atlantic City to the world through rose-colored glasses. According to Heston, "The endless panorama of life upon the water, the strand, and the Boardwalk, constantly in motion and ever changing" made Atlantic City the "queen of watering places."

Heston used his contacts in the publishing world to have his handbooks reviewed and publicized in major newspapers of the day while the railroad subsidized and circulated them. A traveler waiting for a train in Boston, Pittsburgh, Chicago, or in nearly any of the thousands of railroad stations throughout the United States could always find a free copy of the Heston handbook.

As the resort grew in popularity, one of the main themes of its promoters was to dispel the belief that Atlantic City was attractive only in the summer. Not everyone was like Walt Whitman, who found that Atlantic City "suits me just as well, perhaps best, for winter quarters." Whitman enjoyed riding in a horse-drawn carriage along the beach and in January 1879 wrote to a friend, "I have a fine and bracing drive along the smooth sand (the carriage wheels hardly make a dent in it). The bright sun, the sparkling waves, the foam, the view—the vital vast monotonous sea … were the items of my drive … How the soul dwells on their simplicity, eternity, grimness, absence of art!"

But Whitman's prose attracted few wintertime visitors, so the railroad's publicity agents conjured up another law of nature to convince vacationers that Atlantic City had mild winters. Promotional literature claimed that the warm Gulf Stream, coursing its way northward, made a westerly turn just beyond Cape May and swept within a few miles of the stretch of the Jersey coast where Absecon Island was located. The Gulf Stream then, as if guided by an unseen hand, turned out to the sea on its way to the frozen North, thus preventing any other northeastern seacoast town from receiving its warmth. As one early publicist later admitted, "During blizzards or just plain snowstorms, we plastered the metropolitan dailies with *No snow on the Boardwalk* even though sometimes we had to sweep it off before placing the copy."

The Boardwalk, which began as a way to keep the tourists from tracking beach sand all over town, was another marketing tool for the railroads and local merchants. Without any idea of what they were doing, Jacob Keim, a hotelier, and Alexander Boardman, a train conductor—both of whom were annoyed with the sand brought indoors by their patrons—created a novelty that would in time win hundreds of thousands of new converts for Atlantic City. In the spring of 1870, Keim and Boardman called a meeting of other business people at Keim's hotel, the Chester County House. Boardman opened the meeting by stating:

> Gentlemen, we brought you here to present an idea we feel will benefit everyone in this room. Our visitors are no longer satisfied with the rough facilities once offered them here. Today we must supply fine carpets, good furniture and other luxuries. These cost money. Our carpets and even stuffed chairs are being ruined by the sand tracked into our places from the beach. Walking on the beach is a favorite past time. We can't stop this. We propose to give the beach strollers a walkway of boards on the sand, which we believe will overcome our sand problems.

Keim and Boardman presented sketches of their idea and a petition to city council was circulated. It was an easy sell. The first Boardwalk was a flimsy structure, eight-foot wide, in 12-foot sections, so it could be taken up and stored at the end of summer. Extending from the Seaview Excursion House to the Absecon Lighthouse, it turned "tiresome areas of mosquito marsh and soft sand" into a crowded little thoroughfare of tourists eager to prance upon every plank. Stretched out across the dunes, filled with people scurrying about, this little promenade must have been a curious sight.

At the time the Boardwalk was originally built, city council adopted an ordinance prohibiting the construction of any buildings within 30 feet of the walkway on the city side, and prohibited construction entirely on the ocean side. By 1880, after the success of the second railroad was evident, local businessmen saw the potential for locating shops along the Boardwalk. Property owners near the walk-way pressured council to reverse itself to make retail shops available to the strollers. In less than three years after the ordinance was rescinded, the Boardwalk became a busy street with more than 100 businesses facing the beach. As demand for access to the Boardwalk increased it was improved, becoming more elaborate and permanent. In 1884 it was elevated to get it off the sand and moved closer to the shoreline. In 1896, the city made a major commitment, constructing a Boardwalk that rested upon steel pilings driven into the beach sand. After 1896, the Boardwalk was truly a "grand promenade," with nothing like it anywhere in the world. By the end of the 19th century, the Boardwalk was a major attraction unto itself, with many visitors coming to the resort for the first time just to walk on it. There was something magical about being so near the sand and water, yet removed from it, that captured the public's imagination.

The businesses along the Boardwalk helped to foster an emphasis on buying and selling that would pervade the Atlantic City scene for years to come. Every foot of this grand promenade was dedicated to assisting its strollers to part with their money. If the people walking on the Boardwalk weren't gazing at the ocean, they were certain to be looking at something for sale. The Boardwalk merchants under-stood their customers and did everything they could to divert their attention from the surf. The industrialization and urbanization of America were, for the first time, creating expendable income for the masses. Atlantic City played a significant role in fostering the illu-sion that the route to happiness was by way of materialism. The Boardwalk merchants appealed to the impulse to consume and con-vinced their patrons they couldn't have a fun time at the shore unless they purchased some of their goodies. Through the commercializa-tion of the Boardwalk, recreational buying came into vogue. The spending of money as a sort of pleasure was introduced to the work-ing class and became part of popular American culture.

More than conveniences for their strollers, the Boardwalk's shops became a medium of entertainment and a chance to fulfill the American dream, if only temporarily. Hundreds of small stores and kiosk-like structures were constructed in front of the hotels on the city side of the Boardwalk. While there were more refined shops featuring expensive jewelry and furnishings in the hotels, their numbers were few. There were many more stores along the

Boardwalk making sales from nickels and dimes selling trinkets. With the grand hotels as a backdrop, these small stores offered visitors, most of whom could never afford a stay in the hotels, the opportunity to purchase gifts and mementos so they could take home a taste of the high life.

There was no limit to the wonderful junk Boardwalk merchants offered for sale: postcards with sexual innuendoes, paintings on shells, tinsel jewelry, handmade Native American moccasins, kewpie dolls, Bohemian cut glass, and an endless inventory of nonsense that the visitor would never buy any place else except when vacationing in Atlantic City. In addition, the Boardwalk merchants pioneered walk-away eateries offering an incredible array of food and beverages. There was everything from deviled crabs, tutti-frutti, saltwater taffy, caramel popcorn, and pretzels to all the "Natural Saratoga Water" you could drink for five cents.

The Boardwalk became Main Street, Fantasy Island. It was a wonderland of glitz and cheap thrills. "The Boardwalk was a stage, upon which there was a temporary suspension of disbelief; behavior that was exaggerated, even ridiculous, in every day life was expected at the resort." By the beginning of the 20th century, the resort attracted the attention of the *New Baedeker*, a publication for the sophisticated traveler, which remarked, "Atlantic City is an eighth wonder of the world. It is overwhelming in its crudeness—barbaric, hideous, and magnificent. There is something colossal about its vulgarity."

Atlantic City's grand promenade created for its strollers an illusion of social mobility that couldn't be found at other resorts. Elias Howe's invention of the sewing machine in 1846 laid the foundation for the ready-to-wear clothing industry. Its widespread use in the last half of the 19th century produced a fashion revolution in America. The working class could now afford stylish garments. Ready-made clothing blurred class lines and for many of the resort's patrons, the Boardwalk became a showcase for their new clothes. A trip to Atlantic City was an excuse for getting dressed up. Strolling on the Boardwalk made visitors feel they were marchers in a grand fashion parade. The working class craved opportunities to participate in festive occasions and the Boardwalk gave them just such a chance. During the summer months, the resort became a huge masquerade party, with everyone trying to appear as if they had arrived socially. At the same time the resort was growing in popularity, American society was groping toward a popular culture to suit the new industrial world. The average worker wanted to be free of the limits imposed by farm life and small villages. Atlantic City was an outlet for that urge. The Boardwalk created the illusion that everyone was part of a huge middle class parading to prosperity and social freedom. There were no class distinctions while strolling the Boardwalk; everyone was someone special.

For visitors to the Boardwalk, the glorification of the common man reached its peak with the rolling chair. The rolling chair was first introduced to the Boardwalk in 1887 by William Hayday, a hardware store merchant, as a part of Atlantic City's role as a health resort. Invalids could hire a chair and enjoy the pleasures of the view of the surf, the salt air, and the wares for sale in the Boardwalk's many shops. Harry Shill, a wheelchair manufacturer, was so impressed that he began producing rolling chairs in mass. They quickly evolved from an aid for invalids into a means for transporting every visitor from a working stiff into royalty, even if it was only for a short while. What better way to stroke the ego of the working-class visitor than to wheel him around in a beautifully decorated vehicle, thickly padded with comfortable cushions, and driven by an obliging servant? They couldn't get that kind of treatment back home, making the Boardwalk something special in their memories.

The Boardwalk brought resort patrons to the water's edge, but the five amusement piers built on the ocean side lured them farther, overtop the ocean itself. The excitement at the very thought of it was more than most visitors could resist and they spent their money on any attraction offered on the piers. The first three piers that were built didn't last beyond a single summer; winter storms destroyed them all. John Applegate, a Boardwalk photographer, built a sturdier one in 1884, a 670-foot-long pier consisting of an upper and lower deck, with an amusement pavilion at the outer end. Applegate's pier was a profitable investment for its owner but it was small time compared to the success had by John Young, who purchased it in 1891.

John Young understood what Atlantic City was all about. Born across the bay in Absecon Village to an oyster man, he was fatherless at the age of three. He left school early for work to support himself. While working as a carpenter doing repair work on the Boardwalk, he met Stewart McShea, a Pennsylvania baker. McShea had money and Young had ideas. Together, they opened a roller-skating rink and a carousel, both of which were successful. When Applegate's pier went up for sale they grabbed it, with Young in charge of the show.

Young extended Applegate's pier to a length of 2,000 feet, then searched the world over for attractions to lure the masses. His pier was a glittering palace: It contained the "world's largest ballroom," a hippodrome, an exhibit hall with everything from butterflies to mutants, a reproduction of a Greek temple, and an aquarium where he kept special finds from his daily fish hauls. Young held dances, promoted contests, gave away prizes, featured exhibitions, and sponsored productions of both contemporary and classical plays in Young's Pier Playhouse. He even brought Sarah Bernhardt to his pier to star in a performance of "Camile." The Captain had something for everybody.

The pier Young bought from Applegate was destroyed by fire in 1902. Young bought out McShea and rebuilt in time for the next summer, calling his new pier "Young's Million Dollar Pier." His pier was a tinsel palace that dazzled Boardwalk strollers. Highlighted by gobs of gaudy Victorian gingerbread, it housed attractions designed to lure a wide cross-section of patrons. It worked like a charm. At the height of his success, Young was reaping an annual income of more than a million dollars, and all before the income tax.

Young didn't hide his wealth and erected a marble mansion on his pier so he could, to use his own words, "fish out my kitchen window." The home included furnishings from around the world and was recognized by the U.S. Post Office as "No. 1, Atlantic Ocean, U.S.A." Although it was constructed on a pier, there was a formal garden fronting Young's mansion. The garden included statues imported from Florence, Italy. "They were undraped in the classic tradition and considered daring for their time. His Adam and Eve group especially caused a sensation when a bolt of lightning struck Eve in an embarrassing spot. The humor of the situation hit the press. Newspapers and newsreels gave them nationwide coverage." The lighting and landscaping for Young's palace were designed by his long-time friend, Thomas Edison. The Captain and the inventor spent many an afternoon together fishing off the end of the pier behind the mansion. Eventually washed into the sea by a winter storm, Young's mansion was the envy of his customers.

Young and other Boardwalk merchants who modeled themselves after him were, in large part, responsible for institutionalizing the concept of the spending spree in American culture. Thanks to them, Atlantic City developed into a place where visitors came knowing they would part with their money. The tourists did so gladly, because the Boardwalk merchants were able to convince them that they were having the time of their lives.

The counterpart of the Boardwalk merchants were the resort hotel and boardinghouse owners who were pioneers willing to sink their money into the sand in hopes of making a fortune. Many of them came out of Philadelphia and viewed Atlantic City as a new frontier of the hotel industry. For them, the resort was Philadelphia's summertime playground, and they claimed the market as their own. While they participated in the national advertising campaign of the railroads, the resort's hotel and boardinghouse operators knew they couldn't survive without Philadelphia.

The first hotel owner to experience a large success was Benjamin Brown, who purchased the 600-room United States Hotel. Constructed by the Camden-Atlantic Railroad, the hotel had changed hands several times before he acquired it. Shortly after acquiring the hotel, Brown was wooing his visitors with ads stating, "Large rooms, furnished in walnut ... gas in every room ... morning, afternoon and evening concerts by celebrated orchestras." Benjamin Brown was every bit the showman that John Young was. Working together with the railroad, he launched an aggressive campaign toward attracting the rich and famous, using them as a draw for nouveau riche social climbers. He gave well-known visitors all expenses paid vacations, provided he was permitted to use their names in his promotional literature. On one occasion Brown was able to attract President Ulysses S. Grant. "My father's friend, Al, said Grant drank so much when he was in town that he probably doesn't remember being here." A holiday was declared for Grant's arrival and ads were taken in the major newspapers of the Northeast, showing that Cape May wasn't the only resort that could host a president.

Another influential hotelier was Charles McGlade, owner of the Mansion House, which stood at the corner of Pennsylvania and Atlantic avenues. A low, rambling three-story frame structure, the place was floundering when McGlade took it over. He turned things around quickly. McGlade, a restless bundle of energy, supervised every aspect of his hotel. He began by promoting his property and was the first resort hotelier to use bold commercial display print for his newspaper advertising, like the ads run by retailers. Prior to McGlade, hotel advertisements were routinely set in a style comparable to today's classified ads: five or six lines, in modest type, under the heading "resorts" was the conventional practice of the staid Victorian era. McGlade ignored convention. He shouted his message using eye-catching bold print ads in the major Northeastern newspapers. It worked and his competitors soon followed his example, creating a revolution in hotel advertising.

The master of the Mansion House was responsible for innovations that went beyond advertising. Prior to McGlade, most of the town's hotels and boardinghouses were sparsely furnished, creating a sober, almost spartanlike environment—what one might expect to find on a religious retreat. McGlade brought creature comforts to Atlantic City, which local hoteliers hadn't considered worth the investment for businesses operating only during the summer season. The first thing he did was to transform the "parlor" into a sophisticated hotel lobby. Bare walls and sparse furnishings gave way to frescoed ceilings of flowers and figures painted by local artist, Jerre Leeds.

McGlade created an aura of glamour. He installed elegant carpeting, expensive wallpaper, cushioned lounge chairs, crystal chandeliers, polished glass, and mahogany paneling. The bare walls and stiff furniture of McGlade's competitors soon gave way to a whole line of improvements that transformed the resort hotel industry. "The bar, a principal part of all successful hotel operations, was transformed from a saloon to salon" and became a popular meeting place for visitors from the other hotels and boardinghouses. He also installed an outdoor dance pavilion, permitting guests to enjoy the open air rather than a hot dining room, which is where his competitors permitted dancing. More importantly, McGlade set a standard for entertaining his customers that soon became an Atlantic City trademark. He arranged for his guests to be met at the train station by an elegant horse-drawn carriage and had them transported to his hotel where he would personally greet them. He oversaw every service offered his patrons and made them feel as if they were personal guests. Upon their departure, he was there to wish them farewell with "Hope you will return again soon." McGlade set the standard for hospitality. Other hoteliers followed his example. One such hotel pioneer was Josiah White, who started a resort dynasty.

Josiah White III was the great grand-nephew of Josiah White, a Pennsylvania pioneer who had constructed the Lehigh Canal. The Whites were eager to become involved in new businesses in Pennsylvania, much the same way the Richards family did in southern New Jersey. Josiah White could see that Atlantic City was Philadelphia's playground and in 1887, he purchased the Luray Hotel, a 90-room boardinghouse on Kentucky Avenue near the beach. He quickly acquired the land between the Luray and the ocean and, with his sons, John and Allen, expanded the Luray into a hotel of more than 300 rooms. White and his sons built stores along the Boardwalk and erected the resort's first hotel sundeck. The Whites added another first, hot and cold running seawater for those rooms that had private baths.

From the success with the Luray, White and his sons purchased a nearby property used for retreats by the Academy of the Sacred Heart. In 1902, the Whites erected the Marlborough House. A short time later, the Luray was destroyed by fire. Rather than rebuild, White and his sons acquired additional property near the Marlborough and constructed the Blenheim Hotel. It was one of the first fireproof hotels in Atlantic City and the first hotel with a private bath for every room, something unheard of in the hotel industry. Another first of the Blenheim was that it was constructed of reinforced concrete. It was a new process and its inventor, Thomas Edison, was on hand to supervise the construction.

The Whites' hotels, together with several other large hotels that followed them, created a magical aura along the Boardwalk. They were magnificent sand castles that captured the public's attention and enhanced Atlantic City's reputation. The Marlborough, named after the home of the Prince of Wales, was built in the Queen Anne style of architecture. The Blenheim, named after the Blenheim Castle, home of the Duke of Marlborough, was designed in a Spanish–Moorish architecture. While most of Atlantic City's visitors could never afford to stay at the Marlborough-Blenheim, the Whites' properties set a tone of elegance adding to the illusion of Atlantic City and its Boardwalk.

Through the leadership of hoteliers such as Benjamin Brown, Charles McGlade, and the Whites, Atlantic City's hospitality industry gained a reputation as a destination where the vacationer could count on being treated well. They set the standard for the entire hospitality industry, including the smaller hotels and boardinghouses. Regardless of their financial means, upon arrival in Atlantic City, guests knew they would be fussed over. But the pampering of hotel guests—especially before modern conveniences—was labor intensive. The resort's hotel industry couldn't function without large numbers of unskilled workers. Cooks, waiters, chambermaids, dishwashers, bellboys, and janitors were in constant demand. These jobs were filled almost entirely by freed slaves and their descendants who had migrated north following the Civil War. These African-Americans were essential to Atlantic City's surge to prominence as a destination for vacationers. While the money to build a national resort came primarily from Philadelphia and New York investors, the muscle and sweat needed to keep things going was furnished by Black workers, lured north in hope of a better life.

# 3

# A Plantation by the Sea

"Elegant" was a word often used to describe the Windsor Hotel. In the late 1800s, it was one of Atlantic City's most talked about places. Originally built in 1884 as a small boardinghouse called the Mineola, it was combined with the Berkely Hotel several years later under the name "the Windsor." The Windsor was a tony place. A small hotel, noted for its service, it had the city's first French-style courtyard and was a center of social life year-round.

Until the summer of 1893, everyone at the Windsor understood their place in resort society. That June saw the first effort by hotel workers to stage a strike. It failed miserably.

Unhappy with the meal he had been given during break time, a Black waiter in the Windsor's dining room placed an order with the kitchen for himself. When the White headwaiter learned that the meal was for one of his Black staff, the meal was canceled. The workers were told that if they wanted to eat, they could do so in the Black-only help's dining area, which was off to one side in the kitchen. At the next dinner break, the food was inedible. The waiters refused their meals and politely advised the headwaiter they would strike if they didn't receive better food. The headwaiter was unfazed by the threat. He

> … cooly told them to strike out for another job and summoned all the chambermaids attired in their knobby white caps and aprons to wait at supper and the next morning he had a new force of colored waiters.

Typical of the era, the name of the waiter who led the strike remains unknown. To White society, African-Americans, generally, were anonymous. As for the meal that prompted a strike by workers accustomed to third-rate treatment, one can only imagine how putrid it was. White hoteliers viewed Blacks as little more than beasts of burden. They were brought to town in much the same way Northern

35

farmers recruited migrant farm hands. Any worker who questioned a hotel's rules was replaced.

As Cape May had done years earlier, Atlantic City's hotels reached out to the Upper South for domestic servants. In a short time, the resort became a mecca for Black men and women as hotel workers. Between the years 1870 and 1915, thousands of Blacks left their homes in Maryland, Virginia, and North Carolina and ventured to Atlantic City in search of opportunity. By 1915, African-Americans accounted for more than 27 percent of the resort's population, a percentage more than five times that of any other northern city. At the same time, they comprised 95 percent of the hotel workforce. And with the treatment they received, Atlantic City's hotel industry was akin to a plantation.

Atlantic City's evolution into a plantation by the sea is a product of its unique status in the era in which it was growing from a beach village to a major resort. For nearly three generations after the Civil War, as America was shifting from an agricultural-based economy to a manufacturing economy, racial prejudice excluded Blacks from industrial employment. During the years between the American Civil War and World War II, the only occupations realistically available to Black Americans were either as a farm laborer or domestic worker. Domestic work was thought to be peculiarly "Negro work," with the attitude of most Whites being, "Negroes are servants; servants are Negroes."

African-American history is filled with many cruel ironies. Following the Civil War, thousands of skilled Black tradesmen were forced to abandon finely honed skills to become servants. During slavery, many Blacks worked at crafts and became masters. Entire families of slaves were engaged in highly skilled trades, one generation after another. Beyond farm labor, male Blacks were trained as ironworkers, carpenters, wheelwrights, coopers, tanners, shoemakers, and bakers. As for female slaves, they were capable of far more than household chores. Many were skilled at sewing, spinning, weaving, dressmaking, pottery, nursing, and midwifery. Upon emancipation, Black artisans became a threat to White workers.

When freed Black tradesmen were thrown into competition with White workers, there was often open social conflict. White workers, in both the South and North, reacted violently. They wouldn't permit one of their own to be displaced by a Black worker, regardless of how skilled he might be. Despite their newfound freedom, few employers risked hiring skilled Blacks, regardless of how cheap they'd work, for fear of reprisals by White workers. African-American historian E. F. Frazier found that at the end of the Civil War there were approximately 100,000 skilled Black tradesmen in the South as compared with 20,000 Whites. Between 1865 and 1890 the number of Black artisans dwindled to only a handful. That such a large reservoir of talent was permitted to dry up confirms the ignorance and inutility of racial prejudice.

For Blacks who had moved North, their existence was precarious. Ill-equipped to deal with the economic and social realities of post-Civil War America, a disproportionate number of Blacks found themselves in poverty. In Philadelphia, between 1891 and 1896, approximately 9 percent of the inmates in the almshouse were Blacks, although they constituted only 4 percent of that city's population. Unable to gain a foothold in the expanding industries of the region, and the opportunities at farming limited, freed slaves and their children had little choice but to accept domestic work. Shut out of high-paying, skilled jobs, it was domestic work or the poor house.

The situation in New Jersey was typical. In 1903, of the 475 industrial concerns surveyed by the New Jersey Bureau of Statistics of Labor and Industry, only 83 employed Blacks in any capacity, mostly janitorial. An illustration of the closed doors confronting Blacks in New Jersey's industries is Paterson, which was a major industrial center not only in the state but the nation. By 1915, 50 years after the Civil War, the percentage of Black male workers employed in Paterson's factories, at any job, was less than 5 percent.

The distribution of Blacks throughout the American economy is revealing of the prevailing racial attitudes of the day. Prior to 1890, the United States Census did not distinguish occupational classes by race or color, but from that date forward, it did. In the population counts, for 1890 and 1900 upward of 87 percent of all Black workers were employed in either agricultural pursuits or domestic and personal service. The remaining 13 percent breaks down as follows: 6 percent in manufacturing and mechanical pursuits, 6 percent in commerce and transportation, and 1 percent in the professions.

In the North Atlantic region, more than two-thirds of all African-Americans earned their income in domestic work. Most Blacks hired to work in a White household were general servants. Routinely, a family hired a single domestic servant who was required to be a cook, a waitress, and a housekeeper. The work of a household servant was hard and the hours were long. The typical general servant worked a 12-hour day and was responsible for maintaining the household seven days a week. Days off were dependent upon the generosity of the employer. Domestic service was a field of work sought out of necessity rather than choice. For most Blacks, working as a domestic servant was only a small step up from slavery. No other group in the American population—including new immigrants from Europe—had such a large proportion of its members in such menial employment.

But the menial employment in Atlantic City was different. Hotel work was an attractive alternative. There was a crucial difference between the work experience of Blacks in Atlantic City and those of other cities at the time. The work opportunities were more varied and stimulating. The hotel and recreation economy had many types of positions requiring strong backs and quick hands and feet. To keep the resort running smoothly during its peak season, hoteliers, restaurateurs, Boardwalk merchants, and amusement operators relied heavily upon the affordable labor provided by Blacks. While it was often difficult work, an employee was part of something bigger and more dynamic than were Blacks hired to perform domestic work in private homes.

Those Blacks who came to Atlantic City in search of work found they could make four to five times the wages available in the South. The Civil War had devastated the South and left it destitute. The Union Army had scarred the Southern landscape and wrecked its economy. While there was no longer slavery in the Old Confederacy, freedom had simply lifted the Black man from slave to sharecropper. Both Blacks and Whites were unfamiliar with a free-labor, market economy and upward of 90 percent of the Black population fell into the sharecropping and crop-lien system. Sharecropping produced a nasty, feudal-like economy in which the Black man was a loser. Black sharecroppers were tied to the land in the hopes their efforts would produce enough for them to survive. "Wages," per se, did not exist. To many freed slaves, any type of work in the North was better than sharecropping. Domestic service and hotel work were welcomed alternatives.

While the wages of a domestic servant in most Northern cities were comparable to that of hotel employment, work in a hotel was easier than domestic service and more exciting, with the hours fewer and more predictable. Finally, the Blacks who came to Atlantic City found employment as a hotel worker had less social stigma than domestic work. Working as a general servant was synonymous with social inferiority. Unlike other occupations, the individual was hired, not their labor. The use of the word "servant" was a mark of social degradation.

In Atlantic City, Blacks were not *servants* but, rather, *employees* in a hotel and recreation economy that relied upon them heavily for its success. Based upon data available from the late 19th to early 20th centuries, historian Herbert J. Foster concluded that at the turn of that century the weekly wages of hotel workers in Atlantic City compared favorably with other cities and may have been the highest paid at the time. The resort's reliance upon Black workers evolved swiftly following the boom period ignited by Samuel Richards' second railroad. Between 1854 and 1870 Atlantic City's Black population did not exceed 200. But after the narrow gauge railroad in 1877, tourists flocked to town and the hotel industry flourished. Hotel owners recruited Black workers from Delaware, Maryland, and Virginia for the summer season. Working for hotels and boardinghouses, these workers were provided food, lodging, and wages far better than anything they could earn at home. Beginning in the 1880s, Blacks came to Atlantic City primarily for the summer months and then returned to their homes. As the resort grew in popularity and the number of hotels operating year-round increased, Blacks found work beyond the summer months, and many made the resort their permanent home.

Atlantic City became the most "Black" city in the North. By 1905 the Black population was nearly 9,000. By 1915 it was greater than 11,000, comprising more than one-fourth of the permanent residents. During summer, the Black population swelled to nearly 40 percent. Of those Northern cities having more than 10,000 Black residents, Atlantic City was without any serious rival in terms of percentage of total population. These numbers are critical in terms of understanding the status of Atlantic City's Black experience in American history.

Following the Civil War, between 75 and 90 percent of all African-Americans who traveled North gravitated to cities, with most living in larger cities such as New York, Philadelphia, and Chicago. Those who settled in smaller cities and towns found a bitter isolation. Without sufficient population of their own to establish a separate community life, many Blacks had no life but work. This was especially true of the smaller communities in New Jersey where there had been support for the Confederate cause. New Jersey's reaction to Lincoln's election in 1860 included talk of secession. When war broke out, former Governor Rodman Price and other Democrats openly stated that the state should join the South. Local sentiment didn't change during the War. In addition to being the only Northern state where Lincoln failed to gain a majority, New Jersey selected pro-Southern Democrat James Wall to serve in the U.S. Senate in 1863. The same year, Democratic Governor Joel Parker denounced Lincoln's Emancipation Proclamation as an improper trespass on state's rights and the New Jersey legislature adopted legislation banning Negroes from the state. Finally, the Legislature elected in 1864 rejected the ratification of the 13th Amendment to the U.S. Constitution, which ended slavery.

For many years following the Civil War, in the towns and cities throughout New Jersey, there was a deep division between Blacks and Whites. The vast majority of the African-American population was relegated to blighted areas, which were located "across the tracks," "over the creek," "by the dump," or "back of the hill." Nearly all were employed at unskilled labor and domestic work.

U.S. census statistics show that by the beginning of the 20th century the overwhelming majority of Blacks in Atlantic City were "domestic and personal service workers." But the recreational orientation of Atlantic City's economy makes those numbers misleading. The variety and pay of domestic service positions and, consequently, the social structure of the Black community differed greatly from other Northern cities, both large and small. Hotel/recreation work in Atlantic City paid more than domestic service in other cities, not only because of higher wages, but also because Black hotel workers came in contact with tourists and earned tips. Additionally, most employees were provided with regular daily meals in the hotels. Equally important, there was a hierarchy of positions within the hotel and recreation industry. As a result, the Atlantic City tourist economy provided Black workers with the ability to move from one type of job to another. Such mobility in the workplace was unavailable to Blacks in other cities. The result of this phenomenon was development of a Black social structure in Atlantic City far more complex than other Northern cities. By virtue of their higher income, property ownership, and greater responsibility attached to their hotel positions, a substantial portion of Atlantic City's Black residents were, by comparison to other Blacks nationally, part of the middle and upper classes.

The social structure among African-American workers in Atlantic City roughly broke down along the following lines: *Upper*—hotel-keepers, boardinghouse keepers (and owners), headwaiters, stewards, cooks, head bellmen, and rollingchair managers; *Middle*—waiters, waitresses, chambermaids, elevator operators, lifeguards, actors, musicians, entertainers, and performers; *Lower*—bellmen, busboys, porters, dishwashers, kitchen helpers, and rollingchair pushers. Intelligence, experience, and personal initiative counted for much in the hotel and recreation industry. Unlike many other cities where Blacks were simply servants, those in Atlantic City had a realistic chance for advancement in the tourist economy.

But the mobility available in the workplace did not translate into social mobility. As Blacks grew in numbers, the racial attitude of Atlantic City's Whites hardened. While White racism has been a strong force throughout American history, historians have noted that at the close of the 19th century race relations began to develop more formal patterns.

History rarely marches in a straight line. Succeeding generations have a way of retrenching as they reject portions of social changes made earlier. Time and again, positive social advancements are made only to be followed by negative reactions. Weariness of the federal government's role in the South and political expediency prompted Presidents Rutherford B. Hayes and James Garfield to preside passively over the dismantling of efforts to bring about interracial democracy. Northern Republicans, Hayes' and Garfield's attitudes reflected the views of their constituents.

As part of a bargain to hold on to the White House following the disputed Hayes-Tilden election, in which he was actually the loser in the popular vote, President Hayes withdrew the last federal troops from the South and "home rule" was restored. Hayes and the Republicans wanted tranquility and promoted an alliance of "men of property," both North and South. In expressing his views in letters to friends, Hayes stated, "As to the South, the let-alone policy seems now to be the true course." In another letter he advised, "Time, time is the great cure-all." Hayes' successor, James Garfield, was no more eager to confront the South. Shortly after being sworn into office in 1881, he wrote to a friend, "Time is the only cure for the South's difficulties. In what shape it will come, if it comes at all, is not clear."

Upon the federal government's withdrawal from the South, the forces of White Supremacy were unleashed. Following the fall of Reconstruction governments in the South, "Jim Crow" laws became popular throughout the Old Confederacy. The 1890s saw a wave of segregation laws adopted by southern state legislatures. These laws were a constant reminder to Blacks that they were unfit to associate with Whites on any terms that implied equality. Jim Crow laws hastened the migration of Blacks to the North. Although Northern Whites did not institute a legal system of segregation and disfranchisement, they did develop subtle but identifiable discriminatory patterns of employment and housing. This discrimination led to racial polarization and the growth of Black ghettos in most Northern cities. Blacks were forced out of White neighborhoods into segregated areas by so-called neighborhood improvement associations, boycotts, high rents, anonymous acts of violence and intimidation, and, finally, with the help of lawyers and real estate brokers who devised restrictive covenants in housing.

As Blacks thronged to Atlantic City in ever-growing numbers in search of jobs, little thought was given to their housing. Until they could save money and make a place for themselves, newcomers were huddled like cattle at the rear of luxurious hotels on dirt floors in windowless shacks with little or no ventilation and with accesses that formed a labyrinth of alleys. They were forced to live in worn-out abandoned homesteads and poorly constructed houses without baths or modern lighting, most of which were neither sanitary nor waterproof. The worst living conditions were found among the families of the fishing boat helpers. They lived in houseboats hauled up on the marshy islands near the bay, most of which were so low it was impossible to stand upright and so cramped that parents and children had to sleep together in a single bed.

The results of such living conditions were painfully dramatic. The Black infant mortality rate was double that of White children, and the death rate among Blacks from tuberculosis was more than four times that of Whites. The numbers of persons, especially during the summer months, overwhelmed the supply of housing affordable to Blacks. Few Blacks could afford their own homes. In 1905, the percentage of

Black households with their own homes was less than two percent. Decent housing available for rent to Blacks was so expensive that households were forced to double-up. Many of Atlantic City's Black tenants dealt with high rents by taking in boarders with "privilege of the kitchen" during the summer season. As the Black population swelled, the percentage of households that took in boarders increased from 14.4 percent in 1880 to 57.3 percent in 1915. As the number of Blacks grew, racial discrimination created a chronic condition of crowded, substandard housing.

The growth in the size of the Black workforce became a major concern to the local White establishment. Many readings from the time, which express White attitudes, have an unreal quality. It was almost as if White society wished Blacks would disappear at the end of the workday. Blacks were acceptable as hotel workers, but their presence on the Boardwalk and other public places was unwelcome. The thought of mingling with them socially was intolerable.

The irony of it all was cruel to Blacks. They earned a respectable wage, could vote, and own property. They performed the most personal of services and were entrusted with important responsibilities, but they were barred from restaurants, amusement piers, and booths; were denied shopping privileges by most stores; were admitted to hotels only as workers; were segregated in clinics and hospitals; and could only bathe in one section of the beach, but even then had to wait until after dark. An article appearing in the *Philadelphia Inquirer* in 1893 expressed the revulsion felt by Whites:

> What are we going to do with our colored people? That is the question. Atlantic City has never before seemed so overrun with the dark skinned race as this season ... both the Boardwalk and Atlantic Avenue fairly swarm with them during bathing hours like the fruit in a huckleberry pudding ... Of the hundreds of hotels and boardinghouses ... it is improbable that not a dozen could be found in which White help is employed. And when to the thousands of waiters and cooks and porters are added the nurse girls, the chambermaids, the barbers and boot blacks and hack drivers and other colored gentry in every walk of life, it will be easily realized what an evil it is that hangs over Atlantic City.

The "evil" hanging over the resort was a necessity. Take away all the Black waiters, cooks, porters, and chambermaids complained of by the *Inquirer* and there would have been no one to wait on the reporter who wrote the article.

Without Black workers, Atlantic City would have been a very different place. Absent the cheap labor provided by Blacks, a tourist economy could never have developed and Jonathan Pitney's beach *village* would have remained just that. Between the Civil War and World War I, America's economy was exploding with job opportunities for Whites, both skilled and unskilled. Atlantic City couldn't compete for White workers in the economy of the late 19th century. The nearest population center large enough to generate the required numbers of unskilled workers was Philadelphia. The expansion of that city's industrial economy sucked up every able-bodied person and at wages greater than hotels could afford. There was no chance for Atlantic City's hotels to attract the numbers of White workers needed for such menial work.

The resort had no choice but to pursue Black workers. What none of the White hoteliers could foresee as they began recruiting Blacks was the extent to which their operations would come to rely upon them. Nor could the operators envision what a large presence they would have in the city. And, finally, the last thing business owners gave any thought to was how it would all play out in terms of social integration.

During the early years, Blacks were integrated throughout the city. However, as their numbers increased they were forced out of White neighborhoods and into a ghetto known as the "Northside," an area that was literally the other side of the railroad tracks that ran through that section of town. The Northside was bounded by Absecon Boulevard to the north, Connecticut Avenue to the east, Atlantic Avenue to the south, and Arkansas Avenue to the west. Between 1880 and 1915, the pattern of residence made a radical shift. In 1880, more than 70 percent of the Black households had White neighbors, by 1915 only 20 percent. In a single generation the population had diverged, with Blacks to the Northside and Whites to the Southside and other areas. By 1915, Blacks only went to the Southside to work, to walk on the Boardwalk, and to bathe on their restricted section of the beach.

The Northside became a city within a city. As Blacks encountered racial prejudice, they reached inward to construct a social and institutional life of their own. While White racism had created the physical ghetto, it was civic-minded upper- and middle-class Blacks who led their community to create an institutional ghetto in order to provide services that the White community had denied Blacks. The first major institution established by Blacks in Atlantic City was the church.

According to historian and prominent turn-of-the-20th-century African-American leader, W. E. B. Du Bois, "The Negro Church is the only social institution of the Negroes which started in the African forest and survived slavery." In support of his conclusion, Du Bois argued that the transplanted African priest, "early became an important figure on the plantation and found his function as the interpreter of the supernatural, the comforter of the sorrowing, and as the one who expressed, rudely, but picturesquely, the longing and disappointment and resentment of the stolen people." Black historians, such as Du Bois, have noted that the first established Black churches had only "a veneer of Christianity." Over the years, Blacks found in evangelical sects, such as Baptist and Methodist, a set of beliefs and an opportunity for emotional expression relevant to their everyday experiences in slavery. From the beginning of the importation of slaves, Blacks received Christian Baptism. Initially, there was strong resistance to baptizing slaves. The opposition subsided when laws made it clear that slaves did not become free through the acceptance of the Christian faith. As long as they continued to be property of Whites, Blacks were free to develop their own religions, taking from White churches those practices and tenets that they found relevant to their condition.

African-American historians have characterized their church in slavery as the "invisible institution." The chaos brought about by the Civil War caused a major disruption in that institution. Despite emancipation, the African-American's world had been turned upside down. The social disorganization throughout the South was enormous. The dismantling of Reconstruction caused further deterioration for Blacks. Out of this turmoil the "invisible institution" became visible. It began this process by affiliating with existing independent Negro churches in the North; initially, the most prevalent were the Baptist and Methodist Negro organizations. These denominations, and others, grew rapidly and the church became the glue of Black society. The church was the only effective agency for helping Blacks to cope with racial prejudice. Its growth was a product of necessity. Throughout its development, between the Civil War and World War I, the church was shaped by not only the Biblical teachings of White denominations but, more importantly, by the cultural forces and collective experiences of their isolated social world, both as slaves and freed people.

Through no choice of their own, Blacks who decided to make Atlantic City their home became socially isolated. Out of necessity, these new residents clung to their churches, which became the center of social life in the Black community. It was here that Blacks could freely express themselves through worship and attain status and recognition by participation in the hierarchy and social organizations of their churches. It was common during the off-season for Blacks to combine both religion and recreation on Sundays. Families and friends frequently met at church and brought picnic lunches or uncooked meals with them. After the religious services, they walked to the beach, gathering firewood along the way. There, they camped out for the remainder of the day, eating meals prepared over an open fire and spending the afternoon talking, singing, and playing games.

African-American scholars who have studied the development of their churches in Northern cities have argued that there was a relationship between Black social classes and church affiliation. The upper class usually formed the majority of the relatively small Episcopal, Presbyterian, and Congregational churches; the middle class primarily comprised the more numerous Baptist and Methodist churches; and the lower class gravitated toward the small and numerous Holiness and Spiritualist churches.

The first traditional Black church in Atlantic City was the Bethel African Methodist Episcopal (AME) Church founded in 1875. In 1884, it was renamed St. James AME Church. The next traditional Black church came a year later in 1876. That year, Price Memorial African Methodist Episcopal Zion was founded by a group of locals headed by Clinton Edwards, Dr. George Fletcher, and Cora Flipping. Clinton Edwards was the first Black born in Atlantic City. Dr. Fletcher was the city's first Black physician. Cora Flipping and her son, John, founded one of the first funeral homes in Atlantic City. These people were not only leaders of a new church, but also leaders in their community. Their stature attracted many members. St.

James and Price Memorial are only two examples. To this day, both churches remain a vital force in Atlantic City's Black community.

In the two generations between 1880 and 1930, many church organizations took root in the Black community. By 1930, Atlantic City had a total of 15 traditional Black church organizations. In addition, there were numerous storefront churches that served the needs of migrant Blacks newly out of the South.

The migration of Southern Blacks to the urban North was traumatic for many of them. Stripped of the practices and social structures they had created in order to cope with their lowly status in Southern society, many felt lost in a strange land. Without the customs of the invisible church, these new migrants found it difficult to adjust to the tumult of urban life. The loss of the customary religious practices, which had been their only refuge during slavery, produced an ever-present crisis in the life of the average Black migrant. In order for the visible Black church to play the role needed by its followers, it had to be transformed.

The transformation of the African-American church began with secularization. Black churches began to lose their other-worldliness and focused their energy on the conditions of their congregants in this world. Churches became increasingly interested in the affairs of the community as they impacted upon their members. Another transformation that occurred in Black religious behavior was the emergence of Holiness and Spiritualist churches. Originally formed as personality cults, their leaders had a message directed to the post-slavery experience. In Atlantic City most such churches had their inception in storefronts, side-by-side with row houses and businesses. These storefront churches were usually located in the poorer neighborhoods and served the lower class, especially the newly arrived migrants from the South. As was the case in other Northern cities, storefront churches flourished because they adopted the rural church experience to city life by providing the face-to-face association of a small church. Their existence was due partly to the poverty of their members and the fact that congregants could participate more freely in services during prayers by "shouting."

The inability of the more traditional denominations to serve the needs of Black migrants stimulated the growth of storefront churches. These churches made it possible for Blacks to worship in a manner in which many had practiced in the South. Their religious rites were highly emotional, creating a personal form of worship in which all the members of the congregation became involved. Their pastors preached about a very real heaven and hell. Their church services appealed to those Blacks searching for relief from the insecurities of this world through salvation in the next.

The first Spiritualist church in Atlantic City was founded in 1911 by Levi and Franklin Allen. From that church, 10 other churches sprang up almost immediately. While the sermons of their ministers were other-worldly, these tiny sects never lost sight of the hardships their members had to overcome in this world. The Spiritualist church provided material as well as spiritual assistance to help Southern migrants deal with urban life. A fundamental teaching of Spiritualist doctrine was to serve the community by raising funds to help feed and clothe the poor. Like the Spiritualist churches, the Holiness churches of Atlantic City also found support among the lower class, who were as much devoted to the community as to God. A cornerstone of their church doctrine was never to permit a member to be without the bare necessities of food, shelter, and clothing.

Over time, Atlantic City's Black churches became a social safety net for their members in need. But Sunday was only one day in the week. To build what was required to deal with White racism, namely, a city within a city, Blacks needed more than their church.

Confronted by discrimination and forced segregation, Black leaders began to establish social agencies in the Northside at the turn of the 20th century. The first social agency established by Blacks was a home for the elderly. The Old Folks Home and Sanitarium opened its doors shortly around 1900. Its purpose was to provide convalescent care for Blacks in need, regardless of religion, 65 years or older. The home was run by a Board of Managers consisting of 15 persons who investigated and approved all admissions and established charges depending upon need. The home, which was located at 416 N. Indiana Avenue, was managed well and on July 14, 1922, the Board of Managers had a formal ceremony at the Price Memorial Church, where the mortgage was burned in celebration.

Local Blacks were denied access to the city's Young Men's Christian Association (YMCA). Prominent businessman George Walls organized a group that conceived a plan for the Northside YMCA. Walls was a successful bathhouse operator and a dynamic leader of the Northside who spearheaded numerous causes and lent a helping hand to many Blacks. The "Northside Y" was only one of his accomplishments.

The Northside YMCA operated out of a small cottage on North New York Avenue for more than 30 years. In 1930 it moved to a new building on Arctic Avenue, which contained a gymnasium, recreation room, showers, and dormitory accommodations. Funded entirely through private donations, the Northside YMCA was constructed at a cost of approximately $250,000. The Arctic Avenue branch of the YMCA, as it came to be known, was directed by C. M. Cain. In 1930, a staff of seven secretaries carried on a general character-building YMCA program, with a membership of more than 250 young men. The Arctic Avenue YMCA became the headquarters for many Black community organizations and clubs. Among them were the Northside Board of Trade, the Northside Business and Professional Woman's Club, the Lincoln University Alumni Associates, the Young Men's Progressive Club, the Great Building and Loan Association, the Lion's Social Club, two of the four Black Boy Scout Troops, and the Woman's Home Missionary Society.

In 1916 the Northside Young Women's Christian Association (YWCA) was founded by Maggie Ridley, an active civil leader who was co-owner of the popular Ridley Hotel and one of the founding members of the Jethro Memorial Presbyterian Church. The Northside YWCA operated an employment bureau and provided counseling services to young women. Its facilities were too small for recreational programs so young women used the gymnasium facilities at the Arctic Avenue branch of the YMCA.

As the permanent Black population increased, numerous social societies were established. These groups were often "secret societies," akin to the Masonic Order. These secret societies were one of the vehicles used by Blacks to cope with their minority status. As early as the Revolutionary period, free Blacks found it desirable to join together for social and cultural improvement, economic self-help, and mutual relief. They did this through secret societies. These societies provided their members with one of the few opportunities they had for group expression and cooperation outside of the church. By 1900, Atlantic City had more than a dozen secret societies, among which were the Prince Hall Masons, the Independent Order of Good Samaritans, the Grand United Order of True Reformers, and the Elks. Societies such as the Masons and Elks emphasized moral and social uplift of their race through the conduct of individual members and provided charity to the less fortunate. The Good Samaritans and True Reformers took the lead in providing insurance and business loans for their members. All these societies met at Mason's Hall at North Michigan and Arctic avenues.

Meeting places like the Mason's Hall and the Northside YMCA were critical to a Black social structure. But informal opportunities were also needed. Denied access to the hotels, restaurants, and recreational facilities of the Southside, enterprising Blacks created their own places of amusement. The first known amusement house where Blacks could gather to drink and socialize was established by M. E. Coats in 1879. Another early café and dance hall was Fitzgerald's Auditorium on North Kentucky Avenue. Built in 1890, Fitzgerald's grew in popularity, becoming a bar, restaurant, nightclub, and gambling room. During the Depression, Fitzgerald's was renamed "Club Harlem" and became one of the most chic and talked about nightclubs in the Northeast, frequented by stylish Blacks and Whites. In 1919, the "Waltz Dream," a large recreation center and dance hall at North Ohio Avenue, was established by a Mrs. Thomas, a White woman from Philadelphia. There were weekly wrestling and boxing tournaments, as well as basketball games, to sold-out crowds. The Waltz Dream was the site of many Black charity events and when dances were held at the hall, popular Black orchestras played to capacity crowds of more than 2,000, young and old alike.

In time, the Northside became a self-contained, vibrant community with a wide range of successful Black-owned businesses. The main street of the Black community was Kentucky Avenue. In addition to night spots like Club Harlem, the Northside had its own retail stores, boardinghouses, restaurants, funeral homes, and theaters, which provided a rich life serving most of the Blacks' needs. As for the fire safety needs of the densely populated Northside, there was an all-Black fire company. Engine Company #9 with two platoons and Truck Company #6 with two platoons had their own segregated firehouse at Indiana and Grant avenues. Engine Company #9 earned a national reputation for excellence throughout the country. It played a major role in fighting all the city's fires and held the city record for efficiency six years in a row.

Blacks had developed their own city in response to the racism of Atlantic City's White population. However, there remained two areas where Blacks were unable to build their own institutions and continued to be the victims of racial prejudice: education and healthcare.

There was no discrimination in the school system during the early years of the resort. As long as their numbers remained small, Blacks posed no threat. But as the White community hardened its stance on integrated neighborhoods, so too did it shrink from integrated schools as the number of Black pupils grew.

Prior to 1900, the resort had a single school system with Black and White children being educated together, entirely by White teachers. In 1881, community leader George Walls organized a Literary Society and used it as a vehicle to push for improved education for Black children. Walls presented the local school board with a resolution of his group demanding the hiring of a Black teacher. The board responded by adopting a resolution of its own supporting the idea, but waited 15 years until 1896 before finally yielding and actually hiring a Black teacher.

The lengthy gap in time between the resolution and hiring was in large part a product of the controversy in the Black community caused by Walls' proposal. Walls wanted Black teachers for Black children. He was, in effect, promoting an early Black nationalistic policy of separation of the races, which many Black leaders rejected. Those Blacks favoring integration believed that if the cost of securing Black teachers was the loss of integration, then the price was too high. Walls had his opponents. M. E. Coats, owner of a popular Northside amusement house, and C. Williams, secretary of the Price Memorial AME Zion Church Literary Society, were bitterly opposed to Walls' idea. They feared that Walls' proposal would do more harm than good.

As the controversy raged, Coats and Williams organized a mass meeting of all Blacks. According to historian Herbert J. Foster, Walls might have been physically attacked but for several articles in support of Walls, which appeared in the *Atlantic City Review*. One such article stated:

> This young man is right. The child is at a disadvantage with a white teacher because she does not know his history and environment. She does not have the patience and understanding. When a boy's mother leaves home at six o'clock in the morning, her child is not out of bed, at school time he jumps up, rushes to school without his face

washed or his hair combed, a white teacher does not take that boy aside and make him wash his face, she just goes on with the lesson, ignoring that boy, because she does not know that he is not able to get attention from home. If Negro children have Negro teachers, they will have an inspiration, they will have members of their own race, for ideals and not white ideals that are so diligently instructed about in the schools.

Over time, Walls' proposal gained acceptance and the school board hired Hattie Merritt. Merritt was born in Jersey City and was a graduate of Jersey City Teachers Training School. She was assigned to teach an integrated class at the Indiana Avenue School. Things didn't go well.

Miss Merritt found teaching in an integrated system more than she had bargained for. Her problem wasn't the children but rather the parents. The White parents made her job impossible by coming to school and standing outside the classroom, glaring and taunting her as she tried to teach. Many of these parents demanded that the school board remove their children from her class. Merritt complained to Walls and he in turn complained to the school board. The end result of the controversy came in 1900 when the board decided on a policy of separate education for Black children and the employment of additional Black teachers to instruct them.

With the school board's decision made, Black children were moved out of the city school system and into the basement of the Shiloh Baptist Church. This didn't work out, and the following year the Black students were moved into the Indiana Avenue School, one of the older school buildings, which was converted to an all Black school. As the resort's population grew, the building wasn't large enough to handle the number of school-age Blacks. The next move was to divide the New Jersey Avenue School; half for Whites and half for Blacks. There was a door for "White" and a door for "Colored," and separate play yards to keep the children from mingling.

By 1901, W. M. Pollard, Superintendent of Atlantic City School, claimed proudly that separate classes for Black children was a good thing. In his annual report he stated:

> The employment of colored teachers for separate colored classes has worked very successfully in our city. We

> employ ten colored teachers. These teachers occupy
> rooms in the same building where white children attend.
> The separation is continued as far as the seventh grade,
> after that the colored pupils attend the same grades with
> the white children. This plan has been in many respects
> beneficial for the race.

It's difficult to determine who was vindicated by the results—
Walls or his critics. But the outcome was segregation for as long as
it could be maintained.

Unfortunately, there was no one like Walls to lead the charge on
healthcare for the Black community. Health services for Blacks were
as segregated and meager as Whites could make them. Blacks were
not permitted in White doctors' offices and routine medical services
were dispensed out of a separate Blacks-only clinic in a back room
in city hall until 1899. In that year, the first public hospital was
opened, but it would only treat Blacks in wards separate from
Whites. While the hospital hired Blacks for cooking and cleaning,
there were none to care for patients. As late as 1931, nearly 100
Blacks were employed as orderlies, cooks, janitors, waiters, and
maids, but not one was employed as a nurse or doctor. The few local
Black physicians there were could not see their patients in the hospital, and qualified applicants for training as nurses were turned
away by the hospital's administration, forced to go to other cities for
their education. The message was clear: African-Americans were
servants and that was all they could ever hope to be in Atlantic City.

While upper- and middle-class Blacks of the Northside prospered,
the seasonal employment, squalid housing, and poor health services
for a majority of Blacks took their toll on the quality of life. Without
proper food, clothing, shelter, or medical care, many Black babies
didn't make it through the winter months. A large percentage of their
parents contracted tuberculosis at a rate more than four times that of
Whites.

A city that could host millions of tourists refused to provide facilities for combating tuberculosis among its Black population. To
openly admit to such a problem would have been bad publicity for
the tourist economy, and Atlantic City would have none of that.

# 4

# Philadelphia's Playground

Prostitution was a ticklish subject in the resort. The presence of brothels in turn-of-the-20th century Atlantic City was well known, but talked about little. That's why the exposés on the local prostitution trade published in the *Philadelphia Bulletin* in early August 1890 caused such a stir.

August was the resort's busiest month, and the locals felt the *Bulletin*'s timing was deliberate. The summer was going well for the entire community. The weather was cooperating and tourists flocked to town, spending freely. The *Bulletin* was Philadelphia's most popular newspaper, and many of its readers were regular visitors to Atlantic City. The newspaper had tracked down the infamous Lavinia Thomas and Kate Davis, together with dozens of other veteran prostitutes. They had been chased out of Philadelphia for operating "disorderly houses" and found refuge in Atlantic City. In a series of front-page articles, trumpeted by banner headlines, the *Bulletin* listed the names and addresses of more than 100 local madams and their houses, and righteously condemned their presence. A page one editorial scolded the resort, "What community would hail, as a blessing, or as an evidence of prosperity, the establishment of a vile brothel in its midst?" The newspaper continued its scorn adding, "There are more than 100 of these dens of infamy in Atlantic City. Just think of it—100 such places in a city of this size!"

Resort merchants were upset with the coverage their town was receiving at the hands of the *Bulletin*. They worried it might scare away some of the family trade. Everyone knew the resort was a sanctuary for out-of-town whores, especially during the summer, but no one was comfortable reading about them. A few of the merchants panicked and suggested the brothels be closed temporarily until things calmed down.

Despite the uproar, level heads prevailed and business continued as usual amid reports that local police officers were confiscating the *Bulletin* from Boardwalk newsstands as quickly as the papers arrived.

The *Bulletin* responded with more page one editorials demanding city government to wipe out public prostitution, close down the gambling dens, and shut off the illegal booze. The paper preached at Mayor Harry Hoffman and city council members, "Do you gentlemen realize that you are called upon in your official capacity to take some action in these cases that have been brought to your attention? Can you imagine that gambling houses and brothels will bring wealth and prosperity to your city?" But gambling houses and brothels did bring wealth and prosperity to his city, and the mayor knew something the newspaper's editors did not: The coming of fall would fade the *Bulletin*'s exposés and by next summer everything would return to normal.

While Atlantic City could survive without prostitution, it was an important part of the resort's entertainment package and there was no way the whorehouses would be closed. The *Bulletin* could condemn the peddling of flesh if it wanted, but most of the "johns" were from Philadelphia and Atlantic City was giving them what they wanted. Located only 60 miles from Philadelphia, it was inevitable the resort would be drawn into that city's orbit. Despite present-day myths of the old Atlantic City's grandeur and elegance, Jonathan Pitney's beach village had become to Philadelphia what Coney Island would be to New York—a seaside resort dedicated to providing a cheap, good time for the working man. Cape May could keep the rich— Atlantic City welcomed Philadelphia's blue-collar workers who came to escape Quaker Philadelphia.

The City of Brotherly Love has never been known as a party town. Founded in 1681 as a religious experiment by William Penn, a wealthy Quaker from England, Philadelphia was envisioned as a place where Christians could live together in spiritual union. Penn dreamt of a city governed by the rules of a Friends Meeting. He was committed to liberating his new city from the divisive politics and religious wars of Europe and refused to set up a conventional government, relying instead on brotherly love. Penn's vision never became reality, but the mix of Quakers, Anglicans, Presbyterians, and Baptists, drawn to his city by the policy of religious tolerance, produced a God-fearing population with strict standards of social morality. Honesty and success in business, together with a virtuous life centered on one's church and family, were the ideals of Quaker Philadelphia.

Among no group was the principle of blood being thicker than water more faithfully observed than with the Quakers. Persecuted throughout Europe for their religious beliefs, the Quakers were dispersed around the world and could be found in most seaports with which Philadelphia had commercial relations. Quaker tradition required them to share information on pricing and availability of goods, and their merchants prospered. It's little wonder that Philadelphia, which did not exist until a half-century after the founding of Boston, had become the leading city of the colonies by the time of the Revolutionary War. It was also the most successful seaport in the New World. The city's prosperity was in large part based on the exchange of Pennsylvania farm products for finished goods from Europe. During the Colonial period, Philadelphia was famous for its merchants, shipbuilders, and seamen. It was a major port and played a pivotal role in England's relationship with the American colonies. Following the Revolutionary War, Quaker money transformed Philadelphia into America's first industrial city.

The first half of the 19th century saw Philadelphia turn away from the sea, directing its energies inland. By 1825 the City of Brotherly Love was reaping profits from the coal and iron of Northeastern Pennsylvania. Philadelphia merchants cornered the market on the transportation of coal and were the first to excel in iron manufacturing, gaining notoriety for heavy machinery and ornamental cast iron. However, iron and coal were only part of the economy; finished cotton and wool were also major products of the city. By 1857 Philadelphia had more textile factories than any other city in the world. There were more than 260 factories manufacturing cotton and woolen goods. Cheap coal provided ready steam, giving Philadelphia a decisive edge over other cities in supporting its textile and garment industry. During the American Civil War, it was Philadelphia's textile factories that clothed the Union Army.

The period from the Civil War into the new century saw William Penn's experiment grow to be an industrial giant. In 1860 the city's population stood at 565,000; by 1900, it had reached 1.3 million. Turn-of-the-century Pennsylvania was America's foundry, the center of heavy industry—coal, iron, and steel. New York was the melting pot and Chicago the city of broad shoulders, but Philadelphia is where the Industrial Revolution was won in the United States. The factory mode of production was first introduced to America before 1840 in the cotton mills of New England. After the Civil War, the factory system came to full bloom in Philadelphia. For nearly three generations, Philadelphia had the most diversified and extensive economy of any American city. Its workers produced warships for foreign powers and steam engines for railroad companies around the world. They built tractors and trucks, knitted sweaters and dresses, refined sugar, and manufactured countless other products for the booming American economy.

Philadelphia was home to a staggering number of manufacturers in the iron and steel industry. Its foundries produced one-third of the country's manufactured iron, turning out everything from nuts, bolts, rivets, horseshoes, machine tools, and power hammers to cast iron building fronts, ship plates, locomotive turntables, elevators, ice cream freezers, and sewing machines. In addition, the textile and garment industry continued to rank first in the world. By 1904 more than a third of the city's one-quarter million industrial workers were employed in textile plants, processing one-fifth of all wool consumed in the United States.

A flood of unskilled immigrants was absorbed into Philadelphia through the jobs created by the city's factories. The work wasn't always pleasant, and for many employees the adjustment to the industrial age was traumatic. Mass production of the factory system involved the division of labor into a series of simple, repetitive tasks. This process contrasted sharply with the traditional European craft mode of production in which a single worker produced the end product out of raw materials. Bound in service to machines from dawn to dusk, these unskilled workers were part of a system that had no regard for the Old World order of apprentice-journeyman-master. No longer could a worker attain rank and status according to his skill and experience. For most employees, factory work was degrading, having lost all hope of ever gaining independence through being the master of a craft. The new industrial world broadened the gap between rich and poor by emphasizing the role that capital played in the control of one's life.

As Philadelphia grew into an industrial powerhouse many immigrants made their fortunes. But it took more than money to break into Philadelphia society. As one British traveler noted, "The exclusive feature of American society is no where brought broadly out as it is in the City of Philadelphia ... it is, of course, readily discernible in Boston, New York, and Baltimore; but the line drawn in these places is not so distinctive or so difficult to transcend as it is in

Philadelphia." While William Penn's vision of a Christian community never materialized, the religious beginnings produced a conservative and traditional town.

The Philadelphia establishment grudgingly accepted the Irish, Italian, and Jewish immigrants who manned their factories, but it refused to compromise the rules on social behavior. A phenomenon that developed in response to the city's growing blue-collar population was the "corner saloon," which were little more than shacks placed outside the factories. There were thousands of them, and they provided beer and liquor to workers for a penny a glass. A strong temperance movement, fostered by the local establishment, rose up to stamp out the corner saloon. In 1887 the Pennsylvania Legislature was pressured into adopting the Brooks Law, which severely restricted who could hold a liquor license. In a single year, the number of liquor licenses in Philadelphia was reduced from 5,773 to 1,343. Statutes regulating hours and Sunday Blue Laws further limited the flow of booze to the working class. The patricians who ran Philadelphia were determined to keep their town God-fearing and *sober*.

Philadelphia's blue-collar workers soon found out there was a place they could go for a hell-raising good time. Quaker morality had no place in Atlantic City. Prudish standards preaching abstinence from the vices of alcohol, gambling, and casual sex might be observed at home, but while vacationing at the shore, pleasure was the standard and virtue was put in the closet. As Atlantic City entered the 20th century, it acquired a reputation that made it popular with Philadelphia's factory workers. Sharing the commitment of Boardwalk merchants like John Young were saloonkeepers, madams, and gambling room operators, all determined to give visitors whatever it took to make them happy. The resort existed to make its guests happy. As one long-time resident who understood what Atlantic City was all about has said, "If the people who came to town had wanted Bible readings, we'd have given 'em that. But nobody ever asked for Bible readings. They wanted booze, broads, and gambling, so that's what we gave 'em."

Philadelphia's factories were infernos during the summer. After six days of sucking textile dust or dodging burning cinders, most workers were ready to bust out. Hot summer Sundays weren't spent in church; it was onto the train and down to the seashore. When they arrived, tourists found a city bent on providing pleasures to satisfy every taste, whether lawful or not. For many of Philadelphia's workers, the Sunday excursion was their only chance to get away and the last thing they wanted to hear was Atlantic City's bars were closed on Sunday. Like Pennsylvania, New Jersey's laws prohibited the sale of alcoholic beverages on the Sabbath. In Atlantic City, Sunday wasn't a day of worship but rather the biggest day of the week, and when it came to making a buck, state law was irrelevant. The booze flowed seven days a week with bartenders willing to serve anyone except children.

For the visitor who relished the excitement of gambling, there were plenty of opportunities. Gambling had been popular with tourists and a moneymaker for the resort since the 1860s. Roulette, faro, and poker were popular games found in most of the taverns, as well as in hotels and clubs. There was no problem for a gambler to find a game, regardless of the size of his pocketbook. In one of its annual series of exposés a writer for the *Bulletin* reported,

> As to gambling houses, I can only say this, they are run from away down below Mississippi Avenue where they place a $.05 limit, up to Dutchy's on Delaware Avenue where some of the best known politicians and down-grade businessmen of Philadelphia stake their $5 to $10 on the deal of the little cards. The Lochiel (a gambling casino) is the center of the gambling in the resort … Dutchy (a gambler who had been driven from Philadelphia) rules the Roost.

The prevalence of gambling, prostitution, and unlawful sales of liquor were admitted to openly by local officials. Hundreds of local families relied on illegal sources of income and as long as the visitors were happy, no one interfered. This brazen violation of the law created a furor in the Philadelphia newspapers nearly every summer. In time, resort businessmen and politicians built up immunity to the newspapers' criticisms. They learned that being so remote geographically had its advantages. In the years prior to the automobile, other than direct rail service from Philadelphia or New York, Atlantic City was a difficult place to get to. A judge or legal officer sent to enforce the Sunday Blue Laws would have to be dispatched from Trenton. Whether by horseback or stagecoach, such a trip would take an entire day. The powers that be in Trenton were aware of the goings on in the resort, but no one went to the trouble to do anything about it. Thus, the Philadelphia newspapers banged out their editorials condemning the resort, but they never heard from Atlantic City's officials. Resort politicians knew best how to deal with such complaints—ignore them. When it came to negative news articles about their town, the prevailing attitude among Atlantic City's politicians was always, "Newspaper is what you wrap fish in."

Nothing prevented the resort from providing illicit thrills to its patrons, not even a crusading governor in the New Jersey Statehouse. John Fort was elected in the fall of 1907 campaigning on a promise to enforce the Bishops' Law, which prohibited sale of alcoholic beverages on Sunday. In response to the annual summertime exposés of the *Bulletin*, Governor Fort declared war on Atlantic City. In July of 1908 he vowed to clean up the town. He appointed a special commission to investigate the resort's illegal activities and demanded to know why the county prosecutor refused to file complaints against the saloon keepers, gambling room operators, and madams cited by Philadelphia's newspapers.

In August 1908, Atlantic County Prosecutor Clarence Goldenberg appeared before the governor's commission. Goldenberg testified that personally he saw nothing wrong with the way the resort was run, but that if someone had evidence of wrongdoing, he would prosecute the cases. The prosecutor admitted that witnesses had brought complaints to him, but that on each occasion after a "courteous hearing," the grand jury refused to return an indictment. "It has been impossible to get indictments ... the grand juries are representative of the business interests of the city and the county. The people of the city are getting the government they want."

The grand juries were handpicked by the county sheriff, Smith Johnson. Sheriff Johnson understood the legal system and knew how to protect Atlantic City's businessmen. He controlled the selection of the grand jury and saw to it that everyone chosen to serve was "safe." He even chose jurors who were tavern owners themselves or local businessmen who benefited from vice. When asked why he made no arrests, Johnson told Governor Fort's commission that he had enough to do already and saw no need to "go looking for trouble."

The preliminary reports from his commission enraged Governor Fort. On August 27, 1908, Fort issued a Proclamation branding Atlantic City a "Saturnalia of Vice," demanding the city close the

saloons on Sunday and threatening to exercise Martial Law by sending in the state militia. The Governor's Proclamation read in part:

> No one in office or before the Commission questioned
> the fact that street walking, gambling, houses of ill-fame,
> people of ill-repute, and obscene pictures and open viola-
> tions of the Excise laws exist in Atlantic City ... never
> have the notorious street walkers been worse than they
> have been recently. Never has gambling been more open
> and more of it in the city than it is right now and the
> police department and officials of the city all know it.

The resort's political leaders countered the governor with their
tried and true defense—they ignored him. But the business community was incensed and launched a counterattack. On September 8,
1908, a joint letter from the Atlantic City Board of Trade, the Hotel
Men's Association, and the Businessmen's League was sent to
Governor Fort. It amounted to an "Atlantic City Manifesto," arguing
that the governor was being heavy-handed and had treated the resort
unfairly. As for the gambling, prostitution, and illegal sale of liquor,
the businessmen asserted the "peculiar needs" of a vacation town. It
was simply the local custom of entertaining guests and the traditional
way of doing business in Atlantic City. This broadside at the governor appeared in the *Bulletin* and stated in part:

> The Excise Commission came down and substantially
> demanded that the sale of liquor on Sunday should imme-
> diately cease. This demand, coming as it did in the midst
> of the summer season, after 50 years disregard, was not
> complied with ... She (the resort) hopes that the State
> Legislature will not permit to remain longer upon the
> statute books, in their present shape, laws so crudely
> drawn that, in their endeavor to prevent a wrong, they,
> without necessity, have prohibited a right which all con-
> sider it without harm to anyone, and which is necessary to
> the welfare of one of the State's principal industries,
> namely, its seashore business.

Governor Fort's commission never got around to issuing its final
report until late December. By that time, the furor had subsided and
the report's recommendations were forgotten, as were the governor's

complaints. The notoriety didn't hurt any, and by the following summer it was business as usual.

The more popular Atlantic City became, the greater was the need for cooperation between the resort's businessmen and politicians. Everyone in town lived off the profits from the three months of summer. If the season was slow, it could mean a long, cold winter. Without the blessing of the community, the racketeers who provided the "booze, broads, and gambling" would have had a tenuous existence. Atlantic City's residents understood the role of the local vice industry and appreciated the need for protecting it from interference by law enforcement officials. From the beginning, the police were instructed to turn their heads. Whatever the attraction, if it brought visitors to town and helped to generate a few dollars for the local economy without hurting anyone, then it was legal by Atlantic City's standards.

As the resort's economy matured, the vice industry's relationship with the local government became more structured. The politicians saw the easy money being made by the racketeers and demanded a piece of the action. Prior to the beginning of the 20th century, an informal partnership between the politicians and racketeers ran the town with broad-based consent of the community. Day-to-day decisions were made by a three-man coalition consisting of County Clerk Louis Scott, Congressman John Gardner, and County Sheriff Smith Johnson. Scott was the unofficial leader of the threesome. His most trusted lieutenant and protégé was a young hotelier, Louis Kuehnle.

Born on Christmas Day 1857, Louis Kuehnle was tall and broad-shouldered. He had a ruddy complexion, dark brown eyes, and a bald head nearly always covered with a hat. Kuehnle smoked big cigars, wore dapper clothes, and enjoyed a good time with the boys. He also had a fondness for dogs. His terrier, "Sparkey," was his constant companion, following him around town for nearly 15 years. Sparkey went everywhere with his master, including city council meetings, restaurants, and church. Kuehnle's parents were German immigrants from New York, where his father was renowned as a chef. The Kuehnles were attracted by Atlantic City's growing tourist economy.

Kuehnle's father had acquired a small fortune working in New York and quickly made a successful transition from chef to hotel owner. He purchased a large hotel in the mainland community of Egg

Harbor City, the New York Hotel, and another in Atlantic City known as Kuehnle's Hotel. The latter was built shortly after Richards' second railroad and was located in a prime spot on the north side of Atlantic City near the railroad station. It was a typical "hotel," a large boardinghouse, for its day, with a wraparound porch highlighted by Victorian gingerbread and wicker furniture. Kuehnle's Hotel was a popular meeting place year-round for local residents.

By age 18, Louis Kuehnle took over the management of the hotel in Atlantic City. In a short time, Kuehnle was running the hotel on his own, looking after every detail and overseeing everything from changing sheets and cleaning the barroom to waiting on guests in the dining room. Kuehnle was a typical resort hotelier and enjoyed playing the role of host. Through the management of his family's hotel Kuehnle became well known by everyone in town. He was free with his money; he entertained generously and never denied a request for help from the resort's poor. Kuehnle joined the Atlantic City Yacht Club and became active in its affairs, serving as chairman. He earned the unofficial rank of "Commodore," a moniker that stayed with him the remainder of his life. In time, the entire town referred to him only as "the Commodore." During the next 20 years, the Commodore created a loyal crew of supporters by doing favors and offering his hotel as a meeting place for anyone who needed it.

Kuehnle's Hotel became known by both politicians and the general public alike as "the Corner." The ruling coalition of Scott, Gardner, and Johnson met regularly at the Corner to plan their strategy and to hear requests from their constituents. From the porch of Kuehnle's Hotel, these three power brokers dispensed patronage and favors. In time, people seeking political favors had to first clear their petitions with Kuehnle who had the ear of Scott and his partners. Trusted implicitly by the members of this ruling coalition, Kuehnle's voice soon became a potent factor in political decisions. At the time of Scott's death in 1900, his two cohorts had neither the youth nor desire to assume control and Kuehnle became the unchallenged leader. In a short time after Scott's death, the Commodore was *Boss* and nothing was done without his okay; every candidate, employee, city contract, and mercantile license required his nod of approval.

When things got hot everyone turned to the Commodore. The scorching attacks of Philadelphia's newspapers and the threats made by reform governors caused anxious moments nearly every summer.

The Corner was the scene of many late night meetings with Kuehnle calming the politicians' fears by reminding them that publicity of any kind was good for business. One popular story has it that the Commodore assured his lieutenants and the local merchants that if the governor ever did send down the militia, then Kuehnle would have the local whores greet them at the train station.

Kuehnle's closest ally was Smith Johnson, who served as sheriff every other three years from 1890 to 1908. State law prohibited a sheriff from succeeding himself and Johnson was forced to alternate from sheriff to deputy sheriff. When his first term for office was up, Johnson nominated his loyal deputy, Sam Kirby, to run for sheriff. Upon his election, Kirby appointed Johnson his deputy and so on and so on for 20 years. As sheriff, Johnson doled out political patronage and controlled the fees collected by his office. There were charges for such things as serving summonses, conducting real estate foreclosure sales, executing on civil judgments, and housing inmates in the county jail. These fees totaled $50,000 annually at a time when a round-trip excursion ticket from Philadelphia cost $1. The fees were the personal income of the sheriff and he answered to no one except his political allies. Johnson's fees together with the protection money paid by the gambling rooms, brothels, and saloons financed Kuehnle's organization. When the fee system was abolished by state government and the sheriff limited to an annual salary of $3,500, the Commodore squeezed the racketeers harder, making protection money from the vice industry the life blood of the local Republican Party.

The source of Kuehnle's power included more than protection money. The Commodore was embraced by the business community, which supported his efforts to build up the resort. Kuehnle's favorite slogans were "A bigger and better Atlantic City," and "Boost, don't knock." He succeeded in identifying the local Republican Party with the welfare of the community. Any criticism of the Commodore's regime became an attack on the city. Hoteliers and Boardwalk merchants would shudder at reformers complaining of corruption. "It will hurt the town," they said, "don't spoil the season." Success of "the season" was everything to local residents. With tourism the only industry in town, the months of June, July, and August were crucial. Nothing could interfere with the visitors' happiness and the last thing merchants needed was some reformer tampering with things.

The Commodore understood that Atlantic City's business owners would gladly sacrifice honest government for a profitable summer and he gave them what they wanted. Kuehnle protected the rackets from prosecution and worked with the tourist industry to ensure its success. In exchange, the community let him call the shots.

Louis Kuehnle used his power to help transform a sprawling beach village into a modern city. He understood the need for making investments in public facilities to accommodate the growth generated by Atlantic City's increased popularity. He believed the resort needed a larger, permanent Boardwalk and saw to it that a new Boardwalk with steel pilings and girders was constructed. Resort residents, in particular the hotels and shops, were the victims of a telephone monopoly. Kuehnle broke it up by starting an opposing company, which later was controlled by an independent telephone system with reduced rates. The city's electric lighting was inadequate and expensive; the Commodore backed a competing utility and prices came down. Natural gas was selling at $1.25 per 1,000 feet and Kuehnle organized a gas company, which resulted in prices going down to $.90 per 1,000. The local trolley system, important to the convenience of both tourists and residents, was a mess. Kuehnle organized the Central Passenger Railway Company, which was eventually sold to the Atlantic City and Shore Company, that gave residents and visitors alike first-rate street and railway service.

Kuehnle was corrupt, but he had a vision for his town's future and he worked the levers of power to make that vision a reality. Vitally important, the Commodore realized that without a secure source of fresh water, this island community would never become a true city. His foresight was the driving force behind the purchase of several large tracts on the mainland that were used as sites for wells for Atlantic City's water system. (A portion of this acreage would years later become the site of the Atlantic City International Airport.) It was also his regime that established the city's first modern sewage treatment facility. Additionally, street paving, or the lack of it, had been a sore point ever since the resort was founded, with visitors and locals having to constantly dodge mud puddles. Kuehnle went into the paving business, and in a short time the resort had safe and clean paved avenues and streets. Under Kuehnle's reign, all the elements for the infrastructure of a modern city were put into place.

Atlantic City prospered and so did the Commodore. The companies organized by Kuehnle were all sold at handsome profits to buyers who knew they would have no difficulty obtaining franchises and contracts from the city. Kuehnle was one of the owners of the Atlantic City Brewery, and its beer was the most popular in the resort. If a saloonkeeper wanted his liquor license renewed and not be cited for selling brew on Sunday, he bought the right beer. Kuehnle amassed a fortune.

Money was only part of the foundation for the Commodore's machine. As the County Republican leader, Kuehnle had control over the appointment of the county prosecutor and judges. Only loyal party people got into power. Working closely with the county sheriff's office, Kuehnle set up a network that insulated his organization from the legal system. It was the sheriff who selected the persons who served on grand juries. The juries, handpicked by Smith Johnson, would never indict any of the Commodore's people.

During Kuehnle's years in power there was no Democratic opposition. Atlantic City's population accounted for more than 60 percent of the population in Atlantic County. The remainder of the county was populated by people either dependent on the Atlantic City tourist trade or small farmers who tended to vote Republican. The strength of the Republican Party in Atlantic County was typical of South Jersey at that time. For more than 30 years after the American Civil War, the politics of the southern New Jersey counties was dominated by United States Senator William J. Sewell of Camden. Sewell, an Irish immigrant, had served as a major general in the Union Army and fought at both Gettysburg and Chancellorsville. After the war, he entered politics and served as state senator for nine years, becoming president of the Senate in 1880. The next year he was elected by the legislature to the United States Senate, where he served two terms. Sewell's long public service and forceful personality made him a leader of the New Jersey Republican Party and the dominant force of the Republican Party in South Jersey. With Sewell in power, there was no hope for a Democratic Party anywhere in South Jersey. As Jonathan Pitney had learned, Democrats had no chance at real political power.

The Commodore wasn't content just having control of Atlantic City politics. If he were to catch the attention of the state Republican organization, he would need to dominate things totally. In order to do that, he had to run up election margins in a big way. A key ingredient to his strategy was the manipulation of the resort's African-American voters. From the time of the Civil War until the election of Franklin D. Roosevelt during the Great Depression, the overwhelming majority of Blacks who voted in this country voted Republican, the party of Abraham Lincoln. The presence of such a substantial minority, with a predictable voting pattern, made Atlantic City's African-American population a pawn in Kuehnle's rise to power. He exploited them for every vote he could.

The Commodore became enormously popular in the Northside by providing for needy Blacks out of work during the winter months. The off-season could be a harsh struggle for many year-round residents of the Northside, and Kuehnle helped them make it through the winter. Under the Commodore, the Republican Party established its own private welfare system, dispensing free food, clothing, and coal and paying doctor bills. At Kuehnle's prompting, the hotel and boardinghouse owners required all of their employees to register to vote. Any African-American worker who failed to register was harassed until he did. On Election Day, Kuehnle's lieutenants went into the Northside and rousted Black voters out of their homes. Groups of about 20 Blacks at a time were taken in wagons from ward to ward voting repeatedly, for which they were paid $2 a ballot. The scheme of election fraud was denounced by a national magazine of the day as "the rawest ever known in the country."

Republican election-day workers stood outside the polls with their pockets crammed with $2 bills. They each had a list of deceased and fictitious voters whose names appeared on the voter registration rolls. As the African-American voters entered the polls, they were assigned a name and given a sheet of carbon paper, the size of the regular ballot, together with a sample ballot. "There is your name and there is your address. Now, for God's sake, don't forget where you live." The voter then took his carbon and the sample into the booth with him and marked the regular ballot on the carbon over the sample ballot. When he returned outside, if the markings were right, the voter received his $2. Voters who wanted a second try at the same poll would wait for another Black voter and exchange a hat or an overcoat and then receive another name under which to vote.

Atlantic County's small population kept the Commodore's machine from being a major influence in a statewide general election;

however, it often was a decisive factor in a primary. The ability to crank out lopsided votes in a Republican primary made Kuehnle a power broker on the state level. Politicians respect votes no matter how they're gotten and Kuehnle was wooed by every Republican seeking statewide office. Within the first decade of the 20th century, the Atlantic City machine was one of the key political organizations in New Jersey, able to influence the selection of candidates for governor, senator, and congressman. Kuehnle's stature as a statewide leader increased his power at home. But not everyone was a fan of the Commodore.

There was a small but vocal reform movement made up of the owners of family-oriented businesses and the large hotels along the Boardwalk. Some of the large Boardwalk hotel owners, like the White family of the Marlborough-Blenheim, were from Philadelphia with Quaker backgrounds. They opposed Kuehnle's tactics and wanted Atlantic City to be a middle-class family resort without relying on "booze, broads, and gambling." Others—a small minority— continued to dream of Atlantic City as a genteel resort for the upper crust as Jonathan Pitney had envisioned. Both the Quakers and the dreamers felt things had gone too far under the Commodore. They wanted the resort cleaned up and, though a tiny minority, were a source of tension in the community. This reform group made itself heard through the *Atlantic City Review* and its editor, Harvey Thomas. A coldly serious, steely looking, hard-hitting muckraker, cut from the same cloth as Lincoln Steffens, Harvey Thomas had been brought to town by a clique of wealthy Boardwalk hoteliers who resented Kuehnle and wanted him out of power.

There was a definite class distinction between the large hotel owners along the Boardwalk and the smaller hotels and boarding-houses throughout the town. The Boardwalk hotels featured themselves as hosts to the refined elements of society. "Booze, broads, and gambling" were offensive to them and their clientele. But the backbone of the resort were the blue-collar visitors who stayed in boardinghouses. They came to town to let loose and enjoy the pleasures they couldn't find in Philadelphia. The boardinghouse owners were firmly in Kuehnle's camp, while the Boardwalk hoteliers viewed him as a power hungry bully. Their chance to launch an attack on the Commodore came in the gubernatorial election of 1910.

The election of 1910 was a milestone for both Kuehnle and New Jersey. The Republican candidate for governor was Vivian Lewis, a favorite of the Commodore. The Atlantic County Republican Organization was the first to endorse Lewis' bid for governor. Kuehnle was friendly with Lewis and knew his candidate could be counted on to overlook the way things were done in the resort. Lewis' opponent was a scholarly reformer, Woodrow Wilson, who campaigned on a pledge to wipe out corruption at all levels of government.

Woodrow Wilson was the son, grandson, and nephew of Presbyterian ministers. While a religious background was common among politicians of his day, Wilson was a crusader who saw things in black and white. Impersonal in his relations, he attracted supporters in much the same way people latch on to an abstract principle. A visionary and idealist, he never permitted personal feelings to interfere with his policies and couldn't forgive supporters who failed to measure up to his standards.

When Wilson entered New Jersey politics, the state was a prime example of what reformers throughout the country were battling. In New Jersey, according to one observer, "The domination of politics by corporation-machine alliances had reached its full flower." The state was ruled by an oligarchy composed of the captains of industry, in particular, the railroad and utility interests. Republican and Democratic bosses working hand-in-glove had permitted these special interests to become entrenched in New Jersey's political machinery. Throughout the state there was a deep-seated hostility to large corporations and the special privileges they received from state government. There were progressives in both parties who had managed to elect candidates to the legislature, but the governor's office remained a captive of the special interests. By 1910, the party bosses knew the public was primed to elect a reform governor. The state Democrats were desperately seeking a new leader who could carry their party into power on the crest of the progressive wave that was rolling over the country.

Woodrow Wilson was there at the right time. A transplant from Virginia, Wilson had come to New Jersey to serve as president of Princeton University. His background as a Southerner and a minister's son blended well with the contempt for machine politics that prevailed in educated Northern circles. Wilson was a political scientist and a noted author. His book *Congressional Government*, published in 1885, had attracted widespread interest and won lasting acclaim as a classic of American political analysis. From the mid-1880s to 1910, he was recognized as the country's most author- itative writer on political science. Wilson was also the master of the spoken word and used his talents to generate support for the aca- demic community in a way no university president before him had. While at Princeton, he attracted greater attention than any other col- lege president in American history.

Wilson's tenure as president of Princeton University gave him a pulpit from which to speak out on political issues of the day. Shortly after the 1904 election, Wilson emerged as a spokesman for conser- vative Democrats in opposition to William Jennings Bryan. In 1906 he received several votes in the New Jersey Legislature as a minor- ity Democratic candidate for United States Senator. There was even talk of him as a dark horse candidate for President or Vice President in 1908. As spokesman for the anti-Bryan Democrats, Wilson won the attention of a number of Wall Street financiers and politicians who began boosting him as a presidential candidate. Several promi- nent editors, including George Harvey of *Harper's Weekly*, Henry Watterson of the *Louisville Courier Journal,* and William Laffin of the *New York Sun* went out of their way to give Wilson positive exposure.

George Harvey became a loyal supporter of Wilson after hearing him make an address at Princeton. In 1906, Harvey began printing a headline across the cover of each issue of *Harper's Weekly*; it read, "For President—Woodrow Wilson." The publisher wanted to be a kingmaker and assigned a staff writer to begin "advertising" Wilson with a view to making him Governor of New Jersey in 1910 and a presidential candidate in 1912. Harvey took it upon himself to run interference for Wilson's candidacy, making the initial contact with the state's Democratic boss, former U.S. Senator James Smith.

Jim Smith was an old-time political boss, likeable and gentle- manly, who had held a prominent position in both the business and political life of New Jersey for more than a generation. From his headquarters in Newark, he dominated the powerful Essex County Democratic machine and was the state's most powerful Democratic power broker. Smith didn't need much convincing. New Jersey's Democrats were a minority and if they were to have any hope of suc- ceeding in the election of 1910, they had to run a reform candidate.

The nomination for governor was offered to Wilson with no strings attached. If elected, he would have a free hand as governor.

Wilson was a dynamic campaigner. Sounding much like a fire-and-brimstone preacher, he pounded away at his opponent's weaknesses. He reminded voters that his opponent had been handpicked by the Republican machine and would be no more than a caretaker for the special interests. Wilson campaigned against the boss system and asserted he could break it up through political reforms and by helping independent men gain election to the legislature. His candidacy held out the promise of not only the regeneration of the Democratic Party, but of all state government.

During his campaign, Woodrow Wilson appeared in Atlantic City before a group of prohibitionists and reformers. The rally had been organized by Kuehnle critic, newspaperman Harvey Thomas. Speaking before a crowd of 2,000—mostly out-of-towners—Wilson promised that one of the first places he would root out corruption and bossism was in Atlantic City.

The Commodore saw this preacher's son for the very real threat he was. Kuehnle knew that a zealous moralist in the governor's office would be trouble for Atlantic City. It's likely there was more than one all-night strategy session at the Corner presided over by the Commodore. The Republican organization pulled out all the stops in an effort to elect Vivian Lewis. In less than six months time, there were 2,000 new voters registered in Atlantic City and the turnout on Election Day was a record one, with Lewis carrying the town handily. Much to the Commodore's dismay, Wilson was elected together with Democratic majorities in both houses of the Legislature. Upon checking the election returns in Atlantic City, Woodrow Wilson noticed that his Republican opponent had received more votes than the city had registered voters.

Governor Wilson was determined to drive Kuehnle from power. Riding the crest of popularity created by his victory, Wilson had the legislature form a committee to investigate election fraud, focusing on Atlantic City. The "Macksey Committee," named for its Chairman, Assemblyman William P. Macksey, found an abundance of evidence. The committee held 19 sessions at which it took testimony of more than 600 witnesses, producing more than 1,400 pages of sworn statements. The committee's findings could have served as a basis for another political treatise by Wilson.

To no one's surprise, the Macksey Committee learned that votes were purchased on a broad scale, primarily in the Northside. One witness called by the committee testified of his confrontation with a Republican poll worker who was doling out cash to African-American voters outside one of the voting places. "You are getting that man to vote in somebody's name. Every one of you ought to go to prison." To which he was told, "If you don't get out of here they [referring to the Blacks] will trample you to death." The dialogue continued, "I said, 'Before they trample me to death there will be a few dead negroes here.' He says, 'Don't call them niggers.' I said, 'I didn't call them niggers, I called them negroes, but if you are buying your votes you are worse than a nigger for buying votes.'"

There were key leaders of the Northside who were part of Kuehnle's organization. One such poll worker was discussed before the Macksey Committee. "So after that, men came out from the polls and would hand the man a slip; he was a very well dressed darkey, a dude, rather, he was too well-dressed for his color, he walked up the street with them and he would take out his roll and give them money. I saw him do that time and time again."

In all, there were approximately 3,000 fraudulent votes cast in Atlantic City in the election of 1910, but there's more to the story. In one district, two persistent Democratic challengers who protested fraudulent votes were drugged. They were given drinking water with a "shoe fly" in it. Shoe fly is a concoction of tartar emetic, which induces vomiting, and eleatarium, which causes diarrhea. It is colorless, odorless, and tasteless. One drink of a shoe fly and a Democratic challenger was done for the day. New registrants were added to the voter registration books on Election Day by the officials at the polls. Ballot boxes were removed from the view of the general public and challengers who objected were forcibly removed from the polls by local police officers.

Kuehnle's people engaged in a practice known as "colonizing" voters, which involved hundreds of fictitious voters being registered at local hotels. The fraud was so widespread and well organized that it couldn't possibly have occurred without a close working relationship between the Republican organization and dozens of small hotel and boardinghouse owners of Atlantic City. Additionally, many transient seasonal workers of various hotels, restaurants, shops, and arcades, referred to as "floaters," registered to vote in Atlantic City by using their place of summer employment as their address. They returned from out-of-town to cast their vote on Election Day. That year, hundreds of floaters were given train fare and paid to come back to town to vote for Vivian Lewis.

The Commodore himself was called before the committee and was asked what he knew of "the padded registration in Atlantic City last Fall." In response to a question concerning his involvement in voting fraud, Kuehnle replied, "Why my instructions to the workers was that we didn't want any padded lists, because we had enough Republican votes in Atlantic City and county to win the election at any time." Despite the Commodore's testimony, the Macksey Committee had more than enough information to prove widespread voter fraud.

The next step for Governor Wilson was to convert the committee's report into criminal indictments. That wouldn't be easy, and assuming an indictment could be obtained, securing convictions would be even harder. The last line of defense for Kuehnle's machine were key players in the criminal justice system who could be counted on to frustrate the process. Realizing that County Prosecutor Clarence Goldenberg was a pawn of the Commodore, Wilson asked the legislature to enact special legislation enabling the attorney general to go into any county and conduct an investigation, replacing the local prosecutor. The legislature gave the governor what he wanted, and Attorney General Edmund Wilson moved in to put together criminal charges. But there was one more obstacle, the county sheriff. The sheriff was now Smith Johnson's son, Enoch. Sam Kirby had moved on to county clerk. Enoch Johnson had learned how to draw a grand jury from his father and there was no way any grand jury he chose would return an indictment against an Atlantic City politician.

The first presentation of evidence secured by the Macksey Committee was to a grand jury sitting before Judge Thomas Trenchard, a product of the Commodore's machine. After hearing the evidence presented, the grand jury deliberated and found no basis for an indictment. Governor Wilson was incensed and made a move to replace both Sheriff Johnson and Judge Trenchard. Wilson used a vacancy in the court system to appoint Samuel Kalish, an independently wealthy and respected trial attorney from Mercer County. Upon arriving in Atlantic County, Judge Kalish ordered the sheriff to draw a grand jury and to present the members in court to be admonished prior to commencing their duties. When the jurors appeared, Attorney General Wilson noticed that one of them was Thomas Bowman, who had been named in the Macksey Committee report. Bowman was one of the defendants to be charged with election fraud. Judge Kalish dismissed Bowman and the entire grand jury.

Over Johnson's protests Kalish utilized a little known statute to appoint a committee of "elisors" and empowered them to choose a grand jury of 23 men, comprised of Republicans, Democrats, Independents, and Prohibitionists. The Commodore was powerless to stop Attorney General Wilson. With Sheriff Johnson and his handpicked grand jury out of the way, the criminal justice system proceeded.

The new grand jury returned indictments naming more than 120 defendants, many of whom held positions in city government or the Republican organization. There was Kuehnle, Sheriff Enoch Johnson, Mayor George Carmany, City Councilman Henry Holte, City Clerk Louis Donnelly, Building Inspector Al Gillison, Health Inspector Theodore Voelme, Atlantic City Electric President Lyman Byers, and on and on. These indictments all dealt with election fraud and it was naïve for Governor Wilson to expect an Atlantic County jury to return guilty verdicts against officials of the Republican Party. Nearly everyone was acquitted.

One of the defendants acquitted was Enoch Johnson. His trial helped launch him on his way to becoming Kuehnle's successor. Represented by long-time friend and political attorney Emerson Richards, Johnson took the stand in his own defense and arrogantly defied Attorney General Wilson. He referred to the presiding judge by his first name and addressed the jurors directly, many of whom were supporters of the Republican machine. Neither Johnson nor anyone else of importance in Kuehnle's organization was convicted of election fraud.

Simultaneous with the investigation into election fraud was an inquiry of official corruption in Atlantic City's government. It was no secret that Kuehnle and his lieutenants had been personally benefiting from municipal contracts. The requirement of public employees to pay a portion of their salary to the Republican Party and kickbacks on city contracts were common knowledge.

In July 1911, newspaperman Harvey Thomas arranged a meeting between Attorney General Wilson and private detective William J. Burns. Long before criminal lawyers would debate the concept of entrapment, Burns hit upon an idea to smoke out Atlantic City's elected officials, which the attorney general endorsed. Burns had one of his operatives, Frank Smiley, pose as "Mr. Franklin," a successful New York City contractor. Mr. Franklin rented an elaborate suite of rooms at one of the fancy Boardwalk hotels and made a splash around town as a big spender. Mr. Franklin got the ear of the city councilmen and proposed to each of them that what the resort needed was a concrete Boardwalk. He persuaded five council members to adopt an ordinance appropriating $1,000,000 for the project and paid each of them $500 for their vote. The entire transaction with each council member was recorded by the newly invented dictograph. When confronted with the stenographic transcript of their conversations with Mr. Franklin, each of the councilmen confessed.

The other area scrutinized was the Commodore's personal business interests. In addition to the Atlantic City Brewery, Kuehnle was a shareholder in the United Paving Company. It was one of many firms Kuehnle had formed over the years to obtain government contracts. United Paving was successful from its inception and in a short time had contracts totaling $600,000. It was successful on every municipal project it competed for. There might have been lower bidders, but they were never able to comply with the bid specifications, so United Paving got the jobs.

In 1909, the city council let out for bid a contract to install new timber water mains from the mainland to Absecon Island. It was known as the Woodstave Project. Then, as now, Atlantic City received its drinking water from artesian wells on the mainland seven miles over the meadows. For years, the water had been pumped into the city in small pipes. To accommodate Atlantic City's growth, it was necessary to install one large water main. United Paving hadn't bid on the project because Kuehnle was a member of the Water Commission and there was an obvious conflict of interest. Instead, a dummy bidder, Frank S. Lockwood, a clerk in United Paving, was awarded the contract at a bid price of $224,000. On the same day the bid was awarded Lockwood assigned his contract rights to a firm called Cherry and Lockwood, Cherry being William I. Cherry, the Commodore's partner in United Paving. The Woodstave Project only partially involved paving, but Kuehnle and Cherry wanted the entire contract. Their greed caused the contract price to increase beyond $300,000 with all of the extras being approved by Kuehnle as chairman of the Water Commission. The commission's records showed that of the 15 vouchers submitted for payment, 12 had been personally approved by Kuehnle.

This was all Attorney General Wilson needed. The jury had no choice but to return a guilty verdict. The Commodore's conviction and the success at exposing the widespread corruption in the resort made a valuable trophy for Woodrow Wilson on his march to the White House.

The Commodore appealed his conviction and by the time the final ruling came down upholding the verdict, Woodrow Wilson had gone on to become president. Kuehnle was sentenced to a year of hard labor and $1,000 fine. His sentence began in December 1913 and before going to jail, he made arrangements for Christmas gifts of food and clothing to be given to Atlantic City's poor. Surrogate Emmanual Shaner and Louis Donnelly saw to it that several thousand gifts were given out in the Northside.

The Commodore served his time without complaint. Upon his release from jail, he went to Bermuda for a lengthy vacation and then for an extended visit to Germany, his parents' homeland. Nearly a year later he returned to the resort tanned and rested, to a warm but quiet reception from his many friends. He soon learned things had changed during his absence. A new leader, Enoch "Nucky" Johnson, had emerged as the boss of Atlantic City's Republican Party. The Commodore had known Nucky as Smith Johnson's son, and after the elder Johnson's death, the two became close. Kuehnle confided in him as he had his father. Nucky was seen by many as the Commodore's protégé and with his acquittal at the election fraud trial, he was the heir apparent when Kuehnle went off to jail.

After the Commodore's return, he and Nucky had several skirmishes, but there was no doubt about who was in control. Finally, they reached an accommodation with Johnson agreeing to support the Commodore for city commissioner. Kuehnle was elected in 1920 and re-elected each time his four-year term ended, until his death in 1934. A tribute to his popularity was the naming of a local street in his honor. Kuehnle had the undying affection of the public, but Nucky Johnson had the power, and he used it in a way that made the Commodore look like a choirboy.

Steve Buscemi as Nucky Thompson, based on the real-life Enoch "Nucky" Johnson

Paz de la Huerta as Lucy Danziger, Nucky's sometime girlfriend

Michael Pitt as Nucky's protégé Jimmy Darmody

Stephen Graham as the young Al Capone

Steve Buscemi as Nucky

Kelly Macdonald as Margaret Schroeder, a local woman whom Nucky befriends.

Michael K. Williams as Chalky White, the self-styled mayor of Atlantic City's African-American community

Michael Stuhlbarg as Arnold Rothstein

Vincent Piazza as Lucky Luciano

Steve Buscemi as Nucky

Shea Whigham as Nucky's brother Sheriff Eli Thompson (L),
with Steve Buscemi as Nucky and Michael Pitt as Jimmy Darmody

**Stephen Graham as Al Capone**

**Kelly Macdonald as Margaret Schroeder**

**Aleksa Palladino as Angela Darmody**

Michael Stuhlbarg as Arnold Rothstein (L) with Vincent Piazza as Lucky Luciano

Steve Buscemi as Nucky with Dabney Coleman as his mentor Louis "Commodore" Kaestner, based on the real-life Louis Kuehnle

Michael Shannon as Federal Agent Van Alden

Kelly Macdonald as Margaret Schroeder

Paz de la Huerta as Lucy Danziger

A party at Babette's nightclub

Steve Buscemi as Nucky addressing a meeting of the Women's Temperance League

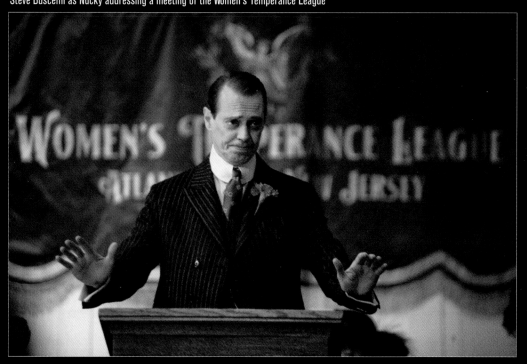

Vincent Piazza as Lucky Luciano

Executive Producer, Writer, and Series Creator Terence Winter

Executive Producer Martin Scorsese, directing a scene from the pilot episode

Michael Pitt with Terence Winter

Martin Scorsese with Steve Buscemi

Michael Shannon as Agent Van Alden

Dabney Coleman as Commodore Kaestner

Michael Pitt as Jimmy Darmody with Steve Buscemi as Nucky

# 5

## The Golden Age of Nucky

Joe Hamilton was the back-up driver. Louie Kessel didn't leave town often but when he did, Joe was first choice to drive the boss around. This night the stops were a baseball game, a wake, and a Fourth Ward Republican Club meeting, followed by dinner at Babette's.

A few innings of the ball game was enough and he was ready to leave. When Joe returned with the limousine there was a young woman with the boss. Joe got out to open the door and was told to drive out of town to Absecon before heading to the wake. The rest is better told by Hamilton. "There I am driving along talking to Mr. Johnson with a pretty little tart seated next to him. The next thing I knew she's got her head in his lap and Mr. Johnson's grinnin' from ear to ear." The boss never missed a chance to mix pleasure with business.

For nearly 30 years, Enoch "Nucky" Johnson lived the life of a decadent monarch, with the power to satisfy his every want. Tall (6 feet 4 inches), trim, and broad-shouldered, Nucky Johnson was a ruggedly handsome man with large, powerful hands, a glistening bald head, a devilish grin, friendly gray eyes, and a booming voice. In his prime, he strode the Boardwalk in evening clothes complete with spats, patent leather shoes, a walking stick, and a red carnation in his lapel. Nucky rode around town in a chauffeur-driven, powder blue Rolls Royce limousine, maintained several residences, hosted lavish parties for hundreds of guests, used the local police as his private gendarmes, had a retinue of servants to satisfy his every want, and an untaxed income of more than $500,000 per year. His antics were reported widely and at the height of his reign he was a national phenomenon, hailed as "the Czar of the Ritz." Despite his notoriety, Johnson was a product of Atlantic City who couldn't have flourished anywhere else.

Enoch Lewis Johnson was born on January 20, 1883, in Smithville, a small bayside farming village several miles north of Atlantic City. The son of Kuehnle ally Sheriff Smith Johnson, Nucky spent his childhood moving between Atlantic City and Mays Landing according to his father's rotation as sheriff. During the years as sheriff, Johnson and his family lived in the sheriff's residence next to the county jail. The years as undersheriff, the Johnsons lived in a rambling frame home in the resort so the sheriff and his wife could enjoy the social life of a booming vacation center.

Nucky's parents, Smith and Virginia Johnson, had used politics to escape the backbreaking work of farming. Election to sheriff was the ticket to an easy life and status in the growing resort. Smith Johnson was a broad-chested bear of a man with a thick black mustache. Standing six-foot-two, weighing 250 pounds, and having paws for hands, he had the strength to lift a wagon. "No one *ever* gave Sheriff Johnson a hard time." Virginia was a tall, slender, beautiful woman with long, auburn hair, and hands with fingers meant to play the piano. She was always exquisitely dressed and was "the kind of woman that comes to mind when you think of an elegant Victorian lady." Virginia was every bit the politician in her own right. "She was big on charity, organizing fundraisers and whatnot, for the poor people, but she always made sure they knew the help came from the Republican Party."

Through his parents, Nucky was immersed in politics long before he was old enough to vote. As a child and a young man, Nucky watched his father make a plaything of government. The law forbidding the re-election of a sheriff was supposed to prevent an individual from accumulating too much power. But the cozy relationship between Smith Johnson and Sam Kirby made a mockery of the re-election ban contained in the state constitution. The sheriff's employees were handpicked solely on the basis of patronage and the fees his office collected were reviewed by no one. Smith Johnson's tactics and the success he attained taught his son early on that government and the electoral process were no more than a game to be mastered for personal power. Nucky also learned that in Atlantic City, a politician would only have power so long as he was prepared to bend the law when needed to help the resort's economy. Smith Johnson and Louis Kuehnle were close friends and the sheriff's favorite hangout was "the Commodore's" hotel. There were many evenings when, while still a boy, Nucky sat quietly next to his father at the Corner and listened to the stories and strategies of Kuehnle and his cohorts. Kuehnle's hotel was the hub of Republican politics in Atlantic City and the place where important political decisions were made. Nucky may not have understood all he heard, but he was there, and while still in his teens began to learn the rules of the game. By age 19, Johnson made his first political speech, and as soon as he was old enough to vote at age 21, his father appointed him undersheriff. He completed high school, attended a year at a teacher's college, and put in a stint at reading law in the office of a local attorney, but it was politics he wanted.

Nucky also wanted the hand of a tall, slender, graceful girl with whom he fell in love at first sight as a teenager. Beautiful and soft-spoken, "Mabel Jeffries was the daughter of the Postmaster in Mays Landing and they knew each other from childhood—Nucky just adored her."

Nucky and Mabel lived in an era when teenage sweethearts married and remained faithful to one another until death. It was Mabel's enrollment at the Trenton Normal School (a teaching college for girls; now the College of New Jersey) that had prompted Nucky to go to college himself. Their schools were near one another and they met each day after class at a campus ice cream parlor where they made plans for their future together. A year of college—away from Atlantic City—was all Nucky could handle. They agreed he should return home and begin his career in politics. Mabel stayed on at school and earned her teaching certificate. After her graduation in June 1906, they were married and moved into an apartment in Atlantic City. By the time of his marriage, Nucky had replaced Sam Kirby as his father's undersheriff. At the next election in 1908, Nucky was elected to sheriff, with his father as undersheriff, at the age of 25, making him the youngest person in New Jersey to hold the post. Like many other locals of their social standing, Nucky and Mabel speculated in the booming Atlantic City real estate market and did well for themselves. They were on their way to a comfortable life together until tragedy destroyed their plans.

Mabel had always been a fragile person, but in the winter of 1913 she came down with a cough she couldn't shake. At Nucky's insistence, she went to a local physician who diagnosed her illness—tuberculosis. The disease was fairly common in the resort, but only the strong or wealthy survived it. On the advice of Johnson's family doctor, he traveled with Mabel to a sanitarium in Colorado. Despite his duties as Atlantic City's new boss, he was prepared to stay until she was well. But it was no use. Three weeks later, Nucky rode home in a railway baggage car, seated next to Mabel's coffin. At the age of 28, she was gone. "My father said that Nucky mourned Mabel for months. Her death, like it was, broke his heart. After she was gone, he was a changed man."

With Mabel's death, politics became his life. While Nucky's term as sheriff was marked by his indictment for election fraud, his acquittal made him a local hero and generated support among the resort's politicians. Instead of smashing the Commodore's machine, Woodrow Wilson helped to make room for a new boss. Rather than continuing in the sheriff's office, Nucky went in another direction—control of the organization. With Kuehnle's blessing and the help of his father, Nucky became secretary to the Republican County Committee. It didn't have a salary, but it was more powerful than being chairman. It was the secretary who called meetings, established the agenda, and made the final call on who was eligible to participate in the organization.

He made his next move in 1913, shortly after Mabel's death. Again with his father's backing, Nucky was appointed county treasurer, one of the offices designated by Kuehnle for funneling graft payments on public contracts. The treasurer's office gave him access to money and, in turn, power over the organization and the selection of candidates. The position paid the same salary as sheriff but was easier to manage. An interesting note to Nucky's selection as treasurer is the fact that there was a minority faction who opposed him. They demanded, as a condition to his assuming this new position, that Nucky be compelled to reconcile the sheriff's account. He had mishandled the funds received by his office and his critics knew he owed thousands of dollars to the county for overcharges. Rather than consent to an accounting, Nucky proposed a single lump sum payment of $10,000, which was paid in cash four days later.

County treasurer was the only political position Nucky held for the next 30 years. As with the Commodore while he was boss, Nucky chose not to seek elected office. He believed that a boss should never be a candidate. Nucky had learned much from Kuehnle and he believed, "Running for election was beneath a real boss."

Crucial to his power and the control of the Republican organization, he learned how to manipulate Atlantic City's Black population. He continued the Commodore's private welfare system, but the assistance he gave Blacks went beyond what Kuehnle had done;

come the winter he was their savior. Long stretches of unemployment in the off-season could be devastating. Johnson saw to it that the Northside had food, clothing, coal, and medical care. "If your kid needed a winter coat, all you had to do was ask—maybe it wouldn't fit but it was warm. If the grocer cut off your credit, the ward leader told you where to shop on the party's tab. The same was true if someone needed a doctor or a prescription filled." In return, he was loved by the Black community and looked on as a "White god." Nucky Johnson "owned" the Black vote and when a large turnout was needed to produce the right election results, they never failed him.

Johnson understood the need for controlling the flow of money to the candidates. With a stranglehold on the money there was no fear of reformers getting into office. To remain boss, he needed an uninterrupted flow of cash. He transformed the system of bribes that existed at the time. Under the Commodore, bribes had been paid in line with a "gentleman's agreement" between the Republican Party and the vice industry. Under Nucky, protection money paid by Atlantic City's racketeers became a major source of revenue for the business of politics. "With Nucky, the payments weren't voluntary. You paid or he shut you down."

The gambling rooms, whorehouses, and illegal saloons were vital to Nucky and his town. Without a flourishing vice industry, Atlantic City would lose an important competitive edge for attracting visitors, and the local Republican Party would lose the money needed to continue its dominance. An important lesson Nucky learned through witnessing Kuehnle's destruction at the hands of Woodrow Wilson also required large amounts of cash. Nucky knew he'd never be safe remaining a local boss. He had to become a force statewide if he and the resort were to avoid future attacks from Trenton. His opportunity came in 1916.

In the gubernatorial election of 1916, Nucky supported the candidacy of Walter Edge. An Atlantic City resident and product of the Kuehnle machine, Edge had served in the state assembly and was elected senator from Atlantic County in the election of 1910: the election made infamous by the Macksey Commission. Edge was as honest as could be hoped for from the Atlantic City organization. He was a capable legislator and in 1912 was selected majority leader of the state senate, having gained the respect of the state Republican organization.

Walter Edge was Atlantic City's answer to Horatio Alger. Born in Philadelphia, he moved to Atlantic City as a child when his father's position with the railroad was transferred. Like other self-made men of his day, Edge pulled himself up by the bootstraps to acquire his wealth through the ownership of a local newspaper and a public relations firm. Edge continued his business success into politics and went on to hold more influential positions than any resort politician, becoming Governor, U.S. Senator, and Ambassador to France. He was an intimate of Warren G. Harding and narrowly missed becoming his vice president. While Edge later disavowed his ties to Kuehnle and Johnson, he needed their support. Despite his personal wealth, he couldn't have been elected from Atlantic County unless he was loyal to the Commodore and his Atlantic City machine; proof is Edge's choice of Nucky as his campaign manager for governor. "Edge was a stuffed shirt, but he knew where to go when he needed something done in politics—Nucky Johnson."

Edge's opponent in the Republican primary was the wealthy Austin Colgate, heir to the toothpaste fortune. The primary was hotly contested and, in a time when there were no campaign finance reports, Colgate spent his money freely. Nucky helped Edge by raising the funds needed to wage a statewide campaign and by using his skill as a powerbroker to gain support for Edge from an unexpected source.

There was no contest in the Democratic primary; the candidate was Jersey City Mayor Otto Wittpenn. A reform mayor, Wittpenn was a headache for Hudson County Democratic boss Frank "I am the Law" Hague, who decided it was time for Wittpenn to move up and out—out of Hague's way. Frank Hague was becoming a force in Democratic politics at about the same time Nucky was making his move to prominence as a Republican. Hague was the son of immigrant Irish parents, born in the "Horseshoe Section" of Jersey City in 1871. Despite having neither an education (he was expelled from school in the sixth grade) nor a family name to bolster him in local politics, Hague became a leader while still a young man. One step at a time, he amassed power as he went from constable to custodian of City Hill to the office of street and water commissioner. Like Nucky, Frank Hague branched out into state politics not because he wanted statewide power, but rather because it was useful to have the influence of state government to safeguard his city's interests.

When the election of 1916 rolled around, there weren't any Democrats whom Hague trusted enough to support for governor, making him ripe for an overture by Nucky. Prior to the 1947 State Constitution, a governor couldn't succeed himself and when Wilson left Trenton for Washington, he was succeeded by James Fiedler, a party hack from Jersey City who happened to be president of the Senate at the right time. Hague controlled Fiedler and supported him in the election of 1913; however, come 1916, Hague could find no one to support. At Nucky's prompting and with a pledge of cooperation from Edge, Hague instructed his people to "crossover" and support Nucky's candidate in the primary. Hague then abandoned Wittpenn in the general election. Wittpenn was a pawn in Hague's and Nucky's game, and Walter Edge became governor. This was the first of many occasions when Nucky and Hague put aside party differences to work for their mutual interests.

As governor, Edge dutifully rewarded Nucky by appointing him clerk of the State Supreme Court. "Can you imagine that, a character like Nucky Johnson, the head clerk to New Jersey's judiciary." Johnson continued serving as Atlantic County Treasurer despite the fact that both jobs were supposed to be full-time. The position of clerk meant little to Nucky, but it gave him an excuse to be in Trenton and to begin making contacts in the state Republican organization. At the age of 33, having a close ally in the governor's chair and the power to dispense favors beyond Atlantic City, Nucky had arrived as a force in statewide politics.

At about the same time Atlantic City was striving to move beyond being merely Philadelphia's Playground into a national resort, the city's popularity and, with it, Johnson's power, were given an enormous boost. In 1919, with Woodrow Wilson in the White House, Victorian morality won a major victory with the adoption of the 18th Amendment to the U.S. Constitution, the Volstead Act. Woodrow Wilson, the reformer, was again unwittingly advancing the career of Nucky Johnson along with hundreds of other racketeers. "Prohibition" banned the manufacture, sale, and transportation of intoxicating liquors—it was doomed to failure. For decades, the Anti-saloon League, and before it, the National Prohibition Party, had been waging a single-minded campaign to shut down the liquor industry. With Wilson as president, the Prohibitionists finally had someone who would listen to them. The 18th Amendment was adopted by the required three-fourths of the states within a single year. The Amendment had been written into the Constitution and scheduled to go into effect in a few months when Hague's candidate, Edward I. Edwards, was elected governor. During the campaign, Edwards pledged, "I intend to interfere with the enforcement of Prohibition in this State." Thanks to Edwards, New Jersey was the last state to ratify the Amendment, doing so after it had been in effect for two years.

That so many people in power could take leave of their senses by supporting a law so utterly unenforceable stands as a monument to the ignorance of single-issue politics. It's the classic example of the "law of unintended consequences." While Prohibition reduced the general availability of alcohol, it greatly increased the money available for political corruption and organized crime. Otherwise law-abiding citizens refused to give up the pleasure of an occasional drink and got their booze from illegal suppliers. An authority on Prohibition, Al Capone once said:

> I make my money by supplying a public demand. If I break the law, my customers, who number hundreds of the best people in Chicago, are as guilty as I am. The only difference between us is that I sell and they buy. Everybody calls me a racketeer. I call myself a businessman. When I sell liquor, it's bootlegging. When my patrons serve it on a silver tray on Lake Shore Drive, it's hospitality.

Selling liquor unlawfully was nothing new in Atlantic City. Resort tavern owners had violated the state's Bishops' Law for years by serving drinks on Sunday. If they could get away with it one day a week, why not seven? "Prohibition didn't happen in Atlantic City." As far as Atlantic City was concerned, the 18th Amendment to the U.S. Constitution never existed. While other cities had speakeasies and private clubs, the sale of alcohol in the resort continued as usual in taverns, restaurants, hotels, and nightclubs. You could buy liquor in drugstores, the corner grocery, and the local farmer's market. The resort was more than an outlet for illegal booze, it was a major port of entry for foreign-produced liquor. Large "mother ships," bearing thousands of cases of whiskey and rum, anchored off the coast where they were greeted by speedboats, which were little more than empty hulls with twin motors. Cases of liquor were unloaded all along the island, with speedboats pulling into the bay near a city firehouse where they were greeted by the local firemen who helped unload the booze. "Everybody helped out. If you worked for the city you could count on one time or another working a night shift and being told to go to such and such place and help unload a boat. You weren't supposed to know what it was but everybody did."

It was the Coast Guard's job to stop the flow of imported whiskey. More often than not, it was unsuccessful. In one incident, four coast guards were arrested on charges of assault with intent to kill for shooting at a rumrunner. Daniel Conover had refused to stop his boat in the Inlet at 2:00 A.M. on a May evening in 1924 when ordered to do so by Chief Petty Officer Edward Robert. Shots were fired and Conover was caught with 75 cases of liquor in the captured boat. Atlantic County Prosecutor Louis Repetto arrested Chief Robert and his three crewmates charging them with abuse of their authority for using firearms. "To my mind" he said, "the Federal men are as guilty as is the individual who uses a pistol without provocation. An officer may fire only in pursuit of persons guilty of felony. Rum smuggling comes under the designation of a misdemeanor." This wasn't an isolated incident. There were dozens of reported occurrences during the 1920s when local law enforcement authorities were used to obstruct federal officials attempting to secure compliance with Prohibition.

The uninterrupted flow of booze enhanced the resort's standing among vacationing businessmen. "You gotta understand, nobody did it the way we did here. Sure you could get booze in New York or Philly, but it was always in a speakeasy you know, hush, hush. Here it was right out in the open, and that made us real attractive to businessmen looking for a place to hold a convention."

As Nucky himself once said, "We have whiskey, wine, women, song, and slot machines. I won't deny it and I won't apologize for it. If the majority of the people didn't want them, they wouldn't be profitable and wouldn't exist. The fact that they do exist proves to me that the people want them."

Because of its willingness to ignore Prohibition, conventioneers flocked to Atlantic City and the resort became the premier convention center of the nation. This enormous success in attracting conventions resulted in the decision to build the present day Boardwalk Convention Center. Architecturally, the old Convention Hall isn't much to look at, but when it opened in May 1929, it was the largest and only building of its kind in the world. For the people of its day, it was one of the wonders of the world. It was hailed across the nation as "the" modern convention facility. The hall was constructed without roof posts and pillars; the building's trusses had a span of 350 feet and at the time were the largest ever used anywhere. The construction materials consisted of 12 million tons of steel, 42,000 cubic yards of concrete covering more than seven acres. Its subbasement is more than 26 feet below high tide level and is anchored with 12,000 30-foot-long pilings. In its day, it was an engineering marvel.

The construction of Convention Hall was Nucky's commitment to a 12-month economy through conventions. Nucky didn't need a market study to know it would be a success. Under Nucky's direction and that of his handpicked mayor, Edward Bader, Convention Hall was constructed at a cost of $15 million. Such an expenditure in 1929, by a city of some 65,000 residents, could not have been made without the stimulation to the resort's popularity caused by Prohibition. And as the resort grew in popularity, so, too, did Nucky's power.

Prohibition raised the political ante in Atlantic City. When a community is thriving, everyone wants power. This was especially true in the resort where the political spoils system was woven into the fabric of the community. With the prosperity stimulated by Prohibition, the competition for local office became intense. One such contest was the city commission election in 1924. It was a pivotal election that affected resort politics for nearly two generations.

The 1924 campaign was a bitter one. It featured two Republican slates: one headed by former Mayor Harry Bacharach and the other by incumbent Edward Bader. Bacharach had been a popular mayor serving from 1916 to 1920. At the end of his second term, he chose not to seek re-election, and Bader became mayor. Bader made thousands of friends while in office and when Bacharach decided to make a comeback, the contest put Nucky on the spot. The hostility between Bader and Bacharach divided the community, and there was nothing Nucky could do to prevent them from clashing. Johnson withheld his support, playing cat and mouse with both candidates; he liked both men and could have worked with either of them. Finally, he struck a deal with Bader and agreed to back him.

Nucky knew the election would be close and went looking for votes outside of the Republican Party. The local Democratic Party had its start with the election of Woodrow Wilson as governor, but it never amounted to much. In the '24 election, the Democratic slate didn't have a chance; their candidates could attract little more than 2,000 votes. Nucky went to the local Democratic leader, Charles Lafferty, and offered to put a Democratic candidate on Bader's slate. At Nucky's prompting, Lafferty chose Harry Headly and the first fusion ticket was formed. Headly was not really a Democrat; he had been a Republican ward worker prior to switching parties to become a candidate. Lafferty and the Democrats turned out for Bader amid Election Day brawling and charges of election fraud. Receiving more than 1,000 illegitimate votes, cast by floaters brought in by train from Philadelphia, the Bader slate was victorious.

The arrangement between Johnson and Lafferty became a permanent fixture in resort politics with Nucky and his successor controlling the Democratic Party for the next 40 years. Headly was in time replaced by William Casey, who likewise was a former Republican having worked as an aide to Harry Bacharach when he was mayor. In later years a second Democrat was added to the city commission slates, but the Republican Party remained firmly in control. The deal between Nucky and Lafferty ensured there would never be a legitimate Democratic Party. As one old time pol has noted, "There never really was a second political party in Atlantic City, just different line-ups of players who ran under different banners. But underneath the uniforms everyone was on the same team."

The "Roaring '20s" were golden years for both Nucky and his town. It was a gay place that reveled in its ability to show its visitors a good time. The liquor flowed and the party seemed as though it would go on forever. In the days before television and widespread home radio, the Boardwalk rivaled New York City's Great White Way as a national showcase for promoting consumer products and introducing new entertainment figures and productions. During the decade between 1920 and 1930, the Boardwalk became known as the "Second Broadway" of the nation. A production didn't go to New York until it first showed in Atlantic City. There were hundreds of Boardwalk theatrical tryouts with famous stage names that drew wealthy playgoers from throughout the entire northeast, many of them arriving in their own private railroad cars.

Typical of the '20s was the year 1920, which saw a total of 168 shows open at the three main theatres: the Apollo, Globe, and

Woods. Victor Herbert started off the year on New Year's Day with his presentation of *My Golden Girl*, followed by Willie Collier in *The Hottentot* and John Drew in *The Catbird*. In March, there was Marie Dresler in *Tillie's Nightmare* with other performances throughout the year featuring the likes of Chauncey Olcott, Helen Hayes, David Warfield, Thurston the Magician, and "Mr. Show Business," George M. Cohan. Also, regulars during the '20s were the prestigious University of Pennsylvania Mask and Wig Club and the Ziegfeld Follies.

The most memorable performance staged during this era was the premier of *The Student Prince* at the Apollo Theatre in 1924. It was a national theatrical event and was the largest production ever staged on the Boardwalk with a cast of 150 players. The resort was more than a try-out town for theatrical productions; it was a showcase for comics, singers, musicians, and dancers. Among those who received their first big break in Atlantic City on the road to stardom were W. C. Fields, Abbott and Costello, Jimmy Durante, Red Skelton, Milton Berle, Martha Ray, Guy Lombardo, Bing Crosby, Bob Hope, Ed Sullivan, Jackie Gleason, Tommy and Jimmy Dorsey, and on and on.

By 1925, Atlantic City had:

- More than 1,200 hotels and boardinghouses capable of accommodating nearly 400,000 visitors at a time.
- Ninety-nine trains in and out daily in the summer, and 65 daily in the winter. Of the 16 fastest trains in the world at the time, 11 were in service to Atlantic City.
- A Boardwalk lined with hundreds of businesses, extending seven miles.
- Five ocean piers with amusements.
- Twenty-one theatres.
- Four newspapers: two daily, one Sunday, and one weekly.
- Three country clubs.
- Three airports—two for seaplanes and one for land planes.
- The Easter Parade and the Miss America Pageant.

The Miss America Pageant got its start in 1921 as the "Intercity Beauty Contest." Conceived as a gimmick for extending the summer season, it was scheduled for the week after Labor Day. In all, eight young girls hailing from the likes of Newark, Pittsburgh, Ocean City, and Harrisburg made up the field. Surprisingly, it was a success and the following year 58 beauties showed. The *New York Times* covered the second pageant during its final two days and reported: "The nation's picked beauties swept along three miles of Boardwalk this afternoon and in the most spectacular rolling-chair parade ever staged here. Crowds packed the borders of the walk, squeezed in the windows of the flanking hotels and stores, and kept up a continuous cheering from the time that King Neptune and his flower-bedecked retinue got underway. Airplanes swooped down and showered the bowered beauties with roses and confetti. Cannons roared and even the breakers boomed forth their tribute to America's prettiest girls." Where else but Atlantic City?

The first host of the City by the Sea throughout this period was Nucky. He wasn't just Atlantic City's boss, he was the town's leading party person. Nucky enjoyed beautiful women and was often in the company of the starlets and showgirls who performed in the many stage productions. When a well-known entertainer was in town he usually threw a party in his or her honor at the Ritz. Throughout his career, there were few parties of any significance held in the resort where Nucky wasn't in attendance.

Damon Runyon would have had a hard time creating a more flamboyant character. His typical day began at 3:00 in the afternoon; awakened at the usual time by his bodyguard and valet, Louis Kessel. Resembling the trunk of a tree, Kessel stood five-foot-five, weighed 260 pounds, and sported a moustache with waxed tips. He had been a wrestler, a bartender, and a cab driver, in that order, before meeting up with Nucky. In his days as a cab driver he often waited outside nightclubs for Nucky and, when he emerged, took him home, undressed him, and put him to bed. Louie was an uncomplicated person looking for a master to serve. Nucky made him his personal servant and their relationship lasted nearly 20 years.

Routinely, Louie started off his boss's day with a rubdown; pounding muscles, snapping loose flesh, and rubbing Nucky with sweet ointments and oil of wintergreen. After Louie had rubbed Nucky's skin pink, he draped his body with a silk robe and escorted him to the breakfast table overlooking the ocean from his view on the ninth floor of the Ritz Carlton. Nucky had leased the entire floor from where he reigned as the "Czar." During Nucky's residence, the Ritz Carlton out dazzled every other hotel on the Boardwalk.

Nucky's presence set a standard of unbridled hedonism; it was a "lavish temple of pleasure."

Once the Czar was fully awake, a Negro maid brought in the breakfast tray, which consisted of a quart of freshly squeezed orange juice, half a dozen eggs, and a ham steak. During breakfast Nucky would read the newspaper and receive reports from local politicos and racketeers. After the boss finished breakfast, Louie picked out one of more than 100 hand-tailored suits and pinned a fresh red carnation to the lapel. In the summer months, Nucky had a weakness for lavender and chocolate-colored suits. If the weather was cold, Louie fetched the boss's full-length raccoon coat. Once dressed and ready to go, it was a dusk-to-dawn performance. Nucky and Louie would leave the Ritz Carlton and walk to the Boardwalk, where the Czar leaned against the railing and held court. Panhandlers begged for, and got, dollar bills and sometimes more; political underlings sought advice and favors; part business, part social, this daily routine lasted an hour or two. Nucky would then go for a long ride in a rollingchair on the Boardwalk or for a stroll on Atlantic Avenue, stopping all along the way to hand out dollar bills to any poor person that looked his way.

Johnson had a passion for Atlantic City's poor people, especially the children. There wasn't a shoeshine boy, flower girl, or paperboy whom Nucky didn't pat on the head and give a dollar or two. If there was a sporting event or another affair at Convention Hall that Nucky thought might excite the children, he saw to it they were permitted in without charge. One lesson Nucky learned well from the Commodore was that the poor have votes just as well as the rich, and if you took care of the poor, you could count on their votes.

Upon completing his daily rounds, Louie then drove the boss in his Rolls Royce to a nightclub, dinner party, an indoor hotel pool—Nucky stayed fit by swimming—a political meeting, and a gambling room or whorehouse, depending on his agenda for the evening. It was common for Nucky to have one of the local call girls accompany him as he made his rounds in the evening, permitting lustful interludes in the back seat of his Rolls.

The Czar of the Ritz was every bit the celebrity on New York's Broadway as he was on the Boardwalk. Despite the fact that there was "never any snow on the Boardwalk," Atlantic City's winter months were longer than Nucky could handle. To cope with the winter doldrums, Nucky rented a large apartment in an exclusive section of Manhattan overlooking Central Park. The rent for his apartment alone nearly equaled his annual salary as treasurer. Evidence of his reputation as a "man about town" is an article by a New York gossip columnist who wrote admiringly that Nucky and oil millionaire Guy Loomis were "among the most liberal and careless spenders of the present day." The reporter noted that when in New York, Nucky was always accompanied by a group of hangers-on, mostly female, whom he took from one nightclub to another, picking up the tabs. On numerous occasions, he'd give a waiter a $20 bill for handing him an extra napkin; tips of $100 were common. Nucky was so popular with restaurant and nightclub help everywhere he went that the waiters' union made him an honorary member—Union card #508—Atlantic City Local.

In addition to fancy nightspots, Nucky loved to be part of major events. He could always be found ringside during a championship boxing match accompanied by a group of friends, and bought whole blocks of tickets for the World Series, inviting dozens of guests. On several occasions, he enjoyed a Broadway play so much that he brought the entire cast to Atlantic City for a weekend at his expense. As an old-time local lawyer recalled, "I went to my first World Series with Nucky. The game was just the beginning of the evening. He sure knew how to have a good time."

Nucky's audacious generosity had no limits. He deliberately made himself a mark for charity solicitors, and when approached by one with a book of tickets to sell, he'd take his silk hat and fill it with tickets; however many it held was what he bought. He was also obliging with the use of his several automobiles. In addition to his Rolls Royce, Nucky owned two 16-cylinder Cadillacs, a Lincoln, and a Ford. This fleet was always available to visiting notables, whether politicians, entertainers, or mobsters. Nucky's lifestyle was the personification of his town's golden years. He was the most colorful player in the World's Playground and was idolized by Atlantic City residents.

The closing years of the Roaring '20s saw Atlantic City's boss attain prestige and power in two different worlds. And as his stature rose, so did his town's. In his own inimitable way, Nucky worked himself into a position in which he was at once the kingmaker in New Jersey Republican politics and a major player in the national family of organized crime.

By the mid-1920s everyone on the public payroll in both Atlantic City and the County owed his job to Nucky. He personally interviewed and okayed every person hired. There wasn't a single employee who wasn't beholden to the boss. He established a practice that was continued by his successor for 30 years more after Nucky was gone. Every successful applicant, regardless of the job's importance and whether the decision to hire had already been made, was required to first meet with the boss to pledge their loyalty and receive instructions on their political duties.

The selection of police officers was most important to Nucky, and he personally screened every applicant to ensure that the police department cooperated in the smooth operation of the vice industry. The elite corps of the department was the vice squad; it was Nucky's right arm for protecting Atlantic City's rackets and collecting the payoffs from bars, gambling rooms, and brothels. A retired detective talked about his hiring. "I was told I had the job but had to go see Nucky before starting work. Nucky was very friendly. He asked me about my folks and said the ward leader liked my family. He told me to just follow my superiors' orders and I'd enjoy being a policeman."

There was no civil service or any type of job security other than to be in the good graces of the organization. In order to keep their jobs, city and county workers had to kick back from one to seven percent of their salary to the local Republican Party, depending on the amount of their wages. This "macing" was done on each of the 26 paydays throughout the year. Every department supervisor was required to keep records of these payments on mimeographed forms that Nucky had distributed. The form listed the scale of payments to be made and provided space for checking them off. Kicking back wasn't an employee's only duty to Nucky. They were also responsible for seeing to it that an assigned number of voters got to the polls on Election Day. Some of those voters were dead, others were out-of-town summer help who weren't in town in November—no matter, they voted, even if it meant a city employee had to vote two or three times in different districts.

In addition to the revenue from macing, Nucky held a tight grip on every contract for public construction jobs and for supplying public institutions with coal, vegetables, milk, and so on. He saw to it that everything had its price and he and his organization profited handsomely. Nucky's organization had become a finely tuned instrument; every part had a function and purpose. There was no one in city or county government or among the contractors, retailers, or professionals who did business with local government—along with the vice industry—who did not have a role to play in keeping the Republican machine running smoothly.

Nucky went beyond what the Commodore had achieved in terms of constructing a formal organization. Kuehnle relied upon his personal popularity and the ability to dispense handouts to the poor, financed through graft and extortion. Unlike the Commodore, Nucky was an organizer. His flamboyant lifestyle camouflaged a calculating mind, figuring angles and planning his moves constantly. Nucky was always talking politics and strategy. He understood human nature and what motivated people, especially the residents of Atlantic City. Under his direction a rigid political spoils system was established. Its hierarchy was based on the four voting wards of Atlantic City. This ward system was the basis for his machine's election victories and cranked out votes, year after year.

Machine politics was the inevitable product of Atlantic City's development. The predominance of a single political party for several generations after the Civil War and Atlantic City's uniquely singular purpose produced a mentality that discouraged pluralistic politics. Atlantic City depended totally on the visitor for its survival. The illicit thrills enjoyed by tourists were a cornerstone of the local economy. Reformers or critics of the status quo couldn't be tolerated. They were bad for business. The resort's singular purpose demanded a single mentality to manage its affairs, a mentality unburdened by political ideologies. The philosophies of the national political parties were irrelevant in resort politics. Success of the local tourist economy was the only ideology.

Nucky seized the opportunity created by such a mentality. He was a professional politician who took his business seriously and understood that the only test he'd ever have to pass was to keep the local economy profitable. One means to that end, the protected violation of vice laws, became the accepted way of doing business. He was able to identify himself with the success of the resort's economy and by doing so elevated himself and the political ward system to the status of a sacred institution.

Nucky's ward politicians were social workers required to keep an eye out for the personal needs of their neighbors; not just at campaign time, but every day of the year. The four wards of Atlantic City were divided into precincts, blocks, and streets with every constituent accounted for. When someone hit upon hard times, Nucky learned about it from one of his lieutenants. More often than not, assistance was offered before it was requested. Whatever the problem, Nucky's organization worked to find a solution. When necessary, Nucky's machine was an employment office, providing a government job of some type or exerting personal influence with private employers.

At Thanksgiving and Christmas everyone in need received a turkey and a basket of vegetables from the Republican Party. During the winter months truck loads of coal were dumped in vacant lots in various neighborhoods and the people in the area were free to take what they needed to keep their homes warm. Should there be a death in the family, the wake was always attended by the block leader and precinct captain, usually by the ward leader, and very often Nucky himself. Nucky was a master at holding the hand of a widow and whispering gently what a fine man her husband was. Always, one of Nucky's several Cadillacs, complete with an obliging uniformed driver, was available to the grieving family should transportation be needed on the day of the funeral. "Remember, there aren't any cemeteries in Atlantic City—it's an island. A ride in a fancy car to the mainland for the funeral made poor people mighty grateful." Funerals were part of the business of politics and Nucky and all who worked with him dedicated themselves to this business every day of the year. By satisfying the personal needs of his constituents, Nucky was able to perpetuate his machine. He had won the hearts of Atlantic City's voters, and they were loyal to him.

Nucky's political clout reached its zenith in the election of 1928. In that year, he supported Morgan Larson for governor and Hamilton Kean for U.S. Senator, both of whom were elected. After the election, a U.S. Senate Committee conducted a formal investigation into a charge that before the primary, Kean had given Nucky a signed blank check, which was cashed for $200,000, with the money used as a slush fund to buy votes. The check was never found but the primary was noteworthy because it was another in which the Democrats in Hudson County crossed over into the Republican primary. The orders went out from Frank Hague and thousands of Democrats invaded the Republican primary to vote for Larson and Kean. Even Democratic election officials themselves voted in the Republican primary. The investigating committee estimated that nearly 22,000 Hudson County Democrats had crossed over. This would never have occurred but for Nucky's relationship with Hague. Kean discounted such talk and attributed his victory to Nucky's magnetism, describing campaign rallies he had attended by saying, "Every speaker began his talk by declaring that he was devoted to God and Enoch Johnson." The following year Larson and Kean offered Nucky the state chairmanship of the Republican Party, but he turned it down. His power was beyond positions and titles.

A vivid illustration of Nucky's power and the manner in which he flaunted it was his encounter with a reformist group known as "the Committee of One Hundred." The committee was an idealistic group of crusaders trying to dismantle the resort's vice industry. Nucky made fools of them.

The Committee of One Hundred was chaired by Samuel Comly, a local attorney. Comly had tried for years to clean up the resort by applying pressure to Atlantic County's criminal justice system. He was frustrated at every turn. Comly and Walter Thompson worked their way through the entire system without making a dent in Nucky's empire. They began by hiring their own private investigators who secured sworn statements of eye witnesses to prostitution, gambling, and the sale of liquor. These affidavits were then submitted to Atlantic County Prosecutor Louis Repetto. This was the same prosecutor who had indicted the Coast Guard officers. Repetto found the committee's proofs lacking and rejected them.

Comly then went to Common Pleas Court Judge William Smathers and asked him to order the closing of a well-known gambling casino, the Golden Inn, on Missouri Avenue. Judge Smathers told Comly, "I'm no reformer. I earn my salary as a judge." Handpicked by Nucky, the judge wasn't about to interfere with the resort's major attractions. Comly then approached State Attorney General E. L. Katzenbach, who refused to get involved. He said, "I'm not going down to Atlantic City unless summoned there by the Supreme Court." Comly made that stop, too, and got the same reception, being advised by Justice Luther Campbell, "I think you're all right legally, but I don't think the community wants anything done." Nucky had influence with all these people, but it was more than his power that accounted for the reception they gave Comly; the people of Atlantic City were happy with the way their town was being run.

Vice as an adjunct to tourism had grown into the resort's major industry and no one was about to tamper with success.

The final humiliation for Comly and the Committee of One Hundred came on January 31, 1930. That night there were two gatherings held in Atlantic City. Comly, Thompson, and several clergymen had organized a rally at the Odd Fellows Hall on New York Avenue. It was the largest meeting of reformers ever held in the resort. There were nearly 600 persons in attendance—mostly religious leaders from out of town—and Nucky and his lieutenants were denounced royally. The resort was likened to Sodom and Gomorrah and the blame for laxity in law enforcement was laid at Nucky's feet. Nucky was unperturbed. He was busy hosting an affair of his own. This was the evening for the gala known as "Nucky's Nocturne."

While the crusaders were condemning the Czar, he was at the Ritz Carlton entertaining the governor, his cabinet, and the entire state legislature, Republican and Democrat alike. Nucky's Nocturne was Johnson's way of once a year showing his appreciation to all his friends in Trenton. Governor Larson had been invited to the Committee of One Hundred's rally and the meeting was rescheduled several times for his convenience, with phony scheduling problems arising each time. A good party was more to Larson's liking than speeches by Prohibitionists and muckrakers, and Nucky's Nocturne was a party no guest could turn down. It was a 12-course meal, beginning around midnight. Nucky served up the best in food, drink, and women the resort had to offer. The state's political leaders were Nucky's playthings and his critics could expect no help from them. But Nucky's political influence was merely a means to an end.

The real business of Atlantic City's boss was protection money from the local rackets. And it was big business, with Nucky personally receiving more than $500,000 per year as his share of the take from Atlantic City's vice industry. The primary source of Nucky's income from the rackets were "tribute" of $6 per case on all liquor brought into Atlantic City during Prohibition, "inspection fees" paid by the proprietors of brothels, "wire service charges" paid by horse race betting rooms, and a percentage of the profits from every gambling room and the numbers writers syndicate.

Nucky's involvement in the rackets extended beyond Atlantic City. In the late 1920s he was taken into the inner circle of Charles "Lucky" Luciano, becoming a trusted member of his family. At about the time Nucky had attained the height of his power, Luciano was a young, ruthless mobster on his way to the top of organized crime. Two of the major forces with whom Luciano had to contend were the Maranzano and Masseria families. Both of them wanted Luciano to join forces with them, and refusing either meant trouble. Luciano eventually sided with Masseria, but interference from Maranzano remained a concern. To strengthen his position, Luciano, on the advice of Meyer Lansky, forged a new interstate crime syndicate comprised of those racketeers he considered his strongest allies. This merger was limited to seven outfits by Luciano, who had a superstition about that number.

The "Seven Group," as it was called, was an infamous bunch that gave the FBI fits and included the following members: the Bug and Meyer gang (Bugsy Siegel and Meyer Lansky), which covered New York City and functioned as prime protectors, enforcers, and shippers of bootleg liquors; Joe Adonis of Brooklyn; Longie Zwillman and Willie Moretti, whose territory consisted of Long Island and Northern New Jersey; King Solomon of Boston, who controlled New England; Harry "Nig" Rosen from Philadelphia; Luciano himself; and, lastly, Nucky Johnson, "the ruler of the South Jersey Coast." The Seven Group was an instant success and by 1929 it had struck cooperative alliances for buying, selling, distilling, shipping, and protecting with 22 different mobs from Maine to Florida and west to the Mississippi River.

In the same year in which Nucky had orchestrated the election of a governor and U.S. Senator and turned down his party's state chairmanship, he became a major player in organized crime. Smith Johnson's son had come a long way from his days as his father's undersheriff.

Lucky Luciano wasn't satisfied with the success of the Seven Group. He wanted to extend his network further. Under Meyer Lansky's tutelage, Luciano encouraged theories and techniques of doing business never before practiced in the world of crime. Luciano promoted the idea of a national convention of the major racket bosses. It took months to make the necessary contacts and establish an agenda, but the selection of the convention site was never in question. Everyone agreed this first underworld conference would be held in Atlantic City. The reasons were simple. Nucky ran the type of town other mobsters envied; his was a wide-open operation, with the rackets immune from the police and courts because Nucky controlled them. In Atlantic City the delegates could come and go as they pleased without attracting attention, knowing their every need would be catered to by Johnson and his people.

The second week in May 1929 was chosen as the date for Luciano's meeting. It was a memorable event. Long, black limousines carrying mobsters arrived in town from all over the country. Al Capone arrived from Chicago, bringing with him Jake "Greasy Thumb" Guzik; Max "Boo Boo" Hoff, Waxy Gordon, and Nig Rosen came in from Philadelphia; from Cleveland came Moe Dalitz and his partners, Lou Rothkopf and Charles Polizzi; King Solomon drove down from Boston; and Abe Bernstein, leader of the Purple Gang of Detroit who was unable to attend, sent a delegate in his stead. Boss Tom Pendergast of Kansas City likewise sent a surrogate, John Lazia; Longie Zwillman and Willie Moretti represented Long Island and Northern New Jersey. Aside from Nucky, who had his entire organization in town, the largest delegation was from New York City led by Luciano, Meyer Lansky (who was honeymooning at the time), Costello, Lepke, and Dutch Schultz.

The original plans for the convention called for the delegates to stay at the Breakers Hotel. At the time, it was one of the most exclusive hotels along the Boardwalk, and Nucky had reserved suites for his guests. Much to Nucky's embarrassment, it was a mistake. Because the Breakers was restricted to WASPs only, the reservations were made in Anglo-Saxon aliases. When the front desk staff took one look at Al Capone and Nig Rosen they refused to admit them. Nucky wasn't present and the manager of the Breakers didn't know who his guests were. What happened after that is best related by Luciano himself (no doubt, with the help of his biographers):

> A hurried call to Nucky Johnson, a quick call by him, and then the fleet of limousines pulled out of the Breakers driveway and headed for the President Hotel. Before they arrived, Nucky Johnson, resplendent as usual with a red carnation in his lapel, joined the cavalcade. When Capone spotted him, he brought the parade to a halt in the middle of the street. Nucky and Al had it out right there in the open. Johnson was about a foot taller than Capone and both of 'em had voices like foghorns. I think you could've heard them in Philadelphia, and there wasn't a decent word passed between 'em. Johnson had a rep for four-letter

words that wasn't even invented, and Capone is screamin'
at him that he had made bad arrangements so Nucky picks
Al up under one arm and throws him into his car and yells
out, "All you fuckers follow me!"

Once the delegates were settled in their rooms, the first order of
business was a lavish party hosted by Nucky. There was liquor, food,
and women in abundance. For those delegates who had brought their
wives or girlfriends, Nucky had presents of fur capes. The party lasted
a full day before they got down to serious business. After breakfast in
their rooms, the delegates wandered out onto the Boardwalk where
they were taken for a ride in rollingchairs. At the undeveloped end of
the Boardwalk, the mobsters abandoned their rollingchairs and headed
for the beach. Once they reached the sand, they took off their shoes
and socks, rolled their pant legs to their knees, and strolled along the
water's edge discussing their business in complete privacy.

All of the decisions involved in the birth of a national network of
crime organizations, operating jointly with decisions made by equals
at the top, were made out in the open on the sand during those daily
walks along the beach. The main topics of the convention were the
need to halt senseless warring of one family with another, nonviolent
alliances against over-zealous police and their informers, and peace-
ful cooperation among gangs in the same business in order to mini-
mize competition and maximize profits. The significance of this
convention was later detailed by Al Capone:

> I told them there was business enough to make us all
> rich and it was time to stop all the killings and look on our
> business as other men look on theirs, as something to
> work at and forget when we go home at night. It wasn't
> an easy matter for men who had been fighting for years to
> agree on a peaceful business program. But we finally
> decided to forget the past and begin all over again—and
> we drew up a written agreement and each man signed on
> the dotted line.

Atlantic City was the birthplace of the first nationwide crime syndicate, and Nucky Johnson was the proud host.

Not all of Nucky's encounters with the mob were as cordial as his
relationship with Lucky Luciano. One winter evening in 1932 Nucky
was "doing the town" in Manhattan. He was giving one of his usual

princely parties in a speakeasy with a showgirl for every one of his guests. Flanked by beautiful women, glutted on rich food, and submerged in champagne, Nucky was having one of the many times of his life when a stranger entered the room and asked to speak with him in private. Nucky thought it was just another person seeking a favor and agreed to step into the next room. The stranger was Tony "The Stinger" Cugino, a hit man from South Philadelphia. The next thing Nucky knew there was a gun in his ribs and he was being whisked away to a dingy tenement in Brooklyn. His lieutenants were notified that he was being held for ransom. Nig Rosen initiated negotiations with Cugino and a ransom of $100,000 was raised and paid within several days, with Nucky released unharmed. There were those who believed Cugino was hired by Rosen so he could pay a phony ransom and win Nucky's gratitude. Regardless of the true reason behind the kidnapping, Nucky rewarded Rosen by giving him a portion of the Atlantic City numbers operation and granted him permission to operate a gambling casino on Iowa Avenue.

Nucky's career as a racketeer and politician sheds light on the complexity of his personality and the town he ruled. Conceived and created as a resort, with the sole purpose of dispensing pleasure, Atlantic City and its residents had no qualms about "ripping off" an out-of-towner. The trick was to keep the visitor smiling as he parted with his money. Johnson was the master of this scheme and local residents loved and admired him. Nucky and his cronies were the idealization of what the resort was all about. During his reign, local racketeers attained a status and prestige they could never find in another city. The easy money from corruption created a perverse sense of community morality. Speakeasy owners, gambling room operators, numbers writers, pimps, whores, policemen on the take, and corrupt politicians who elsewhere would be viewed as lowlifes and crooks were respected members of the community. The more successful ones were heroes and role models. This was the foundation of Nucky's empire: Atlantic City was corrupt to its core.

# 6

# Hard Times for Nucky and His Town

Ralph Weloff and Nucky Johnson entered the lobby of the Ritz Carlton at the same time; Weloff from the street entrance, Johnson from the elevator. Neither expected to see the other. Weloff was on his way to the ninth floor in search of the boss and Johnson was leaving the hotel for his afternoon stroll after breakfast. Nucky had planned to see Weloff later that evening, but Weloff couldn't wait and came by earlier than usual. Nucky could see he was agitated but took the envelope Weloff handed him without a word. Johnson shushed him while he counted the money; it was the regular weekly payment of $1,200. Then he asked Weloff what was bothering him. Weloff wanted to go up to Nucky's suite but Johnson told him that whatever it was, it could be discussed in the lobby.

Weloff was irritated and let Nucky know it. He raised his voice several times and Nucky barked right back at him. Anyone within earshot could hear the conversation. Weloff had been sent to see Johnson by the other members of the local numbers syndicate. An independent numbers writer had opened up without the syndicate's approval and the vice squad had done nothing. Johnson assured him it had to be a mistake. The vice squad members knew their job and kept a list of who was paid up. Johnson asked if he had spoken to Ralph Gold and Weloff said he hadn't. Johnson told him to see Detective Gold and he would straighten things out. Weloff was relieved and shook hands with Nucky. As they parted, Nucky told Weloff to get back to him if Gold didn't take care of the matter.

Nucky's riotous lifestyle and brazen defiance of the law in running his empire should have made him a target for someone's criminal investigation; however, after 20 years as a major powerbroker he intimidated New Jersey's criminal justice system. Not since Woodrow Wilson was there anyone to take him on. As far as state government was concerned, Johnson and the resort's vice industry were above the law. But things changed for Nucky in the 1930s.

The Great Depression brought hard times to Atlantic City as it did for the rest of the nation. Vacations were one of the first things to go when the American economy collapsed. Atlantic City was no longer a national resort. Philadelphia's working class continued coming, but most were day-trippers, with many visiting solely to gamble. The Boardwalk merchants had to scrounge to survive and scores of long-established businesses went under. Nearly all of the major hotels along the Boardwalk were operating in the red and 10 of the 14 local banks were forced to close, bringing financial ruin to many local investors. Real estate assessments had shrunk to one-third of their 1930 high of $317 million and the tax rate was one of the highest in the state, causing many residents to lose their homes at tax sale. By the end of the '30s, Atlantic City's per capita debt was not only the highest for its class of 30,000 to 100,000, but was higher than that of any other city in the country.

The repeal of Prohibition in 1933 made things worse. What was intended as a boost to portions of the nation's economy deepened the resort's financial problems. "Losin' Prohibition really hurt. We lost a lot of our regular customers from Philly." The end of Prohibition stripped Atlantic City of its competitive advantage in attracting conventions that it had enjoyed for 14 years. But through it all Nucky and the local vice industry prospered.

The contrast of the sickly condition of the resort's municipal finances and hotel/recreation industry with the vitality of Atlantic City's rackets became the focal point of criticism by out-of-town newspapers. It was a favorite target of the Hearst newspaper chain, which enjoyed denouncing Atlantic City's corruption. Newspaper magnate William Randolph Hearst had been a regular visitor during Prohibition and he was every bit the lady's man Nucky was. Hearst's steady date during his visits was a showgirl at the Silver Slipper Saloon, a popular local nightclub. Nucky became a little too friendly with her and when Hearst learned of it he made an ugly scene, threatening to destroy Johnson. "A bartender I knew said that Hearst swore he'd get Nucky if it was the last thing he did. Think of it—all that trouble over a broad."

As revenge, Hearst's newspapers ran several exposés of corruption in Atlantic City, which portrayed Nucky as a ruthless dictator. Johnson retaliated by banning Hearst's newspapers from the resort, making an enemy for life. According to intimates of Johnson, Hearst used his influence with the Roosevelt administration to prod the federal government into investigating Nucky's empire. "Hearst was tight with FDR, and when the Feds came to town everyone knew he was the one behind it."

In November 1936, agents of the IRS and FBI led by Special Agent William Frank, who was a lawyer, began undercover operations in Atlantic City. Working out of a furnished apartment, the agents began by locating the gambling casinos, horse race betting rooms, numbers headquarters, and brothels. By making bets in the horse rooms and purchasing numbers slips they determined the odds paid. By observing these activities firsthand and speaking with local residents, the agents learned the names of the key figures in Atlantic City's vice industry.

William Frank and his men found that the resort's underworld was part of the community and made no effort to conceal its business. "These rackets were absolutely wide open." The horse rooms were located on the two busiest streets, Atlantic and Pacific avenues, and their doors were open to whomever walked in off the street. The houses of prostitution were known by everyone and there was no pretense of hiding their activities. The numbers game or lottery, based upon results from several horse races, was played everywhere, similar to the prevalence of today's state-sponsored lottery. "It was difficult to find a store in which numbers weren't written." Finally, the agents confirmed that not only did the police department know about these things, it was involved in regulating and protecting them from outside interference. The results of Agent Frank's preliminary investigation provided Treasury Secretary Robert Morgenthau with justification to launch a full-scale probe of Johnson and his city. The investigation proved to be anything but routine.

Nucky had experience with tax audits from having been audited by the IRS in the past. He developed a practice of managing his money that left behind few footprints. He kept no books or records, maintained no bank or brokerage accounts, and held no assets in his own name—he did everything in cash. Nucky made it impossible for the agents to make a direct investigation of his tax liability. For each of the years preceding the investigation, Nucky had filed timely tax returns and listed his gross income at approximately $36,000. The County Treasurer's salary accounted for $6,000 and the remainder was described as "other commissions," for which neither Nucky, his secretary, nor his accountant would explain the source when questioned under oath. Nucky had created a situation where the government had to prove unreported income in excess of $30,000 per year. By making the entry "commissions," which was permitted by the tax laws of the time, Nucky was able, should the agents prove a single graft payment, to argue that it was included in the amount reported under commissions.

Nucky instructed his lieutenants to handle their taxes the same way. Each year the people of Johnson's inner circle filed timely income tax returns. The politicians stated their positions of lawful employment, while the racketeers referred to themselves as commission agents. They computed the amount needed to cover their verifiable expenditures and savings and used that amount as their gross income in their tax returns. Any unlawful income was included under the undefined heading of "other commissions." This practice forced the government to construct tax liabilities from outside sources.

Another problem for the investigation was the surveillance of the agents themselves. During the first several months of the investigation, while their numbers were small, the agents went undetected. However, as William Frank's investigative team increased in size and intensified their questioning, the agents soon found their every move was being watched. The city police department with its patrolmen, and the county prosecutor's office, with its detectives, were loyal soldiers in Nucky's empire. Once the FBI agents' presence became known, they were placed under strict observation and Nucky received daily reports of whom the investigators were questioning. He kept closer tabs on them than they could on him. In addition to the police, Nucky saw to it that the entire community knew the agents were in town. Anyone who cooperated with them was blacklisted.

One of the first areas examined by Frank and his agents was municipal graft. It was common knowledge that every contract with city hall had its price. Since the time of the Commodore and before, graft was part of every contract let by city and county government. The typical price of doing business was to kickback anywhere from 5 to 33⅓ percent of the contract profits depending on the quantity and nature of the contract involved. This cost of doing business was factored into the contract price, and anyone who refused to play by the rules watched the work go to others. The agents knew they would find unreported income in this area; it was merely a question of whether any of it could be traced to Johnson.

Certain types of public work contracts were more likely sources of graft than others; one was highway construction. John Tomlin had been a local Republican leader for more than 20 years and had served as a member of the county governing body, the Board of Freeholders, where he was chairman of the road committee. With a dual position of authority in the city and county power structure, Tomlin was a prime suspect. He had encouraged his son, Morrell Tomlin, to begin a general contracting firm. Between the years 1929 and 1936, Morrell Tomlin had a virtual monopoly of the road construction and paving contracts let out by the county. In addition to the county work, Tomlin received a large contract from the state for the construction of a portion of the Black Horse Pike, a new major highway linking Atlantic City to Philadelphia. Johnson had obtained federal funding for the road from the Harding Administration. Nucky was a favorite of President Harding, having delivered the Jersey delegation at the Republican Convention. To show his gratitude, Harding invited Nucky to the White House to sleep in President Lincoln's bed. In exchange, Johnson had an Atlantic County portion of a federal highway named in honor of Harding. With his influence in Washington and Trenton, Johnson was able to pick the contractors for his new road, the Black Horse Pike. It was John Tomlin's son.

When subpoenaed by the treasury agents, Morrell Tomlin's records were in shambles; however, he had a checking account for his contracting firm and the agents reviewed the ledger sheets and deposit tickets. But finding these records wasn't easy. Tomlin's bank went under during the Depression, and investigators were forced to spend several weeks in the summer of 1937 holed up in a steamy warehouse going through thousands of closed files and records until they reconstructed his accounts. When finally assembled, the checking account records showed total deposits for Morrell Tomlin for the years 1928 through 1935 of more than $1.6 million. As for John Tomlin, the deposits totaled in excess of $500,000. Morrell Tomlin never bothered to file an income tax return, while his father filed returns showing a nominal income below the taxable minimum.

The money in John Tomlin's account was easily traced from his son's business account. When first summoned to a meeting with the

FBI agents to explain their unreported income, the Tomlins came dressed in rags and stated they were prepared to take a pauper's oath. One of the agents confronted John Tomlin with a photograph from a recent newspaper where he was shown in attendance at one of Nucky's gala political dinners dressed in formal evening clothes. When the agents made it clear they intended to prosecute them, the Tomlins hired lawyers and spent whatever was needed on their defense. Both father and son were indicted and eventually convicted. Despite offers of immunity for their testimony, neither Tomlin would admit that Nucky had shared with them in the profits.

Another public contract scrutinized by Agent Frank's team of investigators was the city garbage contract for the years 1933 through 1935. The individuals involved were Charles Bader, brother of Mayor Edward Bader; James Donahue, a Republican ward leader from Philadelphia; and Edward Graham. The three of them traded under the name Charles L. Bader and Company. This was the simplest case the agents handled. Bader's records proved an obvious case of tax evasion—it was there among the firm's books, banking statements, and canceled checks. The records also showed bribes to Nucky. Bader's daughter, who was the bookkeeper, had carefully made notations of Nucky's initials, "E. L. J.," on the check stubs for the withdrawals of cash made by Bader and Donahue who passed cash totaling $10,000 on to Nucky.

The payments to Nucky were confirmed by the court records of a lawsuit. Bader, Donahue, and Graham had quarreled over the division of the profits from the garbage contract. Their dispute wound up in the Atlantic County Chancery Court. The court ordered an accounting, which, among other things, disclosed the $10,000 bribe paid to Nucky as part of the firm's expenses. The judge hearing the case, as well as the lawyers trying it, all knew a bribe had been paid to secure a municipal contract, yet none of them did anything about it. Nucky's influence was so dominant and Atlantic County's judicial system so corrupt that an extortion payment was a routine business expense. Bader, Donahue, and Graham were all convicted, but a single $10,000 bribe wasn't enough for a case of tax evasion against Nucky.

Special Agent William Frank was obsessed with obtaining more evidence against Johnson. The investigation had taken on a personal flavor, with Frank openly contemptuous of Nucky. He ordered his men to continue looking into public contracts. One project that couldn't be overlooked was the construction of the new railway station for Atlantic City. In 1933 the two railroads that had been servicing Atlantic City were ordered by the New Jersey Public Utilities Commission (PUC) to consolidate into the Pennsylvania Reading Seashore Line. As part of the state's ruling, a new railroad station was to be constructed.

At a time during the Depression when there was little work available for contractors, Johnson secured a $2.4 million contract for A. P. Miller, Inc., the construction company of an ally, Tony Miller. Nucky had control over the key figures who made decisions and was able to handpick the contractor for this project. Under state law the railroad was mandated to pay one-half the construction costs and the PUC the remainder. Mayor Harry Bacharach sat on the PUC as the city's representative, and he followed Nucky's orders to the letter. There was also the need for special legislation from Trenton and approval of the location by city commission. Nucky took care of all the details. As for the railroad, members of the commission were practical people and agreed to go along with Nucky's choice, provided a competent firm did the work. Nucky put together all the pieces and the contract was awarded to A. P. Miller, Inc.

In examining the books of the Miller company, the agents discovered that in 1935, the final year of the contract, the company paid a $60,000 legal fee to a local attorney, Joseph A. Corio. The stated profit on the entire contract amounted to approximately $240,000. The corporation's tax return showed another figure for legal fees for that year, in the amount of $1,150. The $60,000 item was buried among the construction costs of the station. Several checks totaling $60,000 were paid to Corio but weren't deposited in his bank account. He cashed them personally.

Joe Corio was a close friend and political ally of Nucky. He was valuable in delivering the vote in the resort's Italian-American neighborhood of "Duck Town." Over the years, Corio performed many chores for Nucky and was always rewarded. In exchange for his loyalty and success at getting out the vote, Nucky referred clients to Corio, had him elected state assemblyman, county recorder, and finally appointed Judge of the Common Pleas Court. One of the firms that Corio represented prior to going on the bench was A. P. Miller, Inc.

A review of Corio's income tax return for 1935 showed he had reported a gross income of $20,800. Judge Corio agreed to meet with the agents in his chambers. When confronted with the $60,000 legal fee vs. his reported gross income, Corio explained that more than $40,000 of the fee had gone to expenses; however, he had nothing to back them up. When the agents began grilling him asking for proof, Corio donned his robes and stomped around his chambers demanding what right they had to question his integrity. Corio's pompous attitude provoked William Frank, and he instructed his agents to dig into his financial records. Fortunately for the agents, the bank Corio dealt with was one that kept a photographic record of all its customers' checks.

Several days after reviewing Corio's attorney account records, the agents confronted him with proof he hadn't spent anywhere near $40,000 on legal expenses in 1935, whereupon, Corio's judicial dignity collapsed. He admitted his tax return didn't tell the whole story and offered to pay any additional taxes and penalties, which the agents might assess. He told the agents he wanted "to settle the case" and "get it off his mind." But the FBI refused to make a deal. They demanded a full explanation of the $60,000 legal fee and warned Corio that if he didn't cooperate they would seek an indictment for income tax evasion.

Corio refused to talk, and between October 1937 and April 1938 he did everything possible to settle his tax liability and to prevent prosecution. Nucky saw to it that high-powered lawyers were retained, and a personal appeal was made directly to U.S. Attorney General Robert H. Jackson. Despite these efforts, the case against Corio went forward. In May 1938, a federal grand jury indicted him on charges of tax evasion and making false statements to Treasury Agents. With that, Judge Corio reportedly had a nervous breakdown and was hospitalized in a sanitarium the remainder of the year.

Corio's case was set down for trial in January 1939. When he finally realized he wasn't going to escape prosecution, he decided to talk. In exchange for a grant of immunity, he gave a statement to the FBI, which disclosed that the $60,000 he received wasn't a legal fee but rather a distribution of a portion of the profit on the railroad station contract to Miller, Corio, and Nucky. "Joe Corio surprised everybody. We all thought he'd keep his mouth shut and go to jail."

According to Corio, Miller had agreed to give Nucky three-fifths of the net profit after taxes in exchange for receiving the contract. Corio and Miller, who were related, had a side agreement of their own, which called for an equal split of the remaining profits. Nucky didn't trust Miller and insisted their agreement be reduced to writing. Corio represented Miller and Nucky was represented by Atlantic County Judge Lindley Jeffers in the preparation of the agreement. Corio believed the written agreement was destroyed in 1935 when the three of them changed the plan for dividing the profits in order to evade taxes; however, the agents learned that the secretary who prepared the document had kept her steno notes and was able to reproduce a true copy.

Corio gave a statement admitting that in September 1935, when Tony Miller received his first profit payment of $70,000, he suggested a scheme of paying a $60,000 legal fee to Corio. This would permit the corporation to deduct that sum as an expense and avoid taxes on that amount. As originally planned, the corporation would have paid a tax on the profits before declaring dividends to Miller. Tony Miller's scheme called for Corio to report the $60,000 as a fee on his individual return and Miller gave him $13,200 to pay the taxes on the $60,000. This left $46,800 to be distributed among the three of them; of this amount, Miller received $9,400, Corio $9,400, and Nucky received the balance of $28,000. Corio stated that he saw the cash change hands from Miller to Nucky. The total tax saving on the corporation's and Miller's individual return amounted to approximately $25,000.

Corio's greed foiled Miller's scheme. Instead of reporting the full $60,000 fee on his income tax return, Corio took a chance by omitting it and pocketed the $13,200, which Miller had given him to pay the taxes. Corio claimed he did this because Miller had welched on their side agreement. When he learned prior to filing time in 1936 that Miller was holding out on him, Corio decided to keep the $13,200 instead of applying it toward the taxes. He sabotaged the agreed-upon plan without informing Miller or Nucky. The agents made a thorough investigation of Corio's statement and concluded it was reliable. However, they couldn't trace any other payments to Nucky. Although the agreement negotiated by Corio and Jeffers provided that Nucky was to receive one-third of the entire railroad station profit, which totaled more than $240,000, the $28,000 payment was all they could prove.

Despite this major break in their investigation, William Frank wasn't satisfied with the case against Nucky. The $28,000 payment by itself didn't establish a case for tax evasion as Nucky had reported a new loss of $56,000 on his 1935 income tax return. As a result, Frank was forced to recommend a single charge of conspiracy to evade the corporate income taxes of A. P. Miller, Inc.

The federal grand jury returned an indictment against Nucky and Miller on May 10, 1939. But William Frank was far from pleased; after 2½ years of work, Corio's statement was all he had. Frank knew the power Nucky wielded and feared he might find a way to escape prosecution. All he had to do was to silence Corio—that alone would destroy the government's case. Neither Frank nor the U.S. Attorney's office was confident the conspiracy charge would stand up, especially when one of the co-conspirators was the main witness. If they were to be sure of a conviction, they needed more.

Along with the probe into graft, Frank's agents pursued tax evasion cases against the principals of Atlantic City's rackets. Their strategy was to apply pressure on as many racketeers as possible in an attempt to find someone to admit to paying protection money to Nucky. The two main attractions of Atlantic City's vice industry were prostitution and gambling. During the preliminary phase of their investigation, the FBI found eight large houses of prostitution (there were scores of smaller ones, all of which were doing a flourishing business); 25 horse betting rooms and gambling casinos; nine numbers banks; and more than 800 businesses where one could play the numbers. Atlantic City was fertile soil for prosecution of tax evasion. Finding prospective defendants wasn't the problem; the evidence uncovered revealed violations of the law by so many people that hundreds of indictments could have been filed. The agents' task was one of going after the right defendants who might talk under pressure. They began with the madams.

In the summer of 1937, the federal government launched a two-pronged attack on the resort's prostitution business. At about the same time Frank's men began their probe of the madams, a new team of federal investigators appeared in town in response to complaints that large numbers of women were being transported from out-of-state to the resort for purposes of prostitution. On August 30, 1937, the FBI raided all of the brothels, arresting the proprietors, "inmates," and customers. The arrests totaled more than 200, of whom 140 were prostitutes.

The prostitutes were held as material witnesses at various county jails throughout the state. As a result of the testimony, all of the madams and about 30 pimps were indicted for violation of the Mann Act, commonly known as the White Slavery Law. Also indicted were Ray Born, undersheriff of Atlantic County; Leo Levy, special assistant to the Mayor of Atlantic City; and Louie Kessel, Nucky's bodyguard and valet. Born was the bagman to whom the madams paid protection money each week. Levy and Kessel were involved in the initial arrangements for establishing several brothels. Nearly 40 ranking members of Atlantic City's prostitution business were convicted for Mann Act violations, but none of them would cooperate with Frank and his agents. The investigators then proceeded with tax evasion charges for a second series of indictments.

The madams ran their houses on the same exclusively cash basis as everyone else in Atlantic City's vice industry. Because of this the agents were forced to be creative. From interviews with the individual prostitutes who had been held as material witnesses, the agents secured affidavits as to their earnings, which, according to established practice in Atlantic City, represented one-half of the 50–50 split between madams and prostitutes. This estimate of earnings was further refined by a review of the records of local doctors who routinely examined the girls and laundry records, which were a rough reflection of each house's volume of business. By piecing together these bits of evidence, the FBI established fairly accurate figures for the gross income of each brothel. The madams were indicted and convicted a second time for income tax evasion, but they all remained silent. "The whores hung in there—they were tough old girls."

While prostitution turned a profit, it was only entertainment. Gambling was Atlantic City's serious business. Gambling of every type, and at stakes to suit every class of player, had been part of the resort's economy for several generations. The people who profited from gambling were firmly entrenched in the community and were a force to be reckoned with by anyone who sought political power. While Nucky was a cunning politician, it required more to remain boss for 30 years. "Nucky was Boss because he delivered. He made it possible for everybody to make a buck without a hassle. That's why he was Boss so long." If he hadn't protected the racketeers they would have replaced him long before William Frank and the FBI came to town.

What the agents found were gambling rooms operated out of storefronts and as part of restaurants and nightclubs. They were run as if gambling was legal and open to anyone who walked in off the street. The furnishings of the rooms varied from those rooms that were quite austere, with rows of crude benches, to others that were elegantly furnished salons. Some of these casinos operated on two floors; the street floor being cheaply furnished for the $.50 and $1 players, while the upstairs was luxuriously equipped for $5 and $10 players. Complimentary food and beverages were served, and the management of the casinos paid round-trip railroad fare to any player producing a ticket showing they had come to town that day to gamble.

Indicative of the volume of gamblers was that Atlantic City's horse rooms paid "track prices." This meant they paid the same odds as those paid at the racetracks. Without a routinely heavy volume of bets there wouldn't have been enough of a "spread" to justify paying the prevailing odds. Nucky had total control over the horse rooms. He had gone to Chicago in 1935 and made arrangements with the underworld Nationwide News Service for the exclusive agency in Atlantic City for racing results. Each room paid $200 per week for this service. The price charged by Nationwide News was $40 per week with the difference going to Nucky.

Most of the gambling rooms were involved with everything from horse races and numbers to casino games such as blackjack, poker, craps, and roulette. The rooms that emphasized horse races usually provided craps tables or a game of poker so there would be a second chance to grab the money lost on the horses. The higher priced casinos were usually connected with nightclubs, and the accommodations—food, booze, or broads—were equal to any casino in the world. The smaller rooms had average daily winnings of $500 to $1,000 per day, while the larger rooms grossed $5,000 to $6,000 per day.

Those nightclubs/casinos, which flourished under Nucky's reign, were the 500 Club, Paradise Café, Club Harlem, Little Belmont, the Bath and Turf Club, the Cliquot Club, and Babette's, which was one of the most chic gambling casinos of that era, attracting patrons from around the country. "Only the very best people went to Babette's. They had the best steaks and mixed drinks in town, and great entertainment. I saw Milton Berle there when he was first startin' out."

These nightclubs were nationally advertised and well known, featuring name bands and Broadway or Hollywood stars as entertainers. The owners didn't care if they turned a profit on the nightclubs; the main reason for having them was to attract business to their gambling casinos. The owners of Atlantic City's gambling rooms were all underworld figures, most of whom had arrest records and lived a fast life. Many of them used aliases or were known by nicknames: there was William Kanowitz, who was known as "Wallpaper Willie"; Lou Khoury went by "Lou Kid Curry"; Michael Curcio aka "Doc Cootch"; and Martin Michael, known as "Jack Southern." Had Nucky gone by "Enoch" he would have been considered an oddball.

The most prevalent gambling racket in Atlantic City was the "numbers" game. In a city of 66,000 year-round residents and in a game where the average bets ranged from $.05 to $.10, the enormous volume of play is revealed by the fact that the daily winnings for the number syndicate averaged between $5,000–$6,000, or $1.5 to $2 million per year. The numbers game became so popular there were two plays per day, one for daytime and one for evening. As part of their probe, the agents surveyed nearly 1,500 local retail businesses, interviewing the individual owners. Of these, 830 signed affidavits admitting under oath that their place of business was used to sell numbers. Another 200 to 300 admitted to writing numbers but were afraid to sign affidavits. "If you went to the corner store to buy a quart of milk, you could get your change or play a number. Nearly everybody who had a business wrote numbers." Nucky had succeeded in making the entire community a partner with the rackets.

By the spring of 1939 the investigation had produced more than 40 indictments. The first indictment of the racketeers was against William Kanowitz and David Fischer, who were horse room operators. Following them were the indictments of the principals of the numbers syndicates. In approximately the same period, charges were filed on the county highway contracts and the city garbage contracts. In all, nearly 30 of Nucky's lieutenants were awaiting trial. They were continually pressured by the agents and repeatedly called before the federal grand jury in Camden. But there were no cracks in the wall. Rather than testify against Nucky, Atlantic City's racketeers accepted contempt citations and perjury indictments.

The first tax evasion defendant to go to trial was Austin Clark, a numbers banker. With the exception of the judge having to remove three of Nucky's strong-arm men who were sitting in seats directly in front of the witnesses, the trial was uneventful. Clark was found guilty and sentenced to three years in jail but still refused to cooperate. The government had hoped Clark's conviction would cause the other members of the numbers syndicate to reconsider their silence. But the agents had underestimated the resistance of Nucky's lieutenants.

With the conviction of Austin Clark, Nucky and his people began to obstruct the government in the preparation of its cases. Witnesses for upcoming trials were requested to appear at the FBI's office on the second floor in the new Post Office Building on Pacific Avenue. Most of them never showed. Those who did were, immediately after meeting with the government's lawyers, whisked to the offices of the attorneys for the defendants where they were questioned on what they had discussed with the FBI. William Frank was beside himself at the resistance Nucky was putting up. It's best to let Special Agent Frank speak for himself:

> It now became perfectly clear the opposition was well-organized. It was not a case of individuals committing perjury, but the perjury was the result of a gigantic conspiracy and must have been planned by lawyers. Every day that the grand jury sat a group of lawyers hung around in the corridor of the Post Office Building ready to step in and defend anyone who was either cited for contempt or indicted. There is no question but that these lawyers were engaged by the organization and were not representing individual defendants. One Bondsman was always present, and always posted bond, no matter who was indicted.

As Frank learned, his battle with Nucky was only beginning.

The Austin Clark verdict was followed by several guilty pleas and convictions of minor defendants, all who refused to cooperate with the government. The first major trial hitting at the core of Nucky's empire was that of the numbers bankers, totaling 14 defendants.

They were charged with conspiracy to commit perjury and income tax evasion in connection with the numbers syndicate.

The government began its case on April 29, 1940, with high hopes of convicting all 14 defendants. In addition to the testimony of the agents, the prosecution was forced to use as witnesses employees of the defendants. These witnesses didn't know enough to incriminate Nucky and weren't making enough money to risk imprisonment. They gave the government the same statements they made to the grand jury; nevertheless, on cross-examination by the defense they answered "yes" to any leading question put to them. This destroyed the value of their testimony and the government had to rely on telephone records and statements made by the defendants to prove its case. But the jury wasn't convinced, and after two days of deliberating the court declared a hopeless stalemate. William Frank and his agents weren't about to quit and requested the U.S. Attorney's office to move for a re-trial, which was scheduled in July.

Several weeks after the first trial, the judge who heard the case received a letter informing him one of the defense lawyers had bribed several jurors. While the agents were unable to prove a bribe had actually been paid, they later obtained convictions against several of the defendants and one of their lawyers for jury tampering. The lawyer was Isadore Worth, a former Assistant U.S. Attorney. Worth was convicted and disbarred the following year.

A second trial on conspiracy charges against the same 14 numbers bankers began on July 8, 1940. The government's case went in much stronger than the first time and the prosecutors were certain of a conviction. Despite the prosecutors' confidence, the defendants didn't appear the least bit concerned. This time only two of them took the stand in their defense. Their lawyers put up little resistance, almost as if they were conceding the case. The agents, prosecutors, and judge were baffled when the jury returned a verdict of not guilty.

William Frank feared his investigation was at an end and knew Nucky Johnson was behind the acquittal. Judge Biggs, who heard the trial, was troubled by the jury's verdict and urged Frank to have his agents question the jurors. The result was startling. One of the jurors, Joseph Furhman, was a plant, some think, by friends of Nucky's in the Federal Clerk's office. He was personally acquainted with two of the defense lawyers, Carl Kisselman and Scott Cherchesky. Furhman's brother was an attorney associated with Kisselman. It was common for Kisselman and Cherchesky to meet Furhman socially for lunch and to shoot pool together at the Walt Whitman Hotel in Camden. Neither Kisselman nor Cherchesky advised the court of their relationship with Furhman at the time the jury was selected.

Upon questioning the jurors, William Frank learned the prosecution never had a chance. From the first day of trial, Furhman ridiculed the government's case to the jurors and mocked the judge and the prosecuting attorneys. When the deliberations began, the ballot was eight to four for conviction; however, Furhman was a strong personality and badgered the other eight jurors until he succeeded in getting them all to change their votes. The defendants were tried again—on the substantive crimes as opposed to conspiracy—in March 1941, but only after the panel of jurors had been carefully screened and lectured to by the court. This time there was a conviction.

With Austin Clark and several other defendants sitting in jail and a conviction of all 14 numbers bankers in hand, William Frank and his people turned on the pressure. Frank had the U.S. Attorney subpoena the convicted defendants before the grand jury and questioned them concerning the payment of protection money to Nucky. In response to their perjury, Frank threatened them with a second indictment and, if convicted, a second jail term. The pressure was more than they could handle. It wasn't possible for all 14 to remain silent, and several of them agreed to testify in exchange for leniency on their sentences. A critical witness who came forward was Ralph Weloff, one of the partners in the numbers syndicate. Weloff admitted that from 1935 through 1940 he and others personally delivered to Nucky a minimum of $1,200 per week in protection money. That was all the agents needed. The government obtained a second indictment and pressed for trial on both of them, which was scheduled in July 1941.

The tampering with the first two juries to hear the trial of the numbers syndicate haunted William Frank and the prosecutors. Albert Marino, the judge who presided at Nucky's trial, ordered a careful check of the entire jury panel to prevent any meddling by Johnson. Sure enough, several days before Nucky's trial was scheduled to begin, the agents uncovered a third conspiracy to tamper with a jury.

In May 1941, Zendel Friedman, who was a partner in the nighttime numbers game, went to trial and was convicted of income tax evasion. One of the people from the group of prospective jurors for

Nucky's trial had sat on Friedman's case. When questioned by the agents, this juror revealed that Zendel Friedman and Barney Marion had offered him a bribe. Two days later a second and a third juror gave statements that they too had been offered bribes and that one of the persons who made the offer was employed with the Atlantic County Sheriff's office (Nucky's brother, Alf, was sheriff). This person, Joseph Testa, admitted that Nucky's bodyguard, Louie Kessel, had asked him to approach the juror.

The government assumed the publicity given to the other jury tampering matters would discourage Nucky's people from trying it again, but they were wrong. The contempt citations, convictions, and jail sentences of the people involved in jury tampering hadn't deterred Friedman at all. If Nucky went to such lengths to protect a single numbers racketeer, what would he do to save himself? With the trial only a week away, the prosecution was on the verge of panic.

On July 14, 1941, after 4½ years of exhaustive work by William Frank and his team of investigators, Nucky's case finally went to trial. The courtroom was standing room only and had a carnival atmosphere.

Nucky was a national phenomenon and lived up to his reputation, appearing the first day in a vanilla-colored suit, red carnation, and lavender tie, sporting a straw hat and brass-handled cane. His case received so much advance publicity that special press tables had to be set up in the courtroom to accommodate the more than 30 reporters from throughout the nation who attended the trial each day. Hawkers and vendors of all kinds set up shop outside the courthouse to make a buck off the crowds. Despite having the testimony of Corio on the railroad contract and Weloff on the protection money, the prosecutors were ill at ease as the trial began. In preparation for one of Nucky's rumored defenses, the government summoned 125 persons prior to trial whom they believed the defense might call as witnesses to support Nucky's alleged "political expenses." Frank wanted to explain to them the meaning of perjury. Most of the people summoned never showed. Nucky posted one of his goons in the lobby of the Post Office Building where the agents had their office. Those witnesses who did show were told to go home.

Joseph Corio, who had resigned his judgeship, was the main witness in the first half of the government's case. It had been rumored for years that Nucky was Tony Miller's silent partner and A. P.

Miller, Inc. was a front by which Nucky profited on government contracts. Corio's testimony confirmed the rumors and provided the details. According to Corio, Nucky had received 50 percent of all Miller's profits since he was in business, but the kickback on the railway station was 60 percent. There were numerous delays in the final awarding of the contract and Miller became so nervous he might lose it he agreed to increase Nucky's share of the profits.

Miller's contract with the railroad was a "cost plus" agreement. Under the terms of the contract, Miller submitted bills periodically and received payments for the sums expended plus a small portion of the profit to pay for his overhead. The remainder of the profits was retained by the railroad until the job was entirely completed. Should Miller fail to live up to the terms of the contract, the amount retained could be forfeited as a penalty.

When Miller received his first check, Nucky demanded his share of the profits. Miller explained that his money had to wait until the end of the job, but Nucky's greed was too great. In January 1934 the written contract was prepared. Judge Jeffers asked Corio's secretary to destroy her shorthand notes, but without telling anyone, she hadn't. The only two copies that Nucky knew of were his and Miller's, and both of them were destroyed.

Nucky's lawyer, former U.S. Attorney Walter Winne, made repeated inquiries to learn if the government had a copy of the contract, but each time the prosecution denied him. The court rules at the time permitted this and Winne went to the Department of Justice in Washington and offered to plead Nucky guilty if the government would show him the contract. The U.S. Attorney's office refused, and it wasn't until the trial when Corio's secretary produced a copy of the document that Miller and Nucky had signed. Nucky testified to the contrary, but there was no way the jury could believe his denials.

As to the second half of the government's case, the protection money, the government eventually had more witnesses than they needed. Once Ralph Weloff made the decision to testify, he encouraged other members of the numbers syndicate to do the same so that he wasn't alone. Weloff testified that the numbers syndicate began making weekly payments to Nucky in 1933. The purpose of these protection payments was to ensure there were no raids and that no out-of-towners competed with them. Should there be a problem with the police or a renegade numbers operator, the syndicate's contact person was Atlantic City Police Detective Ralph Gold, who was in charge of the vice squad.

Weloff and others testified that between 1935 and 1940, they personally delivered $1,200 in cash to Nucky each week. In all, a total of 12 numbers racketeers testified that protection money had been paid to Nucky. Despite tough cross-examination, their stories held up.

Nucky's lawyer, Walter Winne, began the defense by conceding that his client had received the money. "We admit that we received money from the numbers racket in Atlantic City. We are not too proud of that source, but we deny that we ever received as income any money that we did not report for taxes."

Winne then proceeded to outline his defense. He began by declaring that the numbers operators had approached Nucky and asked for his help. The numbers game was looked on in Atlantic City as something that should be legalized. Weloff and other numbers people had filed a petition with the City Commission containing the signatures of more than 7,000 local residents in which the petitioners requested city government to recognize the numbers game as legitimate. Nucky was just following the wishes of his constituents, and the money he received was used to support his political organization. According to Winne, Nucky's sole profession was that of a politician. All the payments he received were political contributions, which were spent to finance the Republican machine. As Winne stated, his client needed "plenty of oil to run his political machine."

Proof of the money spent was a shoebox filled with more than 800 receipts, which were presented to the court through the testimony of James Boyd, Clerk to the County Freeholder Board. According to the testimony of Boyd and Rupert Chase, a messenger in Nucky's treasurer's office, Nucky had spent more than $78,000 on political expenses during the several years involved on the tax evasion charge. The remainder of the income that the government could prove was included in Nucky's tax return under "commissions."

Nucky took the stand and testified he had taken the money from the numbers syndicate and spent it "to elect candidates that were friendly to my policies and to carry on throughout the year the building up of my organization—taking care of the poor, paying rent, buying coal." Further testimony in support of the defense that all the money had been used for politics came from the mouths of three local newspaper publishers. The newspapermen testified they had received money for the purpose of publicizing Nucky's organization and that their editorial policy was favorable to his candidates.

Finally, Winne produced a legion of character witnesses on behalf of his client. They were led by former Governor Harold G. Hoffman and retired U.S. Senator David Baird, Jr., but it was to no avail. At the age of 58 Nucky suffered his first defeat. He was found guilty of tax evasion. On August 1, 1941, he was sentenced to 10 years in jail and a fine of $20,000.

If Nucky was humiliated, he never showed it. Johnson handled his conviction with the composure of a deposed monarch, maintaining his poise through it all. With his usual flamboyant style, he had one last jolt for Atlantic City before going off to jail. He decided to take a bride.

During the nearly 30 years following the death of his childhood sweetheart, Mabel Jeffries, Nucky never even hinted at a second marriage. He had known Florence "Flossie" Osbeck, a showgirl/actress, for several years and they had become an item, but no one ever imagined they would marry. On July 31, 1941, the day before he was imprisoned, Nucky and Flossie took their vows at the First Presbyterian Church. Following the ceremony in which the groom was attired in a cream-colored mohair suit with a yellow tie and white shoes, the newlyweds were greeted outside the church by thousands of well-wishers. The wedding was followed by a gay party for hundreds of guests at the Ritz Carlton and went on late into the evening. "Nucky sure knew how to throw a party. You'd never know he was leaving for jail the next day." Nucky and Flossie were devoted to one another until his death, but people who knew Nucky intimately believed the only reason he married her was to ensure a regular and safe communication link with his associates in Atlantic City.

Upon his release from jail, four years later, he led a quiet life and took a pauper's oath when pressed by the government for payment of his tax fines. While his name was suggested several times as a candidate for city commission, Nucky shunned any opportunities to return to power. If he couldn't be the boss, it was better to remain on the sidelines. He remembered the humiliation the Commodore had experienced when he tried to regain control of the Republican Party and refused to expose himself to another defeat.

For the next 20 years, Nucky strolled the Boardwalk and escorted children home from school. He went to charity dinners and, occasionally, political fundraisers. Most years his many friends staged a large birthday party in his honor. The local leaders visited him often, soliciting advice, and in a critical election he aided the Republican ticket in a way only he could. But never again did Nucky Johnson wield the power that had made him Czar of the Ritz.

Gradually, Nucky's health deteriorated. He was placed in the county nursing home in Northfield, where he spent his final days holding court and drinking Scotch with his cronies who visited him regularly. Quietly, on December 9, 1968, Nucky died at the age of 85. They say he died smiling. His career personifies the greed, corruption, and high times that were Atlantic City in its days of glory.

# 7

## Hap

As the elevator came to a stop its lone passenger waited impatiently for it to open. When the doors parted, Frank Farley was through them like a shot. At a near run, he was on his way down the hall. Awaiting him daily in the reception area of his office were 14 chairs, each one filled with someone seeking a favor. As he entered the office, Farley greeted everyone and asked his secretary who was first. Then it was into his office where he met with one person after another until they all had a chance to speak with the senator.

Atlantic City's residents had come to expect favors that went beyond politics. Farley's duties were like those of a feudal lord. The calls for help ranged from jobs, licenses, and contracts coming out of city hall to advice with legal or personal problems and pleas for financial aid. No one was turned away without hope. Sometimes it was a telephone call while the person sat there. Often it took the form of a letter that Farley dictated to his secretary, Dorothy Berry, while the person waited. Occasionally there was no solution, but Farley never let on. Instead, he referred them to someone else who gave the bad news. Regardless of the outcome, everyone who left Farley's office was grateful for his help. He was the town's new boss.

The transfer of power from Nucky Johnson to Frank Farley is revealing of both Farley and the organization Nucky had built. The type of control exercised by Johnson wasn't something he could simply pass to another. The cogs in the machine had a say about whom they'd follow. Nor could Nucky's kind of authority be grabbed by sheer force—there were too many competitors, and no one had an edge.

The power structure Nucky Johnson left behind was more complex than the one he inherited from Louis Kuehnle. While the Commodore had cooperated with the local vice industry and used protection money from the rackets to build his political organization, they remained separate spheres of power. Under Nucky the hierarchy of the local crime syndicate was linked to the chain of command of the city's Republican Party. The local power structure was a single, integrated unit comprised of politicians and criminals. The two spheres of power became one. Nucky presided over what had become a perfect partnership, and the person who took his place had to have the respect of the politicians and racketeers alike.

By 1940, several years into the FBI's investigation, Johnson's inner circle knew it was only a matter of time before he'd be in jail. William Frank and his agents weren't going to leave town until they got him. Once Nucky was indicted and awaiting trial, several of his lieutenants began jockeying for position. The two main competitors were Frank Farley and the mayor, Thomas D. Taggart, Jr.

Tommy Taggart was born in Philadelphia in 1903, and his family moved to Atlantic City when he was six. The Taggarts were one of hundreds of Philadelphia families who relocated to the resort at the turn of the 20th century. Thomas, Sr. was chief surgeon at the Atlantic City Hospital for 25 years and was one of the most respected members of the community. Taggart's mother came from old wealth and boasted that her ancestors had arrived in America on the Mayflower. If Atlantic City had an upper class, the Taggarts were part of it.

Tommy Taggart attended Atlantic City High School and then Dickinson Law School. He was admitted to practice in 1927 and with his family's backing opened his own law office. Taggart immediately gravitated toward politics, joining the Third Ward Republican Club, serving the organization faithfully as a campaign worker in several elections. He did everything from writing campaign literature and printing copies, to personally handing them out on the streets. Despite his advantage in education and family wealth Tommy Taggart worked side-by-side with the other ward heelers. But he wasn't "one of the boys." A little known fact about his personal life was that Taggart was a closet homosexual. One well-connected tavern owner spoke of Taggart this way: "What can I say? He liked boys, young boys. Several times I even fixed him up with good-looking young fags. But he was a hell of a politician, even though he was queer."

Taggart was more fascinated with political power than the attraction of handsome young men. He was devoted to the organization. His commitment and loyalty impressed Nucky, and in 1934 Johnson passed over several other people with more seniority and made him a candidate for State Assembly. Upon his election, Taggart was married to Atlantic City politics. "What you had was a solid organization man. Tommy Taggart moved up because he played by the rules of the ward system."

Once elected, Taggart found the campaign never ended. He was expected to devote himself full-time serving the people; however, an Assemblyman's annual salary of $500 didn't begin to pay for the time spent on politics. Nucky supplemented his income with a second office. The position was police recorder. Comparable to today's municipal court judge, Taggart handled minor criminal complaints, disorderly persons offenses, and traffic violations.

The local municipal court was a sensitive part of the political ward system and its judge had to be a team player. "If your uncle got locked up for being drunk, the ward leader would get him out. If your boy happened to get picked up because he was caught in the wrong place, the ward leader would get him off. If your brother was involved in a fight, the ward leader would make sure he wasn't convicted." The ward leader or his precinct captains needed direct access to the court. They had to be able to fix things whenever one of their constituents had a run-in with the law. If the ward leader couldn't deliver, he would lose the loyalty of the voters. The police recorder had to be someone who could be counted on to bend the law when necessary. He had to know what to do when a ward leader walked into his office and dropped several summonses on his desk and said, "Here, take care of these."

Tommy Taggart knew how to take care of things as police recorder. He understood his new position could be a powerful tool in advancing his career and seized the opportunity. Serving in the municipal court brought him daily contact with the ward leaders and precinct captains throughout the city. His position enabled him to build up hundreds of political IOUs among Atlantic City's residents. He was re-elected to the assembly in 1936 and in 1937 won a three-year term as state senator. Taggart was the most popular Republican candidate in town and considered himself the rightful heir to Nucky's power. When the FBI's investigation began to intensify and key people were indicted and convicted, Taggart thought "everything was up for grabs" and began positioning himself to become boss.

Taggart made his move in 1940. That year he ran for yet another office. He was part of the machine-endorsed slate for City Commission. It was understood that after the election he would be chosen mayor by his fellow commissioners. During the selection of the slate Taggart made a miscue. He resisted, unsuccessfully, the party's choice of one of his running mates, Al Shahadi. Taggart feared Shahadi might support another candidate for mayor rather than him. Shahadi became the candidate and after the election supported Taggart for mayor along with the other commissioners. But Taggart had damaged his standing with the organization. He was a little too ambitious. He had shown that he had "plans of his own" and that disturbed Nucky and his key lieutenants. Despite his personal popularity, Taggart began his term as mayor in May 1940, in an atmosphere of resentment.

Taggart's moves didn't go unnoticed by Assemblyman Frank Farley. A young local attorney with none of Taggart's social advantages, Farley was elected to the assembly in 1937 when Taggart moved up to state senator.

Francis Sherman Farley (Hap) was born in Atlantic City on December 1, 1901. He was the last of 10 children born to Jim and Maria (Clowney) Farley in a family that struggled to keep everyone fed and clothed. Farley's family lived on Pennsylvania Avenue in an area that was fast becoming part of the Northside. Only poor Whites lived next to Blacks. And the whores were there, too. The Farley home was around the corner from "Chalfonte Alley," the local red light district. The prostitutes and their neighbors accepted one another, and Chalfonte Alley was part of the neighborhood. As a boy, Hap delivered newspapers and while in high school worked nights as a proofreader for a local newspaper, the *Press-Union*.

Jim Farley was secretary to the local fire department and one of the leaders in the change from volunteers to full-time firefighters. Through being a leader in the movement for a paid fire department and his efforts as a ward worker in the Kuehnle organization, Jim was appointed secretary in 1904. It didn't pay well, but it was secure and provided income 12 months of the year, something most local residents didn't have. The steady income meant a lot to a man with 10 kids. Secretary of the fire department was also a focal point for patronage, and Jim Farley used his power to make friends. Over the years, he helped several of his sons obtain jobs in the city's fire and police departments. The Farleys were an organization family that marched to the music of the Republican Party. In return they were rewarded by the Kuehnle and Johnson machines. Hap learned from his father and brothers that the local political ward system was the most important institution in town.

The most important person in young Frank Farley's life was his sister Jean. There was a 20-year spread between the 10 Farley children. Typical of large families where children oftentimes pair off and become closer to one sibling than the rest, Frank was inseparable from his sister Jean. She was his closest friend, confidant, and supporter his entire life. Jean saw potential in her younger brother and encouraged him to go to college. She sacrificed and did without to help her brother get through college and law school. Throughout his career Hap visited with Jean every morning to seek her counsel. When an important decision had to be made, Hap didn't act until he first spoke with his older sister.

Farley had none of Nucky's flamboyance. "Monastic" best describes his devotion to Atlantic City's politics. He lived for his town. Hap was a big man with an athletic build and large, powerful hands. He combed his thinning hair straight back and wore nothing but double-breasted suits and wing-tipped shoes. His posture was almost stooped shouldered, his gray eyes focused straight ahead, and he walked nearly at a run every place he went. He had the earnestness of a demanding parish priest. Not a gifted public speaker, he was, nevertheless, a persuasive communicator one-on-one. Unlike Nucky and the Commodore, Farley was Irish and Catholic, the first of his ethnicity to rise to a position of power in Atlantic City.

Frank Farley was a joiner and a doer. As a youth, he developed a passion for sports, which he had until his death. In high school, he played fullback in football, catcher in baseball, and forward in basketball. He was an outstanding athlete, exceling in basketball. While in law school, he was a starting player on the Georgetown University basketball team. Farley loved the competition and thrill of athletics, but, more importantly, he reveled in the camaraderie. He was the spark plug who got things moving whether it was practice or a game. His teammates dubbed him "Happy," which became "Hap" when he left his teens.

Farley had a special trait—some might say need—when it came to maintaining friendships. He remained close with every friend he made throughout his life. New acquaintances found themselves part of Farley's network and would discover they had someone who remembered their birthday, dropped them a note when they were ill, or telephoned unexpectedly just to chat.

One such friendship was struck in 1921 during the summer between Farley's years at the University of Pennsylvania and Georgetown Law School. That summer Hap became acquainted with another Georgetown law student who was working as a night clerk in an Atlantic City hotel. That student was John Sirica, who years later gained fame as the judge of the Nixon/Watergate trials. Farley and Sirica maintained their friendship until his death. Judge Sirica spoke of Farley with great warmth and humor, remembering him as "one of the friendliest fellows I ever met. … We met one summer in Atlantic City and became great friends in law school. After that he would call me at different times and we'd talk and talk. I'd never know when I might hear from him. Once we talked about the Watergate defendants and how stupid they all were to think they could get away with perjury. Hell, any first year law student would have known to plead the 5th Amendment before lying under oath. Despite his politics, Hap thought that Nixon crowd were fools." But there was more to Farley than his genial personality.

Hap Farley was a no-nonsense competitor. He thought of every-thing in terms of "the team." You were either part of his team or you weren't. He approached everything he did, whether work or play, with a fierce determination to succeed. If he couldn't do a thing well, he'd rather not get involved. "Whatever you do, do it thoroughly or don't touch it." Farley lived by this rule. A lifelong friend recalls, "Hap was one of those kind, when you're gonna do something, you're gonna do that and nothing else."

Upon returning home after graduation from law school, Farley was more interested in sports than law and politics. He was active in baseball and basketball, playing semi-professional baseball with the Melrose Club and forward for the Morris Guards. He also coached the Atlantic City Catholic Club and Schmidt Brewers basketball teams, both of which won several league championships. Farley's involvement in athletics continued for more than 10 years after his graduation from law school. While other young lawyers were sharp-ening their skills and establishing a law practice, Hap Farley was playing ball and building a network of friends who became the base for his career in politics. Years after he was gone from politics, there were peers of his who remembered him first as an athlete rather than as a politician. However, Farley's teammates weren't the kind of clients who paid large retainers and the little legal work he picked up through sports was hardly the basis for a successful law practice.

Years later Farley would tell "the story" of how he got involved in politics. He always said he had taken up the cause of his basketball team, which had been locked out of the school gym. It's true Hap did lead a movement for better facilities for his young athletes, but that wasn't the impetus for his political career. What really influenced him were years of going nowhere in his law practice and struggling to survive. In contrast, several of the Farley brothers, who had no formal education, had risen through the ranks of the Johnson organization and had well-paying, secure jobs as officers in the fire and police departments. During the Great Depression, these jobs looked good to a lawyer having a hard time paying his rent. Farley realized the political ward system was the road he'd have to follow if he was to make a place for himself in Atlantic City.

At about the same time Farley became involved in politics, he married his high school sweetheart, Marie "Honey" Feyl. Hap and Honey had met when they were teenagers. The Feyl family was socially prominent in the resort, and they discouraged their daughter's relationship with Hap. In their eyes the Farleys were Shanty Irish, proud but poor and common people. "Hap's people were poor, and the Feyls always thought their daughter was too good for him."

For the first several years of their courtship they communicated with one another by exchanging letters, which were delivered by one of Honey's girlfriends. Hap went off to college and Honey went to work as a secretary at a local realtor's office. Their bond was strong, and the correspondence continued while Hap was away at school. After his graduation from law school, they continued dating for another five years, finally marrying in 1929. But Marie Feyl had an illness that plagued her throughout her marriage to Hap. "Honey was an alcoholic for as long as I knew her. I remember the first night after their honeymoon—my apartment was just below theirs—Hap carried her up the stairs, and it wasn't because they just got married. She was too drunk to walk. It was like that most nights." They never had children and Hap was devoted to Honey until his death. Not even his closest friends detected a hint of infidelity.

Honey's job at Fox Realty brought her into contact with Herman "Stumpy" Orman. Stumpy Orman was a real estate salesman and through his association with Honey, he and Farley became acquainted. Orman had little formal education but was as shrewd and streetwise as anyone in Atlantic City. He had done well during Prohibition and was one of Nucky's key lieutenants. Orman knew a comer when he saw one. He became friends with Farley and treated Hap and Honey to dinner frequently. Through his relationship with Orman and observing Nucky Johnson, Farley learned the mechanics of the partnership between the racketeers and politicians. When Farley was given the nod to run for state assembly in 1937, Stumpy Orman was there to support him, providing Farley the money needed to wage his campaign. This investment was the beginning of an alliance that generated benefits to both of them for the next 25 years.

The network of friends that Farley had made over the years showed itself in the 1937 election results. In his first political contest Farley ran ahead of the ticket and came within 127 votes of out-polling the leading candidate, Tommy Taggart. This was Taggart's fourth election, and prior to Farley he was recognized as the Republican's most popular candidate. With his strong showing in the election of '37 Farley became a force in the Republican Party. Farley and his running mate, Vincent Haneman, a popular local lawyer and mayor of neighboring Brigantine, set about making names for them-selves as public servants throughout Atlantic County and in the State House. Farley and Haneman meshed well and quickly became a powerful team, re-elected by large majorities in 1938 and 1939.

Taggart, Farley, and Haneman: They were the most obvious con-tenders to replace Nucky Johnson. Besides them, there were three others who had standing in the party: James Carmack, a local den-tist, well connected socially and politically; Walt Jeffries, a former U.S. Congressman and county sheriff; and Joe Altman, city com-missioner and former assemblyman and police recorder. Farley stud-ied the strengths, weaknesses, and ambitions of each contender and crafted a strategy for each of them. He began with Haneman.

When Taggart became mayor, the party leaders wouldn't permit him to seek re-election to the state senate. Either Farley or Haneman could have been the candidate to replace Taggart. Haneman was pop-ular and more respected for his intellect as an attorney. Had he pushed for the nomination, Haneman probably would have been suc-cessful. Farley knew his friend loved the law more than politics and that he'd prefer a career as a judge rather than a politician. He also believed Haneman didn't have the stomach for a struggle to replace

Nucky. Farley knew Haneman's backing would give him the edge over any other rival who might jump into the fray. In exchange for Haneman's support for senator and party chairman Farley agreed to push Haneman's name for an appointment to the bench. Haneman was appointed to the Common Pleas Court in 1940 and was eventually elevated to the State Supreme Court in 1960 where he had an outstanding career as a jurist. Next was Carmack.

James Carmack was never a serious contender to replace Nucky, but he thought he was, and his money and social ties were a force to be reckoned with. Farley sensed Carmack wanted only to hold an office with prestige. That would satisfy Carmack and keep him out of the race to succeed Nucky. Farley and Haneman supported Carmack for county sheriff in 1941 and the new sheriff closed ranks behind Farley. Then there was Jeffries.

Walt Jeffries was a long-time, loyal Republican and a popular vote-getter in every campaign. He had worked his way up from local office in the down beach community of Margate, to U.S. Congress. Jeffries didn't want power so much as a decent paying position to round out his career. The quid pro quo for backing Farley's bid to become party chairman was Hap's pledge to permit Jeffries to seek the job of county treasurer without competition, after Johnson was forced out. Farley's Senate salary wasn't enough to live on, and he wanted to be treasurer himself. Haneman counseled him to be patient. Jeffries replaced Nucky for a single three-year term when he went to jail in 1941. Three years later, in 1944, Farley had the votes he needed among the county board of freeholders and ousted Jeffries, remaining treasurer until 1970. Finally, there was Altman.

Joe Altman was a clever and experienced politician. "He was as smooth a glad-hander as ever lived" and was popular among the party leaders and the general public. But, Altman wasn't ambitious. He was quite comfortable following Nucky's lead. While the support may have been there, he wasn't about to try to become boss himself. That would have been too much work. Joe Altman preferred playing cards every afternoon at the Lion's Club. Farley could see what Altman wanted was a safe job with prestige. Mayor was what he wanted, provided someone else was the boss. Farley assured Altman he would back him for mayor once Taggart was out of the way. Altman became mayor in 1944 and remained there, following Farley's lead all the while, for the next 25 years.

Another player, without whose support Farley couldn't have risen to power, was James Boyd, clerk of the board of freeholders. Boyd was Nucky Johnson's political right arm and leader of the powerful Fourth Ward. Boyd recognized that of the contenders for Nucky's title, Farley was the only one with whom he could continue to exercise the same control over the organization he had under Nucky. Boyd had no choice but to back Farley. Finally, as for Johnson's support, there were no deals Farley could make. Nucky was preoccupied with trying to keep out of jail, and as he countered the moves of the FBI, his presence faded. Farley had nothing to offer Johnson except a sympathetic ear and quiet support for a job in city government for Nucky's new bride, Flossie. The trick was to remain loyal but still keep his distance.

As the key players in the Republican machine were lining up behind Farley, Taggart set upon the course that led to his ruin. In addition to being elected mayor, Taggart insisted on being named the director of public safety, giving him direct control over the police department. Taggart believed he could use this power to bludgeon the local vice industry into line. He began sporting pearl-handled six shooters on his hips and was tagged by the local media, "Two Gun Tommy." In the summer 1940, while Johnson was awaiting trial, Taggart began making raids on various gambling rooms throughout town. He had a police radio installed in his car and personally took charge of the raids.

Through his raids on the gambling rooms Two Gun Tommy was sending out the message he was now the boss, and that the racketeers had to deal with him or he'd shut them down. Taggart's raids attracted sensational coverage in both the local and national media. Never before had an Atlantic City politician declared war on the rackets. When the vice industry refused to support him, he increased the raids and cast himself as a crusader cleaning up the town. Tommy Taggart, "the solid organization man" who as police recorder had bent the law to advance his political career, was now a reformer.

It may have made good headlines in out-of-town newspapers, but politically, Taggart's actions were a disaster. Two Gun Tommy's power grab failed. Farley's supporters got the word out that in addition to being a grandstanding troublemaker, Taggart was a homosexual. His position was severely damaged and by April 1941 the Republican ward leaders formed a "War Board," making plans to have Taggart removed from office. That May, only one year after Taggart had been sworn into office, the precinct captains were gathering signatures to have Two Gun Tommy removed at a recall election.

There never was a recall election. Instead Frank Farley engineered a coup, which eliminated any chance of the voters doing something unpredictable. At Farley's prompting, the city commissioners adopted two "Ripper Resolutions" that made Taggart a figurehead. While Taggart was out of town, the other four commissioners stripped him of the Mayor's supervision of the police department, municipal court, the building department, and public relations office. Taggart was mayor in name only. The four commissioners issued a joint statement claiming, "We have restrained every effort" to aid the mayor, they said, but "he has been unable to properly discharge the duties of his departments." This was their only public statement. Farley instructed everyone to duck any questions from the media. Farley and his allies followed the political adage of Calvin Coolidge, "I've never had to explain something I didn't say."

Taggart knew who had masterminded the coup, but there was nothing he could do. By May 1942, with Nucky in jail, everyone of any importance had closed ranks behind Farley. Taggart sued his fellow commissioners to regain his powers and lost, being replaced as mayor by Joe Altman in 1944. Later Taggart attacked Farley and harassed him by every means he could, but it was no use. Consumed and frustrated to the end, Tommy Taggart died, most say from nervous exhaustion, in September 1950. He was crushed by a system he only partly understood.

A telling footnote to the transition from Nucky to Frank Farley is Farley's service as legal counsel to one George Goodman. While Taggart was leading his gambling raids and grabbing headlines, Farley was quietly using his talents as a lawyer to assist the local vice industry.

George Goodman was the operator of the horse race information service for the Atlantic City gambling rooms. He had a private wire to his place of business, originating there and going to 23 other places in Atlantic City. In 1940 New Jersey Bell notified Goodman it intended to cut off his telephone service. The telephone company worried it might be prosecuted for giving service to an illegal enterprise. Farley interceded on behalf of Goodman and met with Frankland Briggs,

Bell's general counsel. Briggs later testified in a legal proceeding that "He [Farley] told me Goodman frankly admitted he was in the scratch sheet business but that he [Goodman] was neither a bookmaker or gambler but was merely conducting an information service. Mr. Farley argued that his client could legally furnish such information and was no more liable to arrest than newspapers or radios which dispensed racing news." Farley won several extensions of Goodman's service, but the telephone company prevailed in the end. By representing Goodman Farley gained the respect of Atlantic City's gangsters, which was essential to becoming boss. While he valued the racketeers' support, it was the respect of the state's political leaders that Farley wanted most.

His several years as an assemblyman had made a lasting impression and with his election to the state senate in 1940, Hap Farley was where he wanted to be. The overwhelming majorities delivered by Atlantic County in Republican primaries guaranteed Nucky's successor a prominent position in Republican politics statewide. Farley's dual role as boss and senator brought him into regular contact with the leaders of both parties. At the time, South Jersey was overwhelmingly Republican and Atlantic County was the leading Republican county. It wasn't long before Hap was the acknowledged spokesman for the seven senators from South Jersey.

Farley loved being State Senator and worked tirelessly to become an effective legislator. He studied his 20 colleagues and always knew what issues were important to them. His relationship with his fellow senators was marked by "unfailing courtesy, personal warmth, and complete integrity to every commitment made." As Senator Wayne Dumont, a colleague of 20 years, recalled, "He never made a commitment lightly, but you could always rely upon his word—it was totally good. I knew if I got a commitment out of him I never had to worry because he would keep it." And he expected everyone else to do likewise. "Once you reneged on a deal with Hap Farley, that was it. He had nothing more to do with you."

Frank Farley had a gift for the legislative process: He never forgot the terms of any alliance, he avoided conflicting obligations with remarkable finesse, and *always* knew where he had to be on a piece of legislation at any given time. "He would remember if he shook your hand and said to you that he was going to do something. You could count on it. Hap remembered every horse he ever traded, nothing got by him." He had a parochial view of the legislative process—Atlantic City and County were his only interests. Provided it wasn't harmful to Atlantic County, Farley would support any legislation devised to help another senator's county. He never became involved in statewide issues per se, except for the impact on Atlantic County; then he was out front taking control of the situation. If Hap couldn't help a colleague on legislation important to him, he'd never hurt him, letting someone else deliver the blow.

Unlike most politicians who are forever looking to the next election for another position, Farley had no aspirations for higher office. He could have run for congress, governor, or U.S. Senator on any one of several occasions, but chose not to. He knew the Atlantic City Republican organization was perceived as one of the most corrupt political machines in the state, matched only by the Democratic Hague-Kenny regime in Jersey City. "Hap knew better than to try to be anything more than the boss of Atlantic County." To run for statewide office would have exposed Farley and his organization to scrutiny he'd rather not have. With that in mind, being senator from Atlantic County satisfied his political ego. Farley had attained all he wanted or could safely aspire to from electoral politics. Politically, he was a competitor to no one in Trenton and his fellow senators never suspected his motives, trusting him completely.

Equally important as his relationship with the other senators were his work habits. In 34 years in the legislature, Farley missed a total of three sessions; on each occasion he was in the hospital. He dedicated himself to being on the job and was a full-time legislator who didn't believe in vacations. His work was his relaxation. Hap believed that "If you're going to get things done you have to be there and apply all your energies to the work at hand." He focused his intensity on learning the ropes of the state bureaucracy, mastering the function of every agency, acquiring a thorough knowledge of their budgets. He understood how valuable the administrative branch could be to an elected official in providing constituent services. He cultivated his relationship with the bureaucrats at every level in much the same way he did with his fellow legislators. His commitment to his duties could serve as a role model for any elected official.

Reminiscent of "Nucky's Nocturne," Hap formed the "21 Club," a social organization dedicated to promoting informal gatherings of all 21 senators, Republican and Democrat. The group got together at the close of each legislative session with Hap always hosting the affair. Each year Hap invited his fellow senators, together with their families, for a weekend of entertainment, food, and relaxation in Atlantic City. The senators and their families were put up in style in one of the Boardwalk hotels. While not as lavish as Nucky's parties, Hap saw to it every need of his guests was satisfied without expense. The 21 Club lasted for nearly 25 years and was valuable public relations for both Farley and the resort.

Farley's relationship with his fellow senators wasn't the only one he nurtured. He had daily contact with the ward leaders and precinct captains. He made himself accessible to the public and had his hand on the pulse of the community. When someone was sick, he would send flowers or a get well card; if there was a death, he went to the wake; should a voter be down on his luck and too proud for welfare, Farley arranged an anonymous gift or a loan. Sometimes it was necessary for him to perform free legal services. Hap was doing "pro bono" legal work before the phrase was coined.

For the first 20 years of his legislative career Farley spent every Monday morning representing constituents who had been threatened with loss of their driver's license before the Division of Motor Vehicles in Trenton. He represented six to eight people each morning before reporting to the Senate and never took a fee; the only thing he ever asked for was their vote for the Republican ticket come election time. Hap was the point person in an elaborate social service program, namely, Republican ward politics, and *everyone* did his or her part. Whatever the problem, Hap's lieutenants had orders that he was to know about it.

During the early years of Hap's reign, there were other "lieutenants" in town. They had nothing to do with ward politics, but they were important, too. The United States Army had come to town. Throughout most of World War II, Atlantic City was used as a training center for tens of thousands of American GIs. It was a boon to the resort economy.

The large hotels and Convention Hall were ideal temporary facilities—they were mostly empty anyway because of the war—and Atlantic City became a Basic Training Center for the Army Air Corps. The Army leased Convention Hall and its main arena and meeting rooms were transformed into a training facility. Thousands of recruits did calisthenics, received briefings daily at the Hall, and trained for maneuvers on the beach. While many of the troops partied on their time off, there was no gambling. The Army brass made it clear that they didn't want their men losing money in the resort's gambling rooms. For the first time in nearly 50 years "the slough was on" for more than several days. The "slough" was the term used by locals when the presence of someone in town, or the occurrence of an event, would temporarily force the closure of gambling rooms. It never lasted any longer than necessary. Even during the FBI's investigation of Nucky the "slough" was only intermittent, weeks at a time at most. With World War II, it lasted for years and created hard times for the people operating gambling rooms that weren't part of a nightclub or restaurant.

The war may not have been a good thing for the local racketeers, but it was great for the resort's economy. Many hotels and boarding-houses throughout the resort were converted into barracks and offices. By 1943, the Army had moved into such places as the Traymore, Breakers, Brighton, Shelburne, and Dennis. For many servicemen, basic training in Atlantic City was a pleasant surprise. Their accommodations were far better than the average GI who trained in places like Fort Dix. Many of the soldiers enjoyed their stay so much they returned with their families after the war. For Boardwalk merchants, shopkeepers, barbers, bartenders, and restaurant owners, the Army and its seven-day per week visitors were a blessing. The Army's presence helped many businesses survive the hard times that followed the repeal of Prohibition and the further loss of vacationers and conventioneers caused by the war. World War II was good to Atlantic City and times were very good for Hap Farley, who saw his power enhanced considerably.

In the election of 1943 Farley's career received an unexpected boost. He was transformed from one of the more influential legislators to the dominant force in the New Jersey Senate. At the age of 70, after being away from Trenton for nearly 25 years, Walter Edge, Atlantic City's most distinguished self-made man ever, made a political comeback and was elected governor. Following the term as governor engineered by Nucky Johnson, Edge went on to serve as U.S. Senator and Ambassador to France. From Hap Farley's perspective, the timing of Edge's return to politics could not have been better. As the political boss of the governor's home county, Farley's stock with the politicians in Trenton rose dramatically. With Walter Edge in the governor's office, political leaders from the entire state, not just South Jersey, treated Farley with respect and sought his support. Hap exploited it for all it was worth. In Edge's first year in office Farley was chosen majority leader; the following year he was elected senate president, becoming the undisputed leader of his party's caucus. In terms of statewide power, Hap Farley never looked back.

Hap ruled the Republican Caucus in the state senate the same way a strong-willed coach runs his team. He called all the plays. At the time, the Republican Caucus *was* the senate, and in short order, Farley *was* the caucus. The GOP maintained sizable majorities, consistently controlling 13 to 17 of the 21 counties. The seven southern counties were nearly always represented by Republican senators; these were Farley's votes. As leader of the caucus, Farley set the ground rules for how legislation was handled. He imposed a rule that no bill could be voted on in the full senate unless it had the support of at least 11 senators in the Republican Caucus. Once 11 votes were secured the other senators were expected to follow the rule of the majority and vote for the bill when it reached the senate floor. But 11 votes it had to be. Even if a majority of the Caucus, comprised of, say, seven to nine North Jersey senators, supported a particular bill, it would never see the light of day if Farley opposed it.

Farley's dominance made the senate's committee system meaningless. With Hap in control, the committees had no function except for political window-dressing. The only senate committee of any real importance was Judiciary, which passed upon nominations of the governor. Farley was either chairman of that committee or its dominant member during most of his career. For the next 25 years, Hap Farley was an insurmountable reality with whom every governor, regardless of party, had to contend. He could not be ignored. Farley controlled the senate so totally that it was political suicide to oppose him. "I can remember sitting in on more than one meeting between Hap and a governor. Hap's agenda was always first." The governors either dealt with Hap Farley or had their programs frustrated.

One bill that passed into law in 1945 demonstrates the power that Farley had attained after four years as senator. In September 1944 the Boardwalk was severely damaged by a hurricane. Whole portions of it had been washed away. It was wartime and Atlantic City's government didn't have the finances for the necessary repairs. Farley and Atlantic County Assemblyman Leon Leonard sponsored legislation to create the Municipal Improvement Tax or "Luxury Tax." The Luxury Tax was special legislation designed to permit Atlantic City to levy a sales tax, something neither state government nor any other city in New Jersey had the power to do. The bill would permit a 5 percent tax on all retail sales, including food and drink in public restaurants, hotel rooms, and other services and entertainment. The idea was popular in the resort as the bulk of the revenue raised would come from tourists. It was estimated that the Luxury Tax would gross $500,000 to $800,000 per year and was to expire after a single summer season.

Securing the necessary votes in the senate was routine. Despite the opposition of a lone Republican Senator from Essex County, Farley had 15 votes, four more than required. The problem was in the assembly, where 31 votes were needed, and again the opposition came from the Republicans of Essex County. The Essex County Republicans had campaigned for election the previous year by running against new taxes of any kind. Without the four Republican votes from Essex County, there were only 28 Republican votes available. Farley tried every tactic he could think of, but the Essex County Assemblymen wouldn't budge. Rather than see his bill go down to defeat, Farley turned to Nucky Johnson's old ally, Jersey City Mayor Frank Hague.

Hudson County Democratic boss Frank Hague controlled four votes in the assembly, and Farley had something he wanted. There were two Republican bills aimed at Hague's machine, both of which had the support of Governor Edge. One bill limited the jurisdiction of the Hudson County Traffic Court, reducing the authority of Hague's handpicked magistrates. The other was designed to make the Hudson County Boulevard Commission a bipartisan agency—the commission was a major source of patronage. Hague wanted both bills killed, and only Farley could do that. Farley defied the governor and promised Hague the bills would never reach the floor of the senate. In exchange, Hague delivered his four votes and Farley got what he wanted. More than 50 years later the Luxury Tax is still in effect, generating millions of dollars in revenue.

With each re-election Farley's presence loomed larger in the state house. In 10 years as senator he had become the most respected, and feared, powerbroker in New Jersey. To get anything done in Trenton, you had to see Hap. His power brought attention, and between 1946 and 1950 Farley was subjected to one investigation after another. His role as attorney for both the Atlantic City Race Track and a local contracting firm, Massett Construction Company, were scrutinized, as were the finances of Atlantic City's government and the county Republican organization. In each instance Farley came away unscathed. Rather than tarnish his image, these investigations increased his stature.

One inquiry into Farley's empire that attracted nationwide publicity was the U.S. Senate's investigation into organized crime. In 1951 Estes Kefauver, U.S. Senator from Tennessee, was gearing up to run for President. As part of his campaign he had declared war on organized crime and the rackets. Using his position as chairman of a Senate Committee, Kefauver went from one city to another holding public hearings, exposing the local crime syndicates. During the preceding year there was a rebellion by several Atlantic City police officers, which attracted national attention and placed Farley and his organization high on Kefauver's list.

In the summer of 1950 a group of police officers and firefighters organized themselves in an effort to secure a wage increase. The average police officer received an annual salary of less than $3,000; they were seeking a pay increase of $400 per year. The wage demands weren't taken to Mayor Altman or the city commission but rather to Farley. City hall was filled with people handpicked by Farley. He was the puppeteer, and city government moved as he pulled the strings. When the city commission held its weekly caucus, Farley was always on hand for key decisions. No public contract, tax assessment, fire inspection, liquor license, or Boardwalk concession received approval if Hap said no. The leaders of this group knew they could never get a pay raise without his support.

Farley met with a delegation of employees and heard their requests. As usual he was cordial and assured them he'd "work something out." The employees took this to mean they'd receive a raise. Several city commission meetings came and went with no action taken or any mention of their request. When approached a second time, Farley told the group's leaders they'd have to be patient a while longer. Rather than wait, the group began a petition drive. Their game plan was to force a public question for their pay raise onto the ballot at the November election of 1950. Circulating their petition door-to-door, they gathered more than 16,000 signatures. With that type of public support, they believed Farley and the city commissioners would have no choice but to support them. They were wrong.

Farley went to a mass meeting of police officers and fire fighters and asked them to withdraw their request for the referendum. The leaders of the petition drive refused. Farley responded by having a loyalty oath circulated. The oath amounted to a counterpetition for police and fire fighters to renounce the referendum and to accept a future wage ordinance to be approved by the city commission. City employees who had signed the loyalty oath were expected to show their paper ballots (the election was pre-machine voting) to the poll workers. The intimidation worked. The referendum proceeded as scheduled and was soundly defeated. The question received the support of less than half the number of voters who had signed the petition, humiliating the group's leaders.

Three of the movement's spokesmen were policemen Jack Portock, Fred Warlich, and Francis Gribbin. They were bitter at their defeat and determined to get revenge. They retaliated by hitting Farley's organization where it hurt.

After Nucky Johnson went to jail, and during World War II, the "slough" had been on more often than not. The slough was the term used to describe the closing of the gambling rooms because of outside pressure, first the federal investigators and then the U.S. Army, which stationed thousands of recruits in the resort's hotels during World War II. By 1950 things had returned to normal. While Farley's people were less brazen than Nucky Johnson, the rackets flourished under Hap. Protection money continued to be paid to the organization with Stumpy Orman tending to such matters, keeping Farley one step removed from handling payoffs.

Portock, Warlich, and Gribbin knew the card games, horse rooms, and numbers syndicate were able to exist because the police officer on the beat looked the other way. The rackets were something individual patrol officers had nothing to do with. If there were problems with an operator who didn't have the okay from Stumpy Orman, or if someone failed to pay protection money, then either Lou Arnheim or Arch Witham of the vice squad would be sent out by Orman to apply pressure by either collecting the money or shutting them down.

Several weeks after defeat of the referendum, Portock and company tried to subdue the organization by attacking it head-on. As Tommy Taggart had done 10 years earlier, they began making arrests for violation of the state gambling laws. Atlantic City's racketeers were stupefied. No one could believe what was happening. Farley responded cautiously. Each of the patrol officers were summoned first to their ward leaders and then to Orman and Jimmy Boyd. According to a ward leader at the time, Portock and the others were told they were "creating a lot of bad publicity for Atlantic City" and were ordered to stop the raids. "What are you doing this for? It won't do you any good, and you know you can't fight the organization. Keep it up and you'll be out of a job."

In winter 1951 one of Farley's lieutenants, Richard Jackson, assistant to the commissioner of public safety, arranged a meeting between Farley and the rebel police officers in an attempt to make peace. At the last moment, Jimmy Boyd killed the meeting. Boyd viewed the police officers' willingness to meet as a sign of weakness and advised Farley he could wipe them out. Nevertheless, the arrests continued and Portock and his cohorts became celebrities, of sorts. Between November 1950 and May 1951 Portock and company wreaked havoc on the rackets. Their raids spared no one and enraged Orman, Boyd, and Farley. They were dubbed by the national media as the "Four Horsemen," portrayed as heroes crusading against crime and political corruption. (There never really was a fourth "horseman" per se; William Shepperson and others occasionally accompanied Portock, Warlich, and Gribbin.) When Farley refused to compromise on the wage increase they found they had backed themselves into a corner. The Four Horsemen had no choice but to continue the raids. The best they could hope for was to embarrass Farley.

But the organization had the last say. The Four Horsemen were given remote duty assignments, at odd hours, patrolling on foot areas of the city where police officers didn't usually patrol. They were assigned deserted potions of the Boardwalk during the winter months and to guard the public water mains coming from the mainland reservoir on the outskirts of town. A special traffic squad was created and Portock and friends were ordered to remain in the middle of the street prohibited from moving farther than 20 feet from their post. The traffic squad's hours were from 10:30 A.M. to 6:30 P.M., the hours during which numbers runners and bookies collected and paid off. The rebels persisted by making raids on their own time and found themselves suspended without pay for five days at a time, the maximum then permitted under Civil Service without a hearing.

Eventually each of the Four Horsemen was brought up on charges for misconduct and fired from their positions.

Before they were crushed, the Four Horsemen had their day in the sun as witnesses before the Kefauver Committee. Portock and his supporters appeared before the committee and named the key politicians and racketeers who profited from gambling. They produced a card index file listing more than 300 racketeers. They told how the numbers barons parlayed the nickels and dimes of local residents and tourists into yearly incomes of $150,000. Their testimony detailed the corrupt workings of the police department. Chief of Police Harry Saunders was at best a figurehead and the city commissioner in charge of the public safety department, William Cuthbert, was exposed as a senile old man. Testimony revealed that Cuthbert was routinely driven around town in his city car by a fireman, delivering eggs from a farm he owned on the mainland. The police department was really run by Stumpy Orman and Jimmy Boyd. Orman, the city's leading racketeer, made sure everybody paid up. Boyd was the political enforcer who kept everyone in line. Kefauver's Committee report concluded that it was "inescapable that Stumpy Orman has controlled the Atlantic City Police Department in the interest of the underworld gambling fraternity."

Orman was subpoenaed to the hearings, but the committee learned nothing from him. He alternated between refusing to answer the questions put to him, and taking refuge in what he called "my very bad memory." Farley had given him such free rein of the rackets that Stumpy Orman wasn't used to answering to anyone.

Supporters of the Four Horsemen, such as former Judge Paul Warke and Jack Wolfe, appeared before the committee and told of the punishment meted out to anyone who bucked the system. As a county judge, Warke had given stiff sentences to several gambling operators arrested by state investigators. When he came up for reappointment he found himself out of a job. Farley denied Warke's sentencing practices were the reason he wasn't reappointed, but the denials were hollow. Jack Wolfe, who was not a Lafferty Democrat, had run for state assembly on the Democratic slate and was fiercely critical of the organization. He received increased assessments on the taxes and municipal utilities at his place of business.

The committee's hearings stripped Farley's organization bare. The testimony elicited by Kefauver's Committee produced the following revelations: The traditional alliance between the racketeers and politicians was alive and well with the local Republican Party financed through protection money; Stumpy Orman periodically issued a list of approved gambling operations and had the vice squad close down anyone who didn't have his blessing; Lester Burdick, a Farley lieutenant who served as Executive Clerk of the New Jersey Senate, was also the bagman for racing results payments from horse-room operators; Vincent Lane, an Atlantic County Probation Officer, moonlighted during his off hours as a gambling room operator; those racketeers arrested by the Four Horsemen were routinely charged with a disorderly persons offense, and, if convicted, sentenced to the county jail from which they were promptly released. In one such instance Austin Johnson, a convicted bookmaker, was driven home on weekends during his sentence by Sheriff Gerald Gormley's chauffeur. In response to all the negative publicity Farley made changes in city government, mostly shuffling the players. In time a grand jury was convened but no one of any consequence, other than the Four Horsemen themselves, was prosecuted.

The impact of the Kefauver hearings was felt on two fronts. The first was in the rackets. Post-Kefauver, Atlantic City's gambling operations could no longer be run wide open. Farley and Orman agreed things had to be done at a lower profile and gambling became a minor industry in the resort's economy. There was also political fallout from the Kefauver investigation. Farley's enemies were emboldened by the negative publicity and decided to make a contest of the city commission election held in the May following the hearings.

The 1952 commission election featured Farley's handpicked slate of incumbents headed by Mayor Joe Altman, minus Public Safety Director William Cuthbert, who was forced to step down. An opposition slate headed by former Atlantic County Sheriff James Carmack ran as the "Fusion-for-Freedom Ticket." Jimmy Carmack had fallen out with the organization shortly after becoming sheriff in 1941. As sheriff, Carmack had failed to clear his patronage appointments through Jimmy Boyd. For refusing to be a team player, he was dropped from the organization. Carmack was joined by Marvin Perskie, a pugnacious former Marine officer and brilliant young attorney who had represented the Four Horsemen in their problems with the organization.

With Perskie firing most of the salvos, the Fusion Ticket made one blistering attack after another against Farley and the Republican machine. Portions of the Kefauver Committee transcripts were reprinted, as were articles from the national media condemning corruption in Atlantic City. Cozy relationships between local contractors and city government were exposed. The payment of insurance premiums and vendors' contracts to local politicians were revealed. The details of the lawyer fees paid for a municipal finance bond ordinance were also made public. Of the nearly $100,000 in fees paid by the taxpayers, only $21,000 went to the New York law firm that actually did the legal work for the bond issue. The remaining $79,000 was divided between Farley and 11 of his cronies, with Hap himself receiving $9,500 for having done nothing. Perskie and Carmack named names and criticized the Republican organization like never before. For the first time since becoming boss, Frank Farley had a fight on his hands.

There were the obligatory denials of the charges made by Perskie and Carmack, but there was no counteroffensive or debate on the campaign issues raised by the Fusion slate. Instead, Farley's strategy was to go to his strength. He appealed to the ward leaders and precinct captains in terms they understood: If the Fusion slate won, the ward workers would lose their access to political patronage.

Farley also brought Nucky Johnson out of retirement and turned him loose in the Northside. Hap had no choice but to rely on Nucky. Despite his imprisonment and the passing of time, Nucky remained popular in Atlantic City's Black community. "Farley could never cultivate the Blacks the way Johnson had. When Nucky went to jail everyone in the Black community assumed he'd eventually come back as the Boss. They never really accepted Farley." Nucky stumped for the slate in every Black precinct, being introduced as "the champion of 'em all." The strategy worked. The machine slate carried 49 of the 64 voting precincts. Carmack, the "high man" for the Fusion Ticket, trailed Tom Wooten, the machine's "low man," by nearly 3,000 votes. The revolt had been quelled. The political ward system constructed by Nucky Johnson more than 30 years earlier was still able to crank out the votes when it had to.

Without the political ward system, Farley's slate would have gone down to defeat. Ward politics was the mortar that held things together; its influence was woven into the fabric of the community. The players in the ward system had a devotion bordering on religious fervor. Atlantic City's ward politicians were streetwise foot soldiers, as disciplined and loyal a group as could be found in a well-trained army. And *everyone* was a soldier. A move up in the Republican machine meant not only more power but responsibility. From the lowliest ward heeler on up to Farley, every member of the organization had a job to do. The ward system was not a monolith headed by a dictator but rather a network of savvy politicians who worked at their craft daily. Farley was boss because he was the one at the top of the pyramid, and remained there only because he delivered to those under him. The pressure to deliver was constant. Hap Farley either performed as expected or he would have been replaced.

Farley was boss, but he wasn't the day-to-day ruler of the political ward system. Just as he had insulated himself from the rackets by delegating authority to Stumpy Orman, he did the same with political matters. Farley enjoyed his role as a legislator, manipulating the state senate, more than anything. He couldn't immerse himself into local politics to the extent Nucky had and still have time for his duties in Trenton. Orman's counterpart was James Boyd, Clerk of the County Board of Freeholders.

Jimmy Boyd or "Boydie" had been a protégé of Nucky Johnson. He and Johnson met in the 1920s when Nucky was becoming involved with Luciano and the Seven Group. Johnson needed someone to whom he could assign a portion of his political chores. Boyd was a bellhop at the Ritz Carlton where Nucky lived, and they took to one another almost immediately. Boyd had a knack for politics and manipulating people, whether by charm or intimidation. Johnson recognized his talent and groomed Boyd to take care of political details for him. Starting out as an assistant to Nucky's personal secretary, Mae Paxson, and then, with the boss's help, moving quickly through the ranks to become freeholder clerk and Fourth Ward leader, Boyd was one of Johnson's most trusted lieutenants. Hap Farley inherited Jimmy Boyd. He couldn't have replaced him if he wanted to.

Jimmy Boyd was "the guy where you ran into the NO." Every political leader who relies on the voters for his power needs someone to be the heavy. Letting a supporter know his request can't be granted is dangerous business for a candidate. There has to be a thick-skinned S.O.B. to take the heat when there is bad news to be delivered. "Hap, and Nucky before him, couldn't come right out and tell you NO. He needed someone to do it for him and Boyd was the one." Farley never told anyone no, and rarely gave someone an unconditional yes. More often than not, no matter what the request, Farley would say, "It's okay with me, but you'd better go over and see Boydie. He'll work out the details."

Working out the details could be an unsettling experience. When he wanted to, Boyd had a "personality like a piece of ice." He knew most people were intimidated by the power Farley let him exercise and exploited their relationship for all it was worth. He usually started out by telling the favor-seeker that what he wanted couldn't be done, or to list all the problems granting the request would create. He did this as a matter of routine even when the answer was clearly yes. Boyd knew how to capitalize for political gain on every opportunity. The more difficult it was to grant a favor, the more indebted the constituent would be to the organization.

As the day-to-day leader of Atlantic City's four political wards, Jimmy Boyd was the enforcer, the one who imposed discipline and kept things running smoothly. Boyd arranged all the meetings and scheduled candidates' appearances. He made the ward workers jump to their assignments. If anyone complained that their task couldn't be done, Boyd would say sarcastically, "Sure, that's okay, we'll just postpone the election." But the sarcasm was the only warning. If the job didn't get done, the worker was replaced and quickly found himself an observer with no access to the organization or its patronage. Jimmy Boyd "had the ability to pull things together with an iron hand." Boyd learned well from Nucky and understood that to remain in control, the Republican machine had to be run like a business.

The organization survived on "services provided." Boyd had a disciplined network of political workers who were in daily contact with the community. Every lost job, arrest, illness, death, request for financial assistance, or new resident in the neighborhood was reported to the precinct captain. If the matter was important enough, it would be brought to the ward leader and possibly Boyd or Farley. No matter what the problem, the ward workers had orders to make an effort to solve it. Nothing could be left to chance. Every voter had to be accounted for, especially someone new to the neighborhood, "You had better not let anybody move into your precinct without registering them to vote or you would hear about it." Under Jimmy Boyd, "politics was a business, an absolute business."

The business of politics produced more than votes. It could generate money, and not all of it was from the obvious sources of graft and extortion. A classic example was Jimmy Boyd's ice cream monopoly. During the summer seasons of the '50s and '60s a combine consisting of Boyd, Edward Nappen, and Reuben Perr had a corner on the sale of ice cream on the Atlantic City beach. There wasn't a popsicle or ice cream cone sold from which Boyd and company didn't profit.

The ice cream combine was a natural. Each of the principals brought a special talent to the project. After World War II the state adopted legislation giving veterans priority for the right to peddle goods in public; however, it was a right subject to local licensing and Boyd had absolute control over who received a license. Despite the fact that as clerk to the freeholder board Boyd had no official tie with city hall, his relationship with Farley gave him the undisputed jurisdiction over such matters. During his reign as Fourth Ward leader there wasn't a business license for anything that didn't require Boyd's approval. Ever the conniver, it took Jimmy Boyd no time to see the potential in the situation.

Boyd recruited Ed Nappen because of his ties with the veterans groups. Nappen had been Fourth Ward leader and local magistrate and was active among Atlantic City's veterans. Nappen chose people who could be trusted to play ball with the combine by kicking back a portion of their profits. Perr was a lawyer who had contacts with the Philadelphia ice cream manufacturers. He saw to it no independents were supplied and set up the mechanics for distributing the ice cream. There were more than a few people who knew of Boyd's scheme, but no one ever complained or cried foul. Only in Atlantic City could you find someone like Jimmy Boyd profiting from the sale of popsicles.

Sweetheart setups to line politicians' pockets such as Boyd's ice cream monopoly were accepted as common practice by the community. Corruption was routine. Atlantic City's residents didn't care that their government was dishonest. What mattered was that government, through the ward politicians, responded to their needs. Quite often that need was for a patronage job with city or county government. The Farley and Boyd regime continued Nucky Johnson's practice of doling out hundreds of part-time and no-show jobs. The organization controlled thousands of positions such as lifeguards, health inspectors, couriers, maintenance men, clerks, ticket collectors at Convention Hall, and groundskeepers at the racetrack.

Obtaining one of these jobs began by making contact with your precinct captain. You didn't just drop by city hall and ask for an application. The precinct captain where you lived had to "sponsor" you or you'd never even receive an application. Every position was allocated and filled on a ward-by-ward basis. Appointments to fill vacancies by resignation, death, or dismissal were *always* done on a ward basis. If a person who resigned or died was working in city or county government and came from the Second Ward, then his replacement came from the Second Ward. It was possible for ward leaders to make trades for one position or another, but the rule was that when a vacancy arose the first question asked was where did the person live? "It was a strict system and was absolute law in the Atlantic City political organization. If there wasn't an opening available for your ward you'd have to wait until there was."

Atlantic City's seasonal economy made year-round, full-time employment a precious thing. If you were lucky enough to land a full-time job, such as a police officer, firefighter, or office worker, you were indebted to the Republican Party. As part of your employment, you were required to become active in ward politics and to contribute a percentage of your salary to the party. This usually took the form of buying tickets to political fundraisers. More importantly, any promotions at work were generally dependant on how well you performed as a political worker.

The incentive to work for the party was the chance of upward mobility. The person ahead of you had been where you were and he had worked his way to that position by being loyal to the party. If you did the same, you could move up, too. If you were to amount to anything, either in government or the political organization, you had to get an education in politics. The system guaranteed that, "If you were going to move up politically, you had to know what you were doing in terms of street politics. If you didn't, you simply didn't move up." The ward system was continually renewing itself by breeding new politicians.

An example of a political leader bred by the Atlantic City ward system is demonstrated in the career of Richard "Dick" Jackson. In 1928, at the age of 20, Dick Jackson moved from the Fourth Ward of Atlantic City to the Second Ward. He had two reasons for his move. He was unhappy and poorly paid with his job as a bank teller and was looking for permanent employment as a fireman with the city. The number of applicants ahead of him on the waiting list in the Fourth Ward made any chance of getting a job hopeless. Dick's brother, Howard, was a veteran fireman and encouraged his younger brother to move, because the likelihood of winning an appointment to the fire department would be better in the Second Ward. Howard also had plans of his own. He wanted to become a captain in the fire department but knew it would never happen until he first became a precinct captain. Dick had an engaging personality and Howard recruited his brother to help in expanding his power base. As a precinct captain, Howard would then command the respect of the organization and have the "political standing" needed to become a captain in the fire department.

Although Dick joined the Second Ward Republican Club promptly after moving, he had to wait more than a year for an opening with the fire department. Immediately after moving to the Second Ward he immersed himself in ward politics. "I knew that if I was ever going to advance myself, I'd have to do like my brother, Howard, did. I went to all the political meetings, made sandwiches, served beer, waited on tables and cleaned up after rallies. I handed out political literature, ran errands, drove people to the polls and registered new voters. Whatever my precinct captain or ward leader asked me to do—I jumped to it."

Jackson made himself known by participating in sports and circulating in the community, getting to know everyone in his neighborhood on a first name basis. One of the people he met through sports was Hap Farley, and they became friends and political allies immediately.

At election time, Jackson went door-to-door urging support for the Republican slate. The standard pitch was, "You don't know the candidate, but I do, and he is the one I have to go to when there's something that you need and you come to me for. So if you expect me to be able to help you, you have to vote for this person." Jackson was selling himself and the system more than he was selling a particular candidate. Through their efforts, one election after another, Dick and Howard Jackson paid their dues to the Republican organization. They finally got their opportunity to break into the hierarchy five years later in 1933. The precinct captain where the Jacksons lived was ill and near death when he decided to step down. The person presumed to be his successor was John Lewis, a freeholder. However, the Jacksons demanded a vote on who would be the next precinct captain. According to party rules every registered Republican in the precinct was permitted to vote, not just dues-paying club members. Dick and Howard Jackson called in all their favors and packed the meeting place with their supporters. Howard won easily and within a year's time became a captain in the fire department.

Dick Jackson had to wait five more years to make his move. In 1938 Howard moved from the Second Ward to the Fourth Ward, leaving a vacancy for precinct captain. Jackson succeeded to his brother's job and remained there until 1941 when he found himself in the middle of Hap Farley's maneuvering to become boss. Jackson respected Farley and had committed himself to support Hap as Nucky's replacement. The Second Ward leader, at that time, was Sam Weekly, who was also chief of police. Weekly had ties with both Taggart and Farley and was reluctant to choose between them, trying to remain neutral. To Farley that was the same as being an enemy. By 1941 Farley was gaining control in city and county governments. He began putting out the word in the Second Ward that the person to see for patronage was Jackson. When Weekly was cut out of the spoils system, the ward workers knew he had fallen and wanted no part of his leadership. In ward politics, "everyone is waiting for the person ahead of them to stumble." When the election of ward leader came up the following year, Weekly resigned rather than be humiliated by Jackson.

Shortly after being chosen Second Ward leader, Jackson was appointed secretary to the fire department. During his years as a fireman Jackson had gone back to school and obtained his high school diploma. He had also taken business college courses in bookkeeping, typing, and accounting. He was better prepared to serve as secretary than anyone realized and he did an outstanding job, receiving National Fire Board commendations for his indexing system of logging fires.

As both Second Ward leader and secretary to the fire department, Jackson had clout in the Atlantic City power structure. But Jackson didn't relax. "I never let myself forget that Secretary of the Fire Department is made with the stroke of a pen and can be taken away with a stroke of a pen. I protected my position by taking the tests for captain and Battalion Chief and passed them both." However, at Farley's request Dick Jackson remained secretary until 1950, when Farley had Public Safety Director William Cuthbert appoint Jackson his Executive Secretary. Cuthbert was growing senile and in no time Jackson was performing his duties.

The Kefauver hearings made Cuthbert look like a fool, and in 1952 Farley wouldn't permit him to seek reelection. Much to Jackson's disappointment, he was passed over to run for city commissioner. The candidate chosen was Tom Wooten (a favorite of Jimmy Boyd), who replaced Cuthbert as public safety director and retained Jackson as his executive secretary. Wooten knew nothing about his new job and had to rely entirely upon Jackson. The following year Commissioner Phil Gravatt resigned and Farley saw to it Jackson was appointed to his seat. Jackson was elected and re-elected to city commission in '56, '60, '64, and '68, each time the high vote getter. From 1963 to '67 Jackson served unofficially as acting mayor, assisting Joe Altman who was ill after a serious auto accident. When Altman finally retired in 1967, Jackson became mayor. He had climbed every rung on the ladder.

Despite a federal conviction for extortion in 1972 as one of the "Atlantic City Seven," Dick Jackson is remembered as one of the more effective mayors Atlantic City has had. That his administration was corrupt doesn't diminish his stature. In Atlantic City corruption was the norm; Jackson just happened to be the one in office when the FBI came to town.

While in federal prison, Jackson was offered his freedom in exchange for fingering Hap Farley. "I wasn't there a week when who do you think shows up—the same guys who handled my investigation. They tell me, 'Give us Farley and you can leave now.' I told them, 'I don't know what you're talkin' about.'" Jackson remained silent and served his time. Upon his release he was received well by the community and earned income as a "consultant" to businesspeople needing access to city hall. Jackson often said, "You really do meet the same people on the way down. You had better be good to them on your way up."

Until the time of his death in 1988, Jackson remained a force in city politics and was admired by everyone, greeted by locals as "Mayor." It was loyal foot soldiers such as Dick Jackson who helped make Hap Farley one of the most powerful political bosses in New Jersey's history. Farley's career shows he was worthy of Jackson's loyalty. Hap's success, and with him that of the Republican organization, was the product of a team effort in which every player knew instinctively that true glory is losing yourself in a common good.

# 8

## The Painful Ride Down

It was late afternoon in winter. The office was dark and still, save for one room. Hap Farley and his partner, Frank Ferry, were seated in Ferry's office. They'd both had a hectic day and were catching up with one another before going home. Frank Ferry was more than Farley's law partner; he was like a son. Ferry's father and Hap were lifelong friends. When Farley made his first run for office in 1937, Ferry's father loaned him his car for the entire campaign so the young candidate could get around to see the voters. Over the years, Farley and Ferry's relationship became special and Farley confided in him as he did with few people. They were discussing something that had Farley troubled, and they both knew the problem was beyond their control.

In its prime, Atlantic City had four newspapers: two dailies, a Sunday, and a weekly. Now the resort was a one-newspaper town, and the *Atlantic City Press* had turned on Farley. He was no longer the fair-haired boy who brought home the bacon from Trenton. He was an aging political boss in an era when bossism had become a favorite target for the media. Farley's political machine was also aging, and his presence no longer inspired fear and trembling among his detractors. Week after week there was one negative story after another. The articles ranged from exposés on payroll padding in city hall to front-page headlines every time a critic of Farley attacked him. Farley's enemies now had a sympathetic ear willing to print their complaints. The latest incident wasn't much by itself, but taken together with everything else, Farley knew there was no hope of making peace with the *Press*.

Earlier in the week Farley had been asked to present a ribbon to a prize-winning entry in a dog show at Convention Hall. When the picture was printed in the paper, Farley was left out of the photo and only the dog appeared. The *Press* had decided Farley would receive no more favorable exposure. Hap Farley could dictate to the officials in city hall and manipulate the state senate, but he couldn't control the *Press*. As he spoke about this incident he made light of it, but Farley and Ferry both realized his public image was being eroded.

As Hap Farley's stature was being whittled away, so too was the resort's stature as a resort. With the repeal of Prohibition the resort lost its special position as a "wet town." From then on it was a slow but steady ride downhill. By the time Farley was in a position to influence events, the resort's economic base had already begun to diminish and the trend was irreversible. Things picked up during World War II when there were thousands of soldiers stationed in town, but by the mid-'50s everything had to be perfect throughout the year for local merchants to survive. A canceled convention during the winter or several rainy weekends during the summer could destroy a business. Owning a restaurant, a boardinghouse in the beach block, or a shop along the Boardwalk no longer guaranteed a secure income.

Atlantic City was the victim of postwar modernization. The changes that occurred in American society were subtle, but they were devastating to Atlantic City. The development of air conditioning and swimming pools made it possible for people to enjoy themselves at home rather than travel to the seashore. They also created more competition by Southern resorts. Air travel was now affordable to the masses, and people were willing to save their money for a single vacation to a faraway place, rather than weekend trips to Atlantic City. Finally there was the automobile.

The family car wreaked havoc on the resort. Atlantic City was a creature of the railroad and for three generations rail service to the resort was second to no other vacation spot. The railroad industry had tied the nation together, linking every state from coast to coast. In the process, the American railroad left behind an important legacy. The urge, almost need, for movement was planted firmly into our nation's character. Working with federal and state governments, the railroad magnates established the concept in the American psyche that mobility was paramount. With the increasing affordability of cars, the working person no longer had to worry about train schedules and routes. The American family could simply pile into the car and go where it wished. It was freedom on a scale the middle class had never known. Between 1920 and 1960, with the exception of World War II, the annual production of new cars exceeded the national birth rate. With the widening use of the automobile, Atlantic City's patrons could choose to go elsewhere, and they did just that.

Improvement in personal transportation turned the leisure industry into big business. All across the country new vacation centers
sprang up, competing for tourists' dollars. In contrast, Atlantic City
wasn't accustomed to competing for visitors and was anything but
modern. The Boardwalk, hotels, shops, restaurants, and the city itself
were all showing signs of aging and being dated. Atlantic City had
lost its appeal, and its patrons were lured away to newer attractions.
As one national news magazine observed, "Today, aside from the
conventioneers, the typical Atlantic City tourist is either poor, Black,
elderly, or all three—and the change has depressed almost every
aspect of the city's economy ... the picture which emerges is one of
steady physical, economic, and social deterioration."

Compounding the threat posed by increased competition was the
response of the business community and city planners. During its
prosperous years there had developed a "core area" within the city,
which traditionally had an 8- to 10-month economy. The area
bounded by the Boardwalk and Virginia, Atlantic, and Arkansas
Avenues contained a heavy concentration of family-owned and
-operated hotels, boardinghouses, restaurants, and shops. It was the
most vital section of the town. Within this 20-square-block portion
of the city there were hundreds of prosperous family businesses.
These families were the people who had built the resort's hotel and
recreation industry. This core was the backbone of the economy,
providing a majority of the jobs and paying the bulk of the real
estate taxes.

In an attempt to capture a greater portion of the market traveling
in cars, the city permitted real estate developers to construct new
motels along the highways into town and other parts of the city outside of the core area. It was the traditional Atlantic City response,
"Give 'em what they want." But the decision was shortsighted and
contributed to siphoning off customers from the core area. The new
motels made money at first, but there weren't enough customers to
go around, and over the long haul, everybody lost.

The owners of the hotels and boardinghouses within the core area
saw the gradual decline. For several generations their families had
cultivated regular customers from throughout the Northeast. They
were proud of the service they provided and went out of the way to
please their guests, making an effort to satisfy individual tastes and
wants. Hoteliers kept lists of their regular patrons and did such

things as send greeting cards during the holidays in winter months and special invitations as the summer season was starting up. Each hotel and boardinghouse had its own dining room and amenities peculiar to it. It might be just a pleasant front porch or an intimate cocktail lounge, or a grand ballroom or indoor swimming pool, but each one had its own special character.

A large percentage of Atlantic City's visitors were repeats who enjoyed returning each summer to the familiar surroundings of their favorite hotel. Year after year these patrons vacationed at the resort. It was common for one generation to follow the other and return to the same hotel where they had vacationed as children with the family. But the world changed and Atlantic City didn't, and as these children became adults, they began to view the resort as second rate. When the core area businessmen noticed the fall off of repeat customers they grew uneasy. When things didn't improve, they panicked. By the late '50s and into the '60s many of the local hotel owners began selling out. The owners knew that as the number of visitors dwindled, their town would eventually fade into oblivion. They were going to get out before things got worse.

The resort's third- and fourth-generation hotelkeepers were replaced by investors from out-of-town who still believed in Atlantic City's reputation as a national resort. They got an unpleasant surprise. The volume of patrons they had expected wasn't there. The response of these new hotelkeepers was to slash the overhead. The first thing to go were the hotel dining rooms. Many of the new proprietors did not have the experience needed to turn a profit on serving meals, so they did away with them. This robbed the small hotels of their individuality, contributing further to their decline. The off-season months became slower and slower, and despite past practice, the new owners couldn't justify remaining open year-round. Their operations were curtailed, with a majority of the small hotels and boardinghouses closing down in October and not reopening until May. The core area no longer had a year-round economy. The backbone of the economy was broken.

The hotels not only became antiquated but fell into neglect. Shrinking profits meant less money for maintenance. Vacationers who travel to a resort expect something more than what they have at home, but Atlantic City's visitors had to settle for less. The construction boom of single-family homes during the 1950s and '60s gave

America's middle class a degree of comfort and privacy in their home life that their grandparents never dreamt possible. The vacationer's standards had changed, but the resort's had not. The modern world vacationer refused to share a bathroom with someone else, sleep in a small room without air conditioning, or walk two blocks to park his car when he didn't have to at home. Atlantic City's reputation could still lure first-time visitors, but few of them returned.

The decline in repeat business meant a rise in vacancies, and empty hotel rooms couldn't make money for their owners. To generate income many of the hotels and boardinghouses were converted into either nursing homes for the aged or shelter care facilities for the poor and transient. Atlantic City has always had a shortage of permanent housing, especially for its poor. These boarders couldn't pay the same rates vacationers had, but they made for year-round occupancy. With the presence of long-term, low-rent tenants, maintenance of the smaller hotels and boardinghouses all but ceased. What had once been gay and colorful places were now shabby and broken-down. The old buildings were as sad-looking as their new tenants.

The deterioration wasn't limited to the physical structures of the city. Atlantic City's population base was eroding. More and more Whites were abandoning their town. The out-migration of the city's White population was significant, nearly doubling every 10 years. Between the years 1940 and 1970, the percentage of Whites declined from nearly 80 percent to 50 percent. During the same time, total population dropped from 64,094 to 47,859. The decade of the '60s was devastating with the resort losing a full one-third of its White population. The exodus of Whites, most whom left their businesses and took their money with them, meant that unskilled workers in the tourist economy, particularly Blacks, had to fend for themselves.

The economic well-being of the African-American community had always been tenuous. They were the muscle and sweat needed to run the hotel and recreation industry, and their financial status rose and fell with the prosperity of the tourist trade. When jobs grew scarce, Blacks discovered they had competition from White workers. Hotel employment was no longer exclusively "Negro work." As the resort's fortunes declined, Blacks found themselves trapped in a city that had no use for them. The grandchildren of the Black workers who had played such a crucial role in transforming Atlantic City from a beach village to a national resort were now a burden and an object of scorn. This disdain was a cruel irony for people whose families had been a major building block in developing the town.

Along with the change in its racial makeup, Atlantic City's population was becoming increasingly elderly, with nearly a third of its population over 65. During the '60s the resort became second only to the Tampa-St. Petersburg region of Florida as the area having the highest percentage of senior citizens. While older persons were moving into Atlantic City, younger persons, the wage earners, were moving out. Many of the senior citizens attracted to the resort were former weekend visitors who recalled the glory days of Atlantic City during their youth. They came in search of a retirement of happy weekends seven days a week. Rather than years of bliss, strolling the Boardwalk and enjoying the sea breezes, they found urban decay with its squalor and violence. Some became prisoners in their own homes. The city's housing stock, of which two-thirds was constructed prior to 1940, was becoming physically obsolete and unsafe. For many of the newly arrived seniors, their dream of an idyllic retirement soon became a nightmare.

In 1964 the painful reality of this sad state of affairs was broadcast to the entire nation. In the summer of that year the Democratic National Convention came to Atlantic City. It was a catastrophe for the resort. The 15,000 delegates, newsmen, and technicians found a town unable to meet their needs. Hotel services broke down under the demands of the Convention. "By mid-morning switchboards would collapse and the flustered operators refused to take messages for political guests whose message mating and communication are of the essence; promised television sets did not work, and promised air conditioning proved nonexistent."

To make matters worse, local hotels and restaurants jacked up their prices during Convention week. Out-of-town politicians and media people had never been favorites of Atlantic City. Resort businesspeople viewed Convention week as a chance to grab a few extra dollars from people they would never see again. Their greed had its price—most of the delegates were outraged at having been exploited. The news media transmitted the delegates' tales of contempt for the resort to the entire nation. "Never had a town and a Chamber of Commerce made a greater effort only to end by exposing themselves to ridicule."

Following the campaign, Presidential historian Theodore White summed up the resort's plight:

> Of Atlantic City it may be written: Better it shouldn't
> have happened ... time has overtaken it, and it has become
> one of those sad gray places of entertainment which one
> can find across America, from Coney Island in New York
> to Knott's Berry Farm in California, where the poor and
> the lower middle class grasp so hungrily for the first taste
> of pleasure that the affluent society begins to offer them—
> and find shoddy instead. Frequented now by old people on
> budget, by teenagers who come for a sporting weekend, by
> families of limited means trying to squeeze into cramped
> motel rooms, it is rundown and glamourless.

The resort was used to negative publicity, but this was different. After the Democratic Convention the criticism became derisive. The major magazines and newspapers ridiculed Atlantic City whenever the chance presented itself. Whether it was a snafu at the Miss America Pageant, a weekend visitor who had been ripped off at a Boardwalk auction, or a disgruntled Elk, Moose, Tall Cedar, or businessperson in town for a convention, it found its way onto the wire services. Typically, such stories would contain negative background information for the main embarrassing event and made a mockery of the resort.

A common theme found in these articles was the pseudoanalysis that Atlantic City's problems were of its own making. The resort itself was to blame for its decline. In one way or another, which was never quite explained, the town had stopped doing something that had made it a national success. What these critics failed to comprehend was Atlantic City hadn't fallen; it was abandoned. Time had left the resort behind.

Although his town was caught in a downward spiral, Hap Farley's political power appeared invincible. Following the heated city commission race of '52, the next election in '56 produced token opposition of three independent candidates against the organization slate of five incumbents. Farley's people won handily. By 1960 the opposition had been so thoroughly subdued that there was no contest. Not a single person filed as a candidate to run against Farley's slate.

The understanding between the Republican organization and local Democrats, forged by Nucky Johnson and Charlie Lafferty, continued under Farley. In time, Lafferty was replaced by William Casey and Arthur Ponzio. These "Democrats" were unabashedly Farley supporters. Each time there was a city commission election, the organization ticket consisted of three Republicans and two "Farleycrats." This arrangement also carried over into county elections, insuring Hap never had more than token opposition. And with each re-election, Farley's power in Trenton grew stronger, making him master of the State Capitol.

After more than 20 years as leader of the majority party of the senate, Hap Farley had succeeded in making alliances that transcended partisan politics and any one person's term in office, giving him complete control over the legislative process. As the most powerful person in Trenton, he had a veto over any program sought by the executive branch and rarely had difficulty obtaining the governor's support. When he did, he simply waited until the right issue came along and put up a roadblock until he got what he wanted. The key was in knowing how to pick his fights. There was no one in Trenton to challenge the senator from Atlantic County. To become governor would have meant a loss of power. But there were forces at work that in time scaled him down to size.

One of the keys to Hap Farley's power in the state house was the composition of the senate. Regardless of population, each of New Jersey's 21 counties was represented by a single senator. It was a situation that had prevailed since the original State Constitution of 1776. During his years in the senate, Farley was able to count the votes of his six fellow senators from South Jersey as his own. He never needed more than four votes of the remaining 14 to control the senate. Consistent Republican majorities and his dominance of the GOP caucus ensured Farley's mastery of the senate.

The decade of the '50s saw enormous growth in New Jersey's metropolitan areas. The 1960 census produced numbers that aroused the politicians from the urban counties. The population figures revealed glaring disparities. A study prepared by Rutgers University presented the following conclusions: The senators from the 11 smallest counties, who constituted a majority of the State Senate, represented only 19 percent of the state's total population; Essex County, with the state's largest city, Newark, was 219.7 percent underrepresented in terms of relative population; Cape May County was 83 percent overrepresented using the same standard. With a population of approximately 160,000, Atlantic County was 44 percent overrepresented. These numbers were typical of many state legislative districts throughout the United States, and they added up to trouble for the status quo.

In 1962 the U.S. Supreme Court decision of *Baker v. Carr* established the principal of "one person, one vote," ordering federal and state voting districts to be of equal size. The *Baker* decision had an almost immediate impact. Never before had there been such a flurry of political action in response to a Court's decision. Within hours of the ruling, lawsuits were filed in both state and federal courts challenging the existing schemes of legislative representation. One of the lawsuits spawned by the *Baker* decision was brought by Christopher Jackman, a union leader and Democratic political activist from Hudson County, who later became speaker of the New Jersey Assembly. Jackman was seeking to force the state legislature to reapportion its districts based upon population. The State Supreme Court ruled unanimously that the districts of both the senate and assembly must be based upon population.

One of the Justices was Farley's old ally, Vincent Haneman, whom Farley had recommended for appointment to the Supreme Court. Haneman voted with the Court but didn't join in its opinion, choosing to write one of his own. His opinion begins, "There comes a time in the career of practically every judge when he must embrace a theory of law to which he does not personally subscribe." Haneman continued, tracing New Jersey history from pre-Revolution days when the colony was divided into East and West Jersey. He explained that New Jersey had always had an upper and lower house in its legislature. Representation in the senate had been "based upon territory as distinguished from population" throughout state history. Each time the State Constitution was revised, this practice was preserved. Haneman saw no reason it shouldn't continue but knew he had to yield to the U.S. Supreme Court. Justice Haneman's opinion reads like an apology to an old friend.

The Court's decision was a political disaster for Hap Farley. Being one of 40 with control over no more than a dozen votes was a major setback from being one of 21 with the power to produce a majority for any bill he wanted.

Trenton wasn't the only place where Farley's power was slipping. While on the surface the local Republican organization appeared as potent as ever, with its candidates sweeping one election after another, its foundation was crumbling. The cornerstone of Farley's empire had been ravaged. Gradually, almost imperceptibly, the political ward system was falling apart. Government reforms emanating from federal and state government had finally taken their toll. Nucky Johnson's finely tuned system for dispensing services and patronage, and grooming political workers and candidates was destroyed by social welfare programs and civil service.

The underpinnings of the political ward system were the delivery of constituent services and control of political spoils. The social welfare programs instituted by Roosevelt's New Deal during the Depression grew and multiplied until Atlantic City's downtrodden no longer had to go to the precinct captain every time they had a problem. Unemployment and welfare payments meant Atlantic City's poor could make it through the winter without having to ask the Republican Party for a handout. It took more than a generation for the effects of Roosevelt's social liberalism to make an impact on the ward system, but when they did, the result was permanent. Constituent services were no longer a political plum for voters loyal to the party; now they were a right.

Control over patronage was also a problem. Although Jimmy Boyd and his lieutenants kept a tight rein over every person hired, civil service gave city and county employees a degree of freedom they had never known. At first Boyd worked around civil service by limiting the number of classified positions and manipulating eligibility for promotion tests, but gradually it took hold, and as it did his discipline over the ward workers diminished. A city employee could now thumb his nose at the ward leader. Failure to perform one's political chores no longer meant dismissal. Involvement in ward politics was now voluntary.

The final blow to the power of the ward system was the change in the voting attitude of the resort's Black community. For more than 50 years the Northside could be counted on for large pluralities for the organization ticket. But Hap never had the loyal following among Blacks the way the Commodore and Nucky had. And again, Roosevelt's New Deal played a decisive role. For millions of disadvantaged Americans, in particular African-Americans, FDR was a beacon of hope. Roosevelt's presidency forged a coalition dedicated to making government work for the have-nots, and Black voters were a keystone of this national coalition. Locally, Blacks had no one to vote for other than the organization's candidates. However, as America entered the '60s and African-Americans began the battle for civil rights, Atlantic City's Blacks became involved in partisan Democratic politics. The switch in loyalties came in part as Blacks recognized the racist tactics of the Republican machine. An investigation of county voter registration records, published by *The Press*, revealed that voting cards had been marked to indicate race. When news of this hit the street, the Black community was outraged. African-American voters were now beyond the control of the ward workers. They could no longer be herded to the polls and their votes sold to the Republican Party. Black voters needed only the right Democratic candidate in order to become a threat to Farley and his machine.

Hap Farley knew the world was growing hostile toward his brand of politics, yet he refused to retire or change his methods. In 10 campaigns no one even came close to defeating him. It didn't matter that his opponents were Farleycrats; in fact, the ability to select opposition candidates was proof of how totally he controlled Atlantic City's politics. That kind of power is intoxicating and only an extraordinary person could have given it up voluntarily.

The first real challenge to Farley's reign as senator came in 1965. It was the first election after the *Jackman* decision and the initial plan for legislative reapportionment called for Atlantic and Cape May counties to be lumped together creating a single senate district.

Several years after the 1952 City Commission election, Farley's foe, Marvin Perskie, moved out of town, relocating his law practice to Wildwood in Cape May County. Farley used his influence with the local judges and his contacts in the business community to ensure that Perskie had no future in Atlantic City as a politician or an attorney. Marvin Perskie was not a beaten man, just realistic. There was no point continuing to bang heads with Hap's machine. Perskie left town, but he never forgave Farley. The two were bitter enemies. By 1965 Perskie had established himself in Wildwood and was eager to make another run at Farley. Despite the influence of the Farleycrats, Perskie was certain of gaining the Democratic nomination from the support of the Democrats of Cape May County and mainland Atlantic County.

Farley remembered the campaign Perskie had waged in '52 and wasn't anxious to face him head on. According to one observer, "Farley was scared to death of Marvin." Shortly before the filing date for the primary, the senate gerrymandered the districts and combined

Gloucester County with Atlantic and Cape May counties to create an unusual district. This new voting district was too large to meet the equal population requirement, but Farley solved this problem by having two senators elected from the three counties. Farley chose Gloucester County because at the time it was represented by a popular incumbent, Republican John Hunt. With a running mate like Hunt, Farley had a substantial advantage over Perskie, who had no base of support in Gloucester County. Farley had stacked the deck against Perskie. Rather than go down to defeat in the senate contest, Perskie chose to run for assembly, where he won handily.

Through the efforts of a small but growing number of independent Democrats, Perskie's place on the Democratic slate was filled by Leo Clark, a former FBI agent. Clark was born and raised in Atlantic City, having attended Holy Spirit High School where he was a star athlete. He went on to graduate from Notre Dame University, followed by an impressive career with the FBI. More importantly, Clark wasn't a Farleycrat and he made a strong candidate who was not afraid to attack Farley.

With prompting from Perskie and local attorney Patrick McGahn, Leo Clark banged away at Farley charging him with corruption and conflict of interest. Clark zeroed in on the sad state of the resort's deteriorating economy and blamed one-party rule for the town's ills. Apparently someone was listening and Clark gave Farley the biggest scare of his life. Clark beat Farley by more than 500 votes in Cape May County and made a respectable showing in Gloucester losing by a similar tally. The difference in the election was in Atlantic City where Jimmy Boyd's Fourth Ward could still crank out the votes. Clark lost by little more than 4,000 votes, which was the closest Farley had come to defeat in 28 years. While the Leo Clark campaign ended in defeat, it was the beginning of a legitimate Democratic Party in Atlantic County.

The next election in 1967 was a farce. There had been a second court ruling and another redistricting approved by the legislature and the voters at a general election. Again it had been proposed that Cape May and Atlantic counties would form a senatorial district. Perskie had been chosen as a Democratic candidate and spent that spring and summer attacking Farley. Perskie labeled Farley a "political dinosaur" and charged that he headed "one of the vilest political machines that still exists in the United States." Perskie was on target, but his efforts were for naught. This time it was the State Supreme Court that came to Farley's rescue. In response to a lawsuit challenging the senatorial districts in Union and Passaic counties, the Court inexplicably decided to do a complete redistricting of the entire state. The Court hadn't been asked to consider anything but Union and Passaic counties, but revamped the districts of all 21 counties on its own initiative. As a result of the Court's ruling, Cape May was placed with Cumberland County, leaving Atlantic County by itself. Marvin Perskie was denied again.

The Court's ruling came in July, and neither Leo Clark nor any other independent Democrat would jump into the campaign at such a late date. The Farleycrats were the only ones organized, and they chose a political unknown, Harry Gaines, who dutifully went to the slaughter. Predictably, Farley was re-elected to a four-year term by a margin of more than 13,000 votes.

Farley's re-election didn't frighten his critics. They felt Perskie would have beaten him if the Supreme Court hadn't toyed with the senate districts. Hap was responsible for the appointment of Vincent Haneman and as a longtime member of the Judiciary Committee had reviewed every court appointment for more than 25 years. Rather than being discouraged, Farley's detractors strengthened their resolve. They received assistance from the local media, in particular, the *Atlantic City Press*. In late 1969 and early '70, Atlantic City's only newspaper ran a series of articles based on the investigative reporting of Bernard Izes and John Katz. Corruption had been the norm in Atlantic City's government for so long that bribery, graft, and payroll padding were standard practices of doing municipal business. Three generations of Atlantic City residents had known nothing but dishonest government. The *Press* decided to shine some light on Farley's organization.

Izes and Katz didn't have to be detectives to uncover material for articles on political corruption. The Republican machine was an open book. The reporters began with the city's uniformed employees, where they found that 9 out of 10 Atlantic City firefighters made annual contributions to the Atlantic County Republican Committee. Of the 221 men listed on the 1968 fire department payroll, all but 19 were contributors. In response to these reports, Fire Chief Warren Conover stated that all the contributions were voluntary and said that there was no pressure, with the firefighters merely being told, "If they want to pay, it is time to get it in, but there is not any retribution against anyone who doesn't want to pay." Contrary to Conover, the *Press* investigation revealed that deputy fire chiefs were given lists of names of those who had refused to contribute to the organization. These firefighters were routinely skipped over on the civil service promotion lists. In one instance, a firefighter was passed over for nine years while a vacancy he was qualified to move into went unfilled.

Izes and Katz's investigation revealed that payroll padding with political hacks was rampant in city and county government. No-show employees were found to exist in every department of city hall. The reporters established there was a direct link between the no-show employees and the precinct workers. As had been the tradition for nearly 70 years, the loyalty of the Republican political workers was rewarded at the expense of the local taxpayers. A sampling of the payroll padding exploited by Farley's machine ran the gamut: An investigator in the revenue and finance department spent 100 percent of his time either selling insurance out of his home or working at the Republican Party headquarters; a luxury tax investigator had a full-time job as a bus driver and never reported to city hall except to receive his check; an assistant supervisor of weights and measures had never made a single inspection and spent all his time as a car salesman; a health inspector, who was a loyal precinct captain, worked full-time at a local hotel and had someone pick up his checks for him.

Another area exposed by Izes and Katz was graft on public contracts and extortion of businesses regulated by the city. They revealed that nothing had changed in city hall since the conviction of the Commodore. Everything had its price and if you wanted to do business with city hall, you had to kick back a percentage of your profits or you were blacklisted. Businesses that were regularly inspected for potential health or fire violations didn't get a clean bill of health unless they paid. If you didn't pay the inspector, you were shut down.

If it involved city hall, no business transaction was routine. A liquor license could only be transferred by using Stumpy Orman as the broker for the sale. Eddie Helfant or Ed Feinberg had to be used as the attorney to make the application to the city. If you didn't use the proper people or grease the right wheel, you got nothing out of city hall. Izes and Katz's articles ultimately prompted an investigation by the U.S. Attorney's office resulting in the indictment of Mayor William Somers and several commissioners and city officials.

These defendants were dubbed by the local media as the "Atlantic City Seven" and were all convicted by a federal jury of bribery, extortion, and abuse of the public trust. Each of the convicted defendants remained silent and Farley was never indicted.

The sun was setting on Frank Farley's career, but he refused to accept it. The first half of his life had been devoted to sports, the second half to elective politics, and he was a champion in both worlds. For nearly 70 years the gratification derived from excelling in competitive activities had been Hap Farley's life. He had never known life without the excitement of combat, whether on the playing field or in politics. It wasn't possible for him to step down gracefully. Like an aging boxer who believes he can win one more title bout before retiring, Hap Farley was destined for a knockout.

Farley's fortunes were tied to those of his city. As the boss of his town's politics, he was the one the voters would eventually hold accountable as things got worse for the resort. It was only a matter of time before Farley's constituents would turn on him and seek a new leader in hopes that someone else could turn things around.

In addition to the resort's deteriorating economy and exposure of corruption in its government, there was growing discontent within the Republican organization. The exodus of middle-class Whites from Atlantic City during the '50s and '60s to the mainland communities along Shore Road, namely Absecon, Pleasantville, Northfield, Linwood, and Somers Point, produced a dramatic change in the county Republican organization. These mainlanders didn't have the loyalty to Farley's machine their parents and grandparents had for the political ward system. They were more educated, more affluent, employed at jobs unrelated to tourism, and not beholden to the Republican Party. Atlantic City's influence in county politics had been diluted. The power was now more evenly distributed, and the Shore Road Republicans were growing tired of Farley. They wanted a change in party leadership.

Politicians begin thinking about the next election as soon as the last one is over. Once the polls have closed and the votes are tallied, would-be candidates and their supporters begin vying for position in the next contest. Coalitions are formed and commitments made early in this unending process. The several months after an election may appear uneventful to the general public, but this is the time when politicians make their decisions concerning who will be rewarded or punished for their role in the previous campaign. It's a critical period in the political process. What the public sees later is window dressing. While Hap Farley had worked tirelessly in the 1970 general election and his candidates were all victorious—albeit by slim margins—there were those within the Republican organization who began to view him as a liability to the party. Before the month of November was over, the dissatisfaction that had been simmering for several years boiled to the surface.

Less than 10 days after the '70 election, Farley had a revolt on his hands. It began with a resolution adopted by the Linwood Republican Club. The Linwood group was only one of several mainland Republican clubs that was growing restless with the Farley-Boyd stranglehold on the party. The statement endorsed by the Linwood GOP called for "political and governmental reform in Atlantic County" and warned that their party was "in need of more enlightened leadership to meet head-on the needs of today. Policies of the past must be abandoned." It was a bolt of lightning.

In calling for Farley to step aside, the Linwood faction shattered the public image of unity that Farley had so carefully maintained. Hap was only able to hold the pieces together by consenting to the creation of a countywide executive committee. The committee would have input on the selection of candidates and setting party policy. Sharing power was a major concession for Farley, but it wasn't enough.

While Hap Farley was doing everything he could to keep the lid on his troubles, the county Democrats were finally putting together an organization. The Leo Clark campaign in '65 and the several following elections saw the Democrats begin to make inroads on the local level by electing candidates in several mainland communities. Nevertheless, the growth of an independent Democratic organization was pathetically slow. The Republican Party had held every governmental position in its grip since the beginning of the 20th century. The only persons who would ally themselves with an independent Democratic organization were idealists opposed to boss rule, Democrats who had moved into Atlantic County from out of the area, or disgruntled Republicans who had been rejected by the party power structure. No practical person who might ever want something from city or county government would register as a Democrat. One of the disgruntled Republicans upon whom the Democratic organization was built was resort attorney Patrick McGahn. His rites of passage into the Democratic Party illustrate how stifling Farley's power had become.

Patrick McGahn was born in Atlantic City in 1928. His father was a native of Ireland and was the owner of "Paddy McGahn's," a local bar at Iowa and Atlantic avenues. Hap Farley was the McGahn family's attorney, and both of Pat's parents were strong supporters of the senator. Paddy McGahn was active in the Fourth Ward Republican Club and at the time of his death in 1949, his honorary pallbearers included Nucky Johnson, Hap Farley, Jimmie Boyd, and Mayor Joseph Altman. After graduating from college and starting his first year of law school, Pat McGahn was called up by his Marine Reserve Unit to fight in the Korean War. He served with distinction and was a decorated war hero. Upon returning to the resort in 1953, McGahn gave thought to getting involved in local politics prior to returning to law school. He had grown up under ward politics and the boss rule of Johnson and Farley. He understood the scheme of things and was prepared to become a foot soldier in Farley's organization in hopes of rising through the ranks. At the urging of his mother, McGahn sought a meeting with the senator to get Farley's advice on how he should go about becoming active in the party.

Hap Farley was "very pleasant" to McGahn but advised him that "there were too many ahead of me and that it would be wise if I went to law school and then seek another area out of Atlantic County to start my career." McGahn found Farley "very gracious" as he closed the door on future involvement. "He had to take care of the people that were already involved. There was no room in the inn." Farley rejected McGahn without even knowing what he had to offer. Thus did Pat McGahn become a Democrat; there were many more frustrated Republicans who found their way to the Democratic Party in a similar fashion.

The frustration felt by Atlantic City's residents as their town deteriorated with no end in sight came to a head in 1971. The beneficiary of this emotional tidal wave was Joseph McGahn, Pat's older brother. Dr. Joseph L. McGahn was the ideal candidate to oppose Farley. An Irish-Catholic, born and raised in Atlantic City, McGahn attended Our Lady Star of the Sea School and Holy Spirit High School. He was valedictorian of his college class and received his medical degree from the University of Pennsylvania. Before entering politics, McGahn had played a positive and highly visible role in the greater

Atlantic City community. He had been a Little League Commissioner for more than 10 years, and as an obstetrician/gynecologist, McGahn and his partner had delivered more than 12,000 babies. Intelligent, articulate, witty, and personable to all his patients, his following included thousands of entire families. It was an excellent base for an aspiring politician.

Joe McGahn's first run for political office was for Absecon City Council in 1966. He was elected the lone Democrat on a seven-member council. Two years later he ran for mayor and scored a startling victory, winning by a margin of two to one in a city with almost no registered Democrats. It was a phenomenal accomplishment and made "Doc Joe" a leader among the independent Democrats. With Joe serving as the spokesman and Pat as strategist, the McGahn brothers devoted their time and spent their money building up the County Democratic organization, all the while aiming toward the '71 Senate race. After the 1970 election, there finally was a legitimate second party with the Democrats having four mayors and 25 councilmen holding office throughout Atlantic County. While a far cry from the cohesive unit that the Republicans had assembled over the years, it was all the McGahns needed as a base for their battle with Farley.

The McGahn brothers took their battle right into Farley's backyard. They knew their campaign needed much more than the support of Democrats and Independents. The edge in registered voters was so huge that to be successful, Joe McGahn needed the votes of a large percentage of rank-and-file Republicans. Building on relationships they had made over the years, Pat and Joe McGahn reached into the Republican organization and whittled away at Farley's core of strength. The natural place to begin was on the mainland.

The Shore Road Republicans had little difficulty supporting Joe McGahn. In many ways he was one of them. He had re-established his home on the mainland to escape Atlantic City's urban rot. Like them, he saw no future in a city or political organization dominated by an aging autocrat whose practices were better suited for the old style ward politics of 30 years earlier. These mainlanders wanted a change even if it meant voting for a Democrat. Any reluctance they might have had in supporting McGahn was eliminated by Farley's refusal to step aside. They had given him his chance. He could have bowed out gracefully and maybe even chosen his successor. It's likely someone such as County Freeholder Director Howard "Fritz"

Haneman, son of Hap's crony, Vincent Haneman, would have been acceptable to Farley's critics. But Farley wouldn't consider passing the reins and that left the Shore Road Republicans with no choice. In their view, Farley had to go.

With Shore Road Republicans on board, the McGahns turned to Atlantic City. That front was handled deftly by brother Pat. Both the McGahns were born and raised in the Fourth Ward and had strong ties there, but it was Pat who was his father's son, the bartender who could read his customers in a single glance. As a politician, Pat had much in common with Nucky Johnson. Streetwise and tough nosed, Pat McGahn understood what it took to survive in Atlantic City politics. Like Nucky, Pat was as nasty as an alley cat to his enemies, and generous and loyal to his friends.

There was almost no one in Atlantic City who didn't know Pat McGahn and that he was the force behind his brother's campaign. Their association was comparable to the division of responsibilities that existed between Hap Farley and Jimmy Boyd; Joe was the candidate and good guy; Pat was the tactician and enforcer. As was true with Boyd and Farley, Pat didn't have to confer with Joe before making a commitment. Meeting individually with dozens of precinct workers and ward heelers, Pat exploited the discontent of Atlantic City Republican Party regulars and persuaded them to support the Democratic slate.

He knew that many of them had counseled Farley against seeking re-election, and they saw his defeat as inevitable. Pat McGahn wooed them on terms they understood; this was a watershed election, there was going to be a major transfer of power, and they could be part of the new regime. In short, the train was leaving the station and this was their chance to get on board. His appeal was effective. While there were few publicly announced defections, there were many ward workers who quietly urged their neighbors to dump Farley.

And dump him they did. It was a humiliating defeat. Farley was beaten almost three to two, losing by a margin of nearly 12,000 votes. The entire ticket went down in 18 of 23 municipalities in Atlantic County. Hap lost Atlantic City by more than 2,000 votes. In Jimmy Boyd's vaunted Fourth Ward, where Farley had consistently received pluralities by as much as 5,000 votes, the McGahns fought him to a standoff, with Hap edging Joe McGahn by less than 200 votes. For the first time in his life, Hap Farley had been whipped. It was something beyond his experience and left him numb with disappointment. Despite the hurt, Farley conceded defeat graciously. There were no harsh words nor recriminations. He congratulated Joe McGahn and wished him well. Through it all he remained a gentleman.

If Hap Farley had any regrets about the '71 campaign, he never expressed them. Had he stepped down voluntarily, he could have been the resort's distinguished elder statesman; instead, after his defeat—with the exception of a critical election in 1976—he was shoved aside like a worthless relic. There were still those who sought his counsel, but they were few in number and it was always privately. The stigma of his rejection by the voters ostracized him from the political mainstream; however, Farley didn't permit bitterness to consume him and he accepted his fate. For the next several years, until his death to cancer in 1977, Farley was a booster for his city whenever he had the chance.

Of the three bosses who reigned over the corruption of Atlantic City, it was Francis Sherman Farley who ruled with the most knowledge of government and restraint on unlawful excesses. Hap Farley was a giant. In the history of New Jersey politics, he is in a league of his own.

# 9

# Turn Out the Lights

The windows hadn't been washed in months. The seats were grimy and the entire place had a damp stench about it. The marquee was dark and blank, save for the words "Coming Soon." Only Skinny D'Amato, owner of the 500 Club, could recall the last name act to appear in his nightclub.

Paul "Skinny" D'Amato was a local hero. A grade school dropout, running numbers at age 11, he had his own gambling room by the time he was 16. A successful racketeer since the Nucky Johnson era, D'Amato was held in esteem by the entire community. Skinny seemed to know everyone, from the guy slicing lunchmeat at the corner grocery to entertainers in Hollywood. Handsome, dapper, and charming in a way expected of a nightclub owner, D'Amato was a nocturnal creature. A coffee-drinking chain smoker, Skinny hardly ever awoke before noon and routinely had breakfast in bed. The 500 Club was his life's work, offering all kinds of entertainment, from singers and comedians to women and boys. In its prime, the acts at the 500 Club rivaled the best in Vegas and the Big Apple. Dean Martin and Jerry Lewis got their start there, and Frank Sinatra was a frequent performer. But the 500 Club was no longer a nightclub; it was a seedy bar, attracting a handful of old regulars and a trickle of first-timers lured by its reputation. D'Amato was having trouble meeting payroll and taxes, remaining open for lack of anything better to do. The same was true of most of his customers, especially the female patrons.

Rita was the only woman sitting at the bar. Platinum blonde hair and rings on every finger but her thumbs, she wasn't easy to mistake. Her new jeans were so tight they looked as if she had been poured into them. Her sweater was a gaudy green and despite the money she'd spent on her bra, her breasts sagged unmercifully. The years hadn't been kind and no amount of Maybelline helped. It was a young crowd, most of whom came to the 500 Club out of curiosity, hoping to find the hot times they'd heard about from their fathers. A few of them looked her over, but Rita wasn't their idea of action. Within a couple of hours the bar was empty, but for the regulars, leaving Rita with no choice but Pacific Avenue in search of a score.

By 1974 Atlantic City was one with Rita—a broken-down old whore scratching for customers. What once was a prosperous and bustling seaside resort was now a sleazy saltwater ghetto struggling to get by on a hollow reputation. No one who knew better, or who could afford to go elsewhere, would choose Atlantic City as a place to vacation.

Jonathan Pitney's dream had become a nightmare, and his town was collapsing. The core area, once the bustling center of the hotel industry, was a squalid, decaying embarrassment. In the off-season, the town was dead. There were days between September and June when a bowling ball could have rolled from one end of Atlantic Avenue to the other without hitting anything. The profile of the streets leading to the beach resembled a garbage pile. Beginning with the battered, towering hotels along the Boardwalk, and sloping to the grungy motels of the beach block, the streets continued across Pacific Avenue lined with abandoned churches, rundown boarding-houses, discount liquor stores, and greasy-thumb eateries that closed by dark. Across Atlantic Avenue and onto Baltic and Mediterranean, the buildings blurred into a huge pile of rubble making up a vast ghetto. Most of the residential neighborhoods looked like Dresden after World War II. But there had been no bombs, just decay. Street after street, there were thousands of row houses needing painting and repairs, some occupied—the occasional home to vagrants—most vacant, punctuated by burned out ones.

The spirit of the community was burned out, too. As the middle class made its exodus, the town's social fabric unraveled. Schools and churches closed or were forced to consolidate. Service clubs disbanded as their members relocated to the mainland, sapping the city of civic leaders. Little League baseball, teenage basketball, and youth clubs saw their numbers dwindle until many dissolved. The city was rife with street crime. Corner grocers and family-owned clothing, jewelry, and hardware stores packed it in as robberies gobbled up their profits. Barbers and beauticians retired and no one took over their shops, leaving "Sale or Lease" signs all over town. Movie theatres closed for lack of customers and vandalism, and every office building in town had space for rent. With no prospect of a turn-around, despair was the dominant mood.

For nearly a generation Atlantic City's leaders were helpless in dealing with the deterioration. Between 1950 and '74, tourist income shrank from more than $70 million annually to less than $40 million; thousands of hotel rooms were torn down or boarded up, reducing the rooms for visitors from nearly 200,000 to less than 100,000, hardly any of which could be considered modern. "How could you get anyone to stay in a hotel where the mattresses were 40 years old and guests had to share a bathroom?"

As the grand hotels were pulled down, they left gaps along the Boardwalk as startling as missing teeth in a smile. Instead of a grand promenade and showcase for popular culture and industry, the Boardwalk was home to schlock houses, gyp joints, and panhandlers. The unemployment rate was about 25 percent for nine months of the year, with a full one-third of the population on welfare. More than 90 percent of the housing stock had been built prior to 1939, with the majority substandard. Of the nine New Jersey cities included in the Federal Model Cities Program, Atlantic City had the highest percentage of families (33.5 percent) earning less than $3,000 per year. A report prepared by a local antipoverty group disclosed that the resort had the highest divorce, venereal disease, tuberculosis, and infant mortality rates of any city in the state. According to the FBI's Uniform Crime Report, among 528 American cities in the 25,000 to 50,000 population group, Atlantic City had the highest total number of crimes in the seven standard categories. The criminals were poor people stealing from the less poor. No new money of any kind was coming to town. There had been no major construction for nearly a generation. The only activity on the rise was arson.

In an attempt to revive the resort's sagging economy, advertising agencies for some of the hotels tried promoting Atlantic City as a "family resort." The wide-open days were gone, and Atlantic City was now supposed to be a place where mom and pop could bring the kids. What a joke. People like Skinny D'Amato who could still remember Atlantic City in its glory days knew better. They understood their town could never compete as a family resort.

As early as 1958, the resort's Women's Chamber of Commerce, at the urging of local hotel owner Mildred Fox, had gone on record in support of legalized gambling. A feisty little redhead with an Italian temperament—she was Fox née Logiovino—Mildred was forever banging heads with the local power establishment. Politically active, she was a dyed-in-the-wool FDR-JFK Democrat, not a Farleycrat. Atlantic City was her home and she wasn't leaving. Plucky but savvy, Mildred pushed the idea of legalizing gambling to anyone who would listen. "It was our only hope for saving the city. We were on our way to becoming a ghost town." Fox, the mother of four, was the owner and operator of the Fox Manor, a small Pacific Avenue hotel specializing in honeymoon packages. At the time, there was still a small network of backroom gambling operations and for her efforts, Fox and her children received death threats. The FBI took the threats seriously and, with her permission, tapped her phone but were unable to trace any of the calls. For half the year special agents escorted the Fox children to and from school.

By the early 1960s, the gambling rooms were gone, and gradually there developed a mentality that argued that if Atlantic City was ever to regain stature as a national resort, it needed an edge, the only logical one being casino-style gambling. Las Vegas had casinos and look what they were able to do in the desert. Think of what could be done with gambling in a town with the ocean and the Boardwalk, or so the logic went.

Toward the end of his career when the idea was first suggested, Hap Farley refused to sponsor casino gambling. It may have been the only instance in which Farley put his political interests ahead of his city's, or maybe he was weary with the battles to hold onto power and pessimistic there was any one cure. People intimate with Hap believe he was concerned over the scrutiny that would be brought to bear on his regime. Were the resort to become the Las Vegas of the East, state and federal law enforcement agencies would pay even closer attention to Atlantic City's corruption, and Farley wanted none of that.

With Farley gone, Fox's idea was able to surface. She and like-minded business people kept the hope alive. But bringing gambling to the resort was a major undertaking. The legalization of casino-style gambling could only come about by means of an amendment to the New Jersey Constitution, which required approval at a statewide referendum. And there could be no referendum without an act of the legislature and support from the governor's office. That took serious clout, something Atlantic City was short on with Farley gone from the scene. To make matters worse, the governor's chair was occupied by a priggish former Superior Court Judge who, as a criminal prosecutor, had established a reputation as a "Mr. Clean." Brendan Byrne was hardly what Atlantic City needed in the way of a governor to help bring in legalized casino gambling.

Brendan Byrne's first run for political office was his election to governor in 1973. Plucked from the Superior Court bench, he was the handpicked candidate of a group of wealthy North Jersey Irish Democrats, the same clique responsible for the election of two other governors. Byrne was the ideal candidate: trim, handsome, well-spoken, and well-connected; Princeton University undergraduate; and Harvard Law School. He was the antithesis of the Farley-style politician. Upon graduation from law school he served as a clerk to a Superior Court Judge. From there he became assistant prosecutor in the Essex County Prosecutor's office and eventually prosecutor and judgeship. During his days as prosecutor, Byrne gained a reputation as a crime fighter and was referred to by the mob as someone who "couldn't be bought." He savored his reputation and effused self-righteousness.

With the traditional problem of corruption in New Jersey, Byrne would have been welcomed by either political party in much the same way Woodrow Wilson was 60 years earlier. The leading Democrats supported him and he won the primary easily. His campaign was short on substance and consisted essentially of a pledge to "restore integrity" to New Jersey government—a tall order for anyone. Byrne's opponent was Congressman Charles Sandman of Cape May. Charlie Sandman was a perennial candidate and wannabe governor most of his career. In June 1973, he upset incumbent Governor William Cahill in a bitter primary dividing the Republican Party. Sandman would later be Richard Nixon's most loyal supporter during the Watergate hearings, and his uncompromising conservative message had limited appeal. He was no match for Byrne and the election was a landslide. As Brendan Byrne began his first year in office, legalizing gambling wasn't one of his priorities. It wasn't even on his agenda.

But gambling was a priority for the resort's legislative team. 1974 was the year Atlantic City was to begin its comeback. State Senator Joe McGahn took his cue from the local media as well as business and civic leaders. They had one item on their legislative agenda. This was the year casino gambling was to become a reality. For the first time in Atlantic County's history, its legislative delegation was entirely Democratic and there was a Democrat in the governor's chair. As the year began, hopes were high. The *Atlantic City Press* took the lead in expressing confidence: "Governor Brendan Byrne has said he is receptive to a referendum aimed at removing the present constitutional ban on gambling, and a newly elected legislature presumably is willing to vote it onto the ballot. Public approval is regarded as certain." But Joe McGahn knew better.

Joe McGahn had spent most of his life watching his hometown crumble. Now as senator, he had a chance to reverse the downward spiral. While having none of Farley's gifts as a horse-trader, he could think on his feet and had the personal maturity needed to stay focused on a single issue. McGahn's partner, in truth the leader in pursuing a constitutional referendum, was Democratic Assemblyman Steven Perskie. On his first election to the assembly in 1971, at age 26, Perskie was the youngest state legislator ever elected from Atlantic County, having been swept into office on McGahn's coattails in his win over Farley. Upon arriving in Trenton, the young assemblyman needed no one's coattails and learned his way around quickly. Nephew of Farley nemesis Marvin Perskie, Steve Perskie was a third generation attorney from a family of respected lawyers, the son and grandson of judges. Of medium height and build with shaggy black hair and thick horn-rimmed glasses, he was the picture of intensity. Perskie exuded confidence—almost cocksure—and had an innate ability for the legislative process. Brilliant, fast-talking but articulate, and with an engaging personality, he was a tireless advocate of casino gaming and the resort's best spokesperson for the cause. More importantly, Steve Perskie had ingratiated himself with Brendan Byrne. He was one of Byrne's earliest supporters in the Democratic primary and raised the gambling issue with Byrne early on. After the election he visited the governor's office frequently, building important ties with Byrne's staff. Between McGahn and Perskie, the resort had as effective a legislative team as it could hope for.

As the city launched its drive for a constitutional referendum, the watchword was "don't oversell our case." The prevailing mentality produced a caution and restraint in presenting the case for gambling, which could come only from overconfidence. Atlantic City and its leaders felt all they had to do was keep a low profile and things would just fall into place as they planned.

At that time, New Jersey was struggling with statewide tax reform. A State Supreme Court decision on the funding of local public schools had made an income tax inevitable. Some proponents of gambling spread the word that legalizing gambling might eliminate the need for an income tax. To preclude such talk, the *Atlantic City Press* in almost lecturing tones told its readers, especially the politicians, "The state can expect to profit very little, if at all, directly, and gambling opponents and proponents alike know it ... it should not even be mentioned in the same breath with an income tax. It must be sold on the very sound argument that it is a much needed stimulant for the capital investment that can bring Atlantic City back to its days of glory."

Another pitfall was the specter of Atlantic City becoming a "Las Vegas of the East" with a casino on every corner and slot machines in supermarkets, drugstores, and gas stations. Somehow, Atlantic City was supposed to be better than Vegas. The reputation of mob influence and the garishness of Las Vegas were something to be avoided in a statewide campaign. With an almost fairy tale quality, Atlantic City's leaders hoped to present a more dignified image. They talked of gambling in terms of class and elegance comparable to the low-key operations in the Bahamas and Monte Carlo. According to its supporters, Atlantic City was above doing business like Las Vegas. There would be no glitz or glitter or slot machine grind joints. Upon gambling being legalized, it would be quiet and sophisticated—civilized games of chance for gentlemen and ladies only.

A final concern for gambling proponents was the fear that were it limited to Atlantic City alone, other communities in the state might resent it and sabotage the referendum. The resort was prepared to share the opportunity with other communities in the hopes no one else would be interested. In an attempt to neutralize potential opposition, McGahn and Perskie proposed a referendum that would permit gambling casinos throughout the state. Upon approval of the initial constitutional amendment, gambling could be permitted in any community where the voters of both the municipality, and the county in which it was located, approved a second referendum. To prevent mob infiltration, casinos would be owned and operated by state government; no matter that no one in state government was experienced in operating a casino. They would simply adopt regulations and everything would go smoothly. As for new private construction, there wouldn't be much. Casinos would be located in existing hotels or state-owned properties. Additionally, advertising would be prohibited and only properly attired patrons would be permitted to gamble. By creating such a frame in which to view their proposal, Atlantic City's leaders hoped the opposition would have little basis for an attack.

In the report of a study released by the staff of the Senate Conference Committee in May 1974, the Byrne administration's view of how casino gambling should work was outlined for the legislature. It was envisioned that the first casino would be built on the Boardwalk at the state's expense. Following the initial casino, two others would be located in space leased from existing hotels. The hours of operation would be from 8:00 P.M. to 4:00 A.M. The sale of alcoholic beverages would be prohibited as would credit for betting by casino patrons. Private investment of any kind would be prohibited. A rosy picture typical of government, it was assumed the casinos would be staffed and operated by state employees—just one more task for the bureaucracy. The potential of gambling everywhere didn't have the initial support of Governor Byrne and as the constitutional amendment began making its way through the legislature, Byrne made his thoughts known. Prompted by his Attorney General William F. Hyland, Byrne questioned the language of the referendum.

The governor suggested that gambling should be limited to Atlantic City. He went so far as to threaten opposition to the referendum legislation if gambling was permitted anywhere other than Atlantic City. Some observers believe Byrne was looking for a face-saving way out and hoped that by limiting gambling to the resort, he would alienate other regions of the state, killing any chances of the referendum's approval. The resort's leaders were beside themselves, but Steve Perskie refused to quit. Relying upon his personal relationship with Brendan Byrne, Perskie launched a private campaign that resulted in the governor's modifying his position. Byrne agreed to support the referendum as proposed, provided that for the first five years after its approval, casino gambling would be confined to Atlantic City alone. It was a major concession, which only Perskie could have obtained.

With Byrne's support, McGahn and Perskie were successful in obtaining the legislature's approval for a constitutional referendum.

In all, it took less than five months to get the question put on the November ballot. While McGahn and Perskie made their moves in Trenton, the folks back home did nothing. When the year began, the pro-gaming forces knew they would have 10 months to organize their campaign for the November referendum. They also knew they could expect opposition.

The *New York Times* and *Wall Street Journal*, together with most of the local newspapers throughout New Jersey, as well as the New York and Philadelphia television networks, had editorialized against legalizing gambling. Senior U.S. Senator Clifford Case, State Senators Anne Martindell, Raymond Bateman, and John Fay, and Assemblymen James Hurley and Thomas Kean had all fought the question whenever it was discussed in the legislature. Kean, the Assembly Minority Leader, was a vocal opponent. "You are talking about changing the very character of New Jersey. Gambling would become our primary business, we would become known as the gambling state, and all legislation would be discussed in terms of how the gambling interests feel about it." Additionally, the state's two highest law enforcement officials, Attorney General William Hyland and U.S. Attorney Jonathan Goldstein, spoke against the measure.

Jonathan Goldstein was a forceful spokesman for the opposition. Together with clergymen from the New Jersey Council of Churches, he spoke at hundreds of gatherings throughout the state. Goldstein barnstormed across the state with the local newspapers and radio stations spreading the word. Everywhere he went he warned that the only group that would benefit from the legalization of gambling was organized crime. "I am concerned that the very same interests which have allowed Atlantic City to deteriorate will be those who will be the sole beneficiaries of casino gambling." Goldstein was one of the prosecutors of the Atlantic City Seven, and he had a keen grasp of the traditional partnership between local politicians and the racketeers. He played on the suspicions of the average voter that all gambling was controlled by the mob. To the average person, Goldstein's comments had a ring of truth and with the exposure they received, it damaged the resort's cause.

Aside from the crime issue, there was a second basis for opposition expressed by State Senator Anne Martindell. The resort didn't deserve special treatment. According to Martindell, the State Constitution shouldn't be amended to satisfy the needs of one city.

Statewide referenda and the amendment of New Jersey's most basic legal principles should be limited to issues of statewide concern. Martindell argued that if Atlantic City wanted to make a comeback, it should pull itself up by its bootstraps. Let it diversify its economy. Let it seek out light industry and commercial uses other than resort-oriented businesses. The resort wasn't entitled to a quick fix. It should battle urban decay just as every aging city in the Northeast was battling to do. Speaking at a press conference on the Boardwalk several weeks prior to the referendum, Martindell stated, "I am concerned with the future of Atlantic City. I want the city redeveloped on a solid future, not the dangerous shifting sands of gambling. Plans, real plans, have to be made to attract a diversity of industry and investments in order to create new jobs to solve Atlantic City's deep-rooted economic and social problems."

To the resort's leaders, Martindell's comments read like something out of a fantasy. They understood their town's singular purpose. If the resort didn't have a gimmick to revive vacationers' interest, all would be lost. Unfortunately, Martindell's pitch appealed to voters throughout the state, especially those in New Jersey's decaying urban areas. Many politicians from other cities could see no reason why Atlantic City should be the lone beneficiary of a Constitutional Amendment.

The opposition found the media sympathetic to their views and despite the lack of resources—the pro-gaming effort outspent them 20 to 1—Goldstein, Martindell, and others were able to spread their message without the need of financing. An example of the message sent to the voters by the New Jersey's media is an editorial of the *Vineland Times Journal,* which was reprinted in newspapers throughout the state:

> Once again the public is being conned, though this one must rank as one of the great con jobs of all time. What we're being asked to believe is that by making it easier for farmers, wage earners, business owners, housewives, and retirees to lose their shirts at the crap table, the roulette wheels, the blackjack games, or slot machines (now, one must fly all the way to Nevada) this will be a stronger, healthier state, a better place in which to live.
>
> The big promotion of this colossal swindle comes from Atlantic City, whose politicians assert with a straight face that a century of racism, political and police corruption, exploitation of the poor, prostitution, and

general sleaziness all will be reversed by the installation
of gambling. Why, the finest folks in the country will all
flock to Atlantic City, and Absecon Island will be restored
to the ranks of the noble and the pure and well-fed.

Ignoring such vocal opposition, the supporters of gambling squandered the first six months of the campaign. Despite the tinsel and glitter, and the hype and hustle of Atlantic City's past, it was still a laid-back town. Seventy years of corrupt one-party rule had produced a complacent mentality; whatever the problem, the Republican machine, in partnership with the racketeers and hotel owners, would solve it.

Grassroots-level social activism was nonexistent in Atlantic City. As far as resort voters were concerned, politics was the work of professionals like Kuehnle, Johnson, and Farley. With the disintegration of the Republican political ward system, there was nothing to hold things together. With no one to take charge, Atlantic City couldn't find its way.

When things finally did get organized in mid-July, it was a feeble effort. A pollster hired by the campaign organization warned that the election would be close, but no one was listening. The initial fundraising goal of $1 million was never reached; half that amount was spent. A first-rate public relations firm to sell the issue wasn't retained and, more importantly, a statewide, county-by-county organization was never formed. Steve Perskie, Joe McGahn, and others criss-crossed the state debating Goldstein and the ministers, like a traveling vaudeville show, but there was no follow-up. The audiences who attended the debates received no mailings or phone calls from the supporters of gambling. No doors were knocked on and there was no coordinated effort to get out the vote. The pro-casino forces didn't establish a single campaign headquarters outside of Atlantic County. Finally, the campaign had no soul, no theme, no rallying cry. There was nothing to grab the voters to make them vote YES.

The referendum failed miserably. It was defeated by a margin of more than 400,000 votes, carrying only two counties, Atlantic and Hudson. The question was crushed everyplace else. It was like a kick in the ass to a tired old whore who had lost her charm. A wave of despair washed over the city. For many area residents it was hard to imagine a future for their town.

There were brave statements of how the resort would have to move onto other ideas, but for many of Atlantic City's residents, the defeat loomed as the final chapter of their town's history. Those who could afford to relocate their businesses and homes out of the area were making plans to do just that. It seemed all was lost. In the weeks that followed, a bumper sticker summing up the town's plight became popular. It read, "Last one off the island, turn out the lights."

# 10

# A Second Bite at the Apple

It began to rain as she was getting off the bus, and her umbrella was at home. The walk was only two blocks, but her hip slowed her down and by the time she reached city hall she was drenched. Lea Finkler was a transplant from New York City, but everyone knew her and respected her commitment to Atlantic City's senior population. Hunched over by age yet slender, almost petite, she was a frail, bespectacled, shabbily dressed woman with an ashen complexion and short gray hair. Despite her appearance Lea's eyes gave her away; she was no one to mess with.

Lea Finkler was a "gray panther" long before the term was coined or senior citizens organized into interest groups. Her contempt for politicians was notorious, and Atlantic City's elected officials cringed at the thought of confronting her. She had come to the city commission meeting and, as usual, bullied her way onto the agenda demanding to be heard. She was there to complain about street crime. Two days earlier, one of her friends was beaten and robbed outside her apartment house at mid-afternoon by several teenage thugs. Lea was in a rage. "We're prisoners. It's been years since we've been able to walk the street or stroll the Boardwalk after dark. Now we can't even leave our homes to buy bread and milk. What are you bums going to do about it?"

They heard her, but no one was listening. They were used to Lea and tuned her out the instant she opened her mouth. When she was finished one of the commissioners asked her to be patient and promised he'd speak with the police. He told her there were no easy answers but that the long-term solution was to rebuild the resort's economy through casino gambling. A second referendum was being prepared, and after it passed, the streets would be safe for everyone. Rather than hurling insults, she was told to organize her friends to support gambling. Lea was unimpressed and left grumbling in disgust.

For those people serious about rebuilding Atlantic City, there never was a thought of abandoning the quest for casino gambling. While the first referendum was a debacle, it was a valuable learning experience for the pro-casino forces. The months following the 1974 defeat were spent analyzing the campaign, and in a short time most people realized what had gone wrong. Joe McGahn and Steve Perskie had misread the voters' fears about gambling. They were overly sensitive to the public's perception of Atlantic City, concerned that singling out the resort as the only community to be permitted gambling would appear to be greedy. Nevertheless, polls taken shortly after the election revealed that was what the voters feared most, namely, the potential of gambling everywhere. The voters had visions of slot machines in drugstores and gas stations in every community and they were turned off to the idea. They wanted gambling restricted to Atlantic City.

Another misconception dealt with the private ownership of casinos. It was thought that by proposing state-owned and -operated casinos, voters would have more confidence that they'd be run honestly and efficiently. But the voters knew better. They didn't want bureaucrats running casinos and believed the only people who would invest any serious money in Atlantic City were private developers. Thus, by narrowing the focus of their new question to Atlantic City alone, and permitting private development of casinos, it was felt that the resort would be able to face the state's voters a second time on more favorable terms. But McGahn and Perskie knew these changes weren't enough.

For several months prior to the 1974 referendum, New Jersey's clergy went to their pulpits each Sunday and preached against the evils of gambling. The ministers and priests were tough adversaries and their dire warnings of moral decay had a heavy impact, especially among the senior citizens, most of whom went to the polls to oppose casinos.

In a stroke of genius, as clever as anything conjured up by Nucky Johnson, McGahn and Perskie wrote language into their proposal that would not only win the support of senior citizens, but eventually neutralize the churches' opposition as well. The language of the second referendum required the tax revenues generated from Atlantic City's new casinos to be earmarked for a special fund. The money would be used exclusively for subsidizing the payment of utility bills and property taxes of New Jersey's senior citizens and handicapped persons. On the second time around, a vote against casino gambling would be more than a vote against moral decay and special treatment for Atlantic City; it would be a rejection of aid to the elderly and the disabled. The old and the handicapped would be used as a rallying cry in the campaign. Atlantic City couldn't have anyone better to run interference.

There was a sense of urgency to the second gambling referendum from its inception. It was like nothing else in the Atlantic City's history. When the pro-casino forces proposed a second run at New Jersey's voters, long-time residents viewed it as a life or death proposition, and it was. This was their town's last hope to keep from sinking into oblivion. If Atlantic City failed again, there wouldn't be a third chance.

Packaging and timing are everything in politics. McGahn and Perskie decided 1976 would be the year to make another pitch to the voters. Presidential elections traditionally draw more people to the polls, and the pro-casino forces were confident that a larger turnout would benefit their cause. Politicians know there is a class of voter who typically abstains from state and local elections, choosing to vote only for national office. This voter is generally uninformed, having no real grasp of most campaign issues, the kind of person who probably didn't even know about the '74 Casino Gambling referendum. A well-delivered message to such an unsophisticated group could make a difference in the outcome of the next election. In 1976 this block of voters totaled nearly three-quarters of a million persons. When combined with more than one-quarter million senior citizens and handicapped voters, the pro-casino forces had the basis for a turnaround on the second referendum.

The only other ingredients needed for success were money and a well-engineered campaign. By reframing the issue from government-operated to privately owned casinos, financing was no longer a problem. In the '74 campaign there were only eight large contributors of $5,000 or more. In 1976 there were 33 such contributors. More importantly was the amount of new money coming from outside of Atlantic City. The total of out-of-town contributions exceeding $100 in the first referendum was a mere $10,150. In the second referendum drive that class of contributors donated more than $518,000. Some 43 percent of the money raised came from out-of-town businesses speculating on what casino gambling could do for them.

The largest single financial source was a little-known firm based in the Bahamas, Resorts International, which contributed more than $250,000. In all, the pro-casino forces more than doubled their campaign fund, from less than $600,000 in 1974 to more than $1.3 million in 1976. With that kind of money available, there would be no difficulty finding a slick promoter to peddle Atlantic City's new package to the state's voters.

The search for a professional campaign strategist began in earnest once the legislature approved the final wording of the ballot question in early May. With commitments for the necessary financing assured, a steering committee was appointed. Within a week's time it evolved into the Committee to Rebuild Atlantic City. There were no dilettantes among the members of "C.R.A.C.," as it became known. It was a talented group, which quickly became a potent force.

In addition to McGahn and Perskie, some of the people included in this bipartisan alliance were James Cooper, a respected attorney and the president of Atlantic National Bank; Murray Raphel, a former county freeholder and merchandiser par excellence; Charles Reynolds, publisher of the *Press* and a shrewd and capable person, whose newspaper was the second-largest contributor at nearly $50,000; Mildred Fox, a long-time hotel operator and one of the original proponents of casino gambling; Pat McGahn, the senator's brother, who had contacts of his own in Democratic circles statewide; Frank Siracusa, an insurance broker who could hold contributors by the ankles and shake loose every last dollar; and finally Hap Farley, who had been shut out of the '74 campaign.

Hap became involved with C.R.A.C. in an unlikely manner. Steve Perskie reached out to Atlantic County Republican Chairman Howard "Fritz" Haneman, son of Farley's friend and ally, retired Supreme Court Justice Vincent Haneman. A date and time for a meeting between the three politicians was scheduled by Fritz Haneman. At the last moment, Haneman was ill and, knowing the importance of getting Farley involved in the campaign effort as early as possible, Perskie went to meet with Hap on his own. Farley received Marvin Perskie's nephew better than Steve Perskie had hoped. "He was most gracious and advised me that we should let him work where he could help the most—behind the scenes, working privately with his contacts throughout the State." Perskie and C.R.A.C. were only too happy to have Hap's help. This time

## Jonathan Pitney

Jonathan Pitney was a country doctor who yearned to be more. He dreamt of fortune and fame through the development of a "beach village" for the wealthy. Photo taken 1840.

## Samuel Richards

Samuel Richards was part of South Jersey's aristocracy in the mid-19th century. He was a mogul in lumber, bog iron, and glass. Richards latched on to Pitney's plans, and with his wealth and political influence, made the dream a reality, and then some. Photo taken 1884.

### Atlantic City "Pre"-Railroad
This was the virgin landscape out of which Pitney and Richards carved their beach village.
Photo taken 1850.

### Camden-Atlantic Railroad
The first train station built in 1854.

### The Petrel
One of the early trains crossing the bridge connecting Atlantic City with the mainland.
Photo taken 1866.

### United States Hotel
Built by the Camden-Atlantic Railroad in 1854. At the time of its construction,
its 600+ rooms made it the largest hotel in the country.

### Atlantic & Vermont Avenues

View of the early inlet area from atop the Atlantic City Lighthouse in 1866.

### Atlantic & Vermont Avenues

The same view, 20 years later, illustrates the impact
of Samuel Richards' second narrow gauge railroad.

### Tent City

The second railroad launched a period of growth that lasted
nearly 50 years. Each spring of the late 19th century a "Tent City" arose
some place in the town. These provided temporary housing for hundreds
of craftsmen and laborers needed to build Atlantic City. Photo taken 1912.

### The Boardwalk

The early years, circa 1875.

### The Boardwalk
Construction of the first permanent structure with the walk raised above the beach, 1884.

### The Boardwalk
Erection of the first steel-supported Boardwalk, 1896.

### "Captain" John Young

John Young was Atlantic City's answer to
P.T. Barnum. He made a fortune off nickels
and dimes and dazzled patrons with his
"deep sea net haul." Photo taken 1891.

### Hauling the Net

John Young's "creatures of the deep" left his customers gaping
and gave them something to talk about back home. Photo circa 1910.

### Young's Million Dollar Pier
It was a gingerbread castle that offered everything
from popcorn and tutti-frutti to dancing girls and sea monsters.
Photo circa 1905.

### No. 1 Atlantic Ocean
John Young's home at the seaward end of the Million Dollar Pier. Young and his pal
Thomas Edison spent many afternoons fishing out the window. Photo circa 1910.

### John Young Entertaining President Taft
Young loved to entertain at No. 1 Atlantic Ocean.
This dinner honored President Taft and members of his cabinet.
Photo taken 1910.

### Hotel Windsor
This was the site of the first walkout/protest by African-American workers.
It failed miserably. Photo circa 1890.

### Ready to Serve

This group photo is typical of Atlantic City's hotel work force, which was comprised of more than 95 percent African-American workers.
Photo by Fred Hess; donated by Robert Gross, circa 1920.

### The Cakewalk

This was a contest for Black participants only.
The best dancing couple received a cake. Photo circa 1910.

### Colored Excursion Days
At the end of each summer, African-Americans from throughout the Northeast region frequented Atlantic City visiting relatives and friends working in the hotel industry. Photo taken 1886.

### Castles by the Sea
The hotels along the Boardwalk were grand, but their rooms were rarely sold out, running a fairly high vacancy rate. Photo circa 1930.

### Boardinghouses

Built side-by-side, beginning the first block inland from the Boardwalk, these cottages/ guest houses/hotels, i.e., *boardinghouses*, were the backbone of the town. During the summer season there were few, if any, vacancies in the resort's boardinghouses. Photo taken 1900.

### Louis "the Commodore" Kuehnle

The first "Boss" of the Boardwalk. Despite his hunger for power and money, the Commodore had a vision for his town and led in the creation of the infrastructure needed to make the resort a modern city. Photo circa 1910.

### Kuehnle's Hotel

The Commodore's hotel was the birthplace of the partnership between
the local Republican party and Atlantic City racketeers. Photo circa 1910.

### Kuehnle and Friends

The Commodore accompanied by Congressman John Gardner,
County Clerk Louis Scott, and Sheriff Smith Johnson. Photo circa 1910.

### Alfred M. Heston
Atlantic City's No. 1 cheerleader. For more than 20 years he published annual handbooks describing a life of enchantment waiting for all who came to the resort. Photo circa 1900.

### Enoch "Nucky" Johnson
The master at wearing two hats, Nucky was both the most powerful Republican in New Jersey who could influence the destinies of governors and senators, and a racketeer, respected and trusted by organized crime. Photo circa 1938.

### Enoch L. Johnson Benevolent Society

With the help of his supporters, Nucky maintained an elaborate social service program, which provided a safety net for Atlantic City's working poor. Photo taken 1935.

### Birthday Boy

Nucky celebrating his birthday and having one of the many times of his life. Photo taken 1949.

### Francis S. "Hap" Farley

Possibly the most powerful legislator in the history of New Jersey. Despite being deeply involved in the workings of a corrupt organization, Hap exercised restraint and is remembered as a master of the Trenton legislative process. Photo taken 1937.

### Hap and the Governor

Hap's agenda *always* came first. Seen here with Democrat Governor Richard Hughes. Farley had an excellent relationship with Hughes and every governor he worked with. He wielded more power than they did and they knew it. Photo taken 1966.

### Greetings from Richard Nixon

Hap was a key supporter of Richard Nixon at the 1968 Convention. Here he proudly waives a telegram announcing Nixon's commitment to appear at a fundraiser.

around, Farley hosted dozens of private meetings, placed scores of phone calls, and made many one-on-one visits with political leaders of both parties from throughout the state, calling in IOUs he had built up during 34 years in the legislature.

The '76 effort would be led by a powerful nucleus. Once the key players were assembled, C.R.A.C.'s first job was a national search for someone to manage their campaign. Their choice was right on target.

Sanford Weiner was a modern-day Captain John Young. Like Young, he could sell anything. Rather than pandering to the tourist trade, Weiner made his living packaging candidates and causes. Located in San Francisco, he had been introduced to C.R.A.C. by Pat McGahn, who knew of Weiner through his efforts for Congressman Paul McCloskey of California. McGahn and McCloskey were old Marine buddies. It was Weiner who engineered McCloskey's upset victory over Congresswoman Shirley Temple Black. Now, rather than destroying a fantasy, Weiner was being called on to create one.

At the time, there were few people equal to Sanford Weiner at manipulating the electorate. In 18 years as a political consultant he had orchestrated 172 campaigns, all but 13 of which were successful. On 54 political referenda his record was perfect. An incessant chain smoker, his speech was rapid but deliberate. Weiner was a brilliant strategist capable of pushing aside generalities and focusing on what it took to get his message across to the masses. Sanford Weiner was the professional needed to tie everything together for C.R.A.C. A reporter who covered Weiner's role in the 1976 referendum campaign observed:

> The challenge, when Weiner took it on, was a heavy one: to repeddle a tired and unpopular cause—tainted still further through its image as a loser—and to present it somehow as fresh and palatable. But this is where Sanford Weiner has earned his stripes: in altering attitudes, manipulating appearances, reshaping realities to reflect the positive. He is a master of the science of collective persuasion. His success at it suggests a modern axiom: that the public can be induced to swallow any pill, so long as it is skillfully coated.

Sanford Weiner began his work by getting the lay of the land. He directed a team of volunteers and paid staff workers in compiling a vast amount of knowledge on the entire state, including financial information, demographics, and traditional loyalties among the voting public. From this research he made statistical overlays and ran them through a computer to analyze voting patterns in past New Jersey elections, i.e., what the turnout was and how various areas tended to vote. These facts plus Census Bureau information for individual regions gave him a generalized voting profile of every county and city in the state. Finally, through the use of sophisticated telephone polling techniques he learned the general attitude of the public toward the legalization of gambling. Financed by money from Resorts International, these polls were conducted throughout the campaign up to Election Day, and were relied on in the formulation of a week-by-week campaign strategy.

Weiner had to know what the voters were thinking prior to making his sales pitch. The ordinary person votes his prejudices; an effective campaign is one that appeals to what the voter already believes in, rather than trying to reshape his opinion through educating him. By early summer, weeks before he began his media blitz, Weiner learned that 34 percent of New Jersey's voters supported the idea of casinos in Atlantic City; 31 percent opposed it, with the remaining 35 percent undecided. The first group would vote YES no matter was type of campaign was waged. The second group was a lost cause and there would be no effort wasted on them. It was the undecided voter who was the target.

Generally, it's easier to get people to vote against someone or something than for a particular candidate or issue. When it comes to political elections, people are more strongly motivated by negative feelings. The voter who has made up his mind to oppose a person or question is more likely to get to the polls than someone who supports a cause. The only thing pro-casino forces were running "against" was Atlantic City's poverty, hardly an issue that inspired strong feelings outside of the immediate region. Weiner knew he had to get to the undecided voters before someone else gave them a reason to vote NO. Thus, the appeal couldn't be made to a negative attitude. If the campaign was to be successful, it had to be based upon a preconceived notion of the electorate strong enough to make the undecided voter go out and vote YES.

Weiner found what he was looking for in his early polling surveys. In reviewing his telephone polls Weiner learned that nearly eight out of 10 New Jersey voters believed that casinos had the potential to generate large amounts of revenue for state government. While the average voter didn't know just how much revenue gambling would produce, they felt strongly it had to be a lot of money. After all, didn't Nevada have one of the lowest tax rates in the nation? This was the core attitude upon which to build a sales campaign. The voters already believed gambling could be a positive thing to their wallets by minimizing the taxes they would have to pay to state government. Weiner had a ready-made audience. All he had to do was to bolster the voters' faith with the right numbers.

One of several consulting firms hired by Weiner to reinforce his strategy was Economic Research Associates of Washington, D.C. Their study projected the economic impact casinos would have on Atlantic City. It didn't matter that the figures could possibly have been different—they were good ones, and Weiner ran with them. According to the study, were gambling approved, the first five years would see $844 million on renovation and new construction in the resort, 21,000 permanent new jobs, 19,000 construction-related positions, and $400 million new wages. Equally important was the estimate that gambling would generate $17.7 million for senior citizens and the disabled by 1980. Having the numbers he wanted, Weiner proceeded to weave a wonderful tale: With the approval of casino gambling, Atlantic City would be reborn and the state treasury would overflow with money for the aged and the handicapped. The campaign was off and running.

By mid-summer Weiner moved into high gear, and C.R.A.C. was right in step. When the national political parties held their presidential nominating conventions, the resort's politicians seized on the opportunity to court New Jersey's power brokers. A contingent screened and prepped by C.R.A.C. was sent to each convention. There was a series of lavish receptions sponsored by Resorts International where the state's leading politicians were stroked. The message delivered to Democrats and Republicans alike was the tack Hap Farley had used for years: "I *need* your support, but if you can't help, whatever you do, please don't hurt me." Typifying the gains derived from such contacts was an exchange for benefit of the media between Pat McGahn and State Senator Anne Martindell. McGahn: "She said she's made her last speech against casinos." Martindell: "I didn't say that." "Then you said you would be too busy working for Jimmy Carter to campaign against it." "That's it."

The state's political leaders weren't the only ones wooed by C.R.A.C. One of Weiner's criticisms of the 1974 failure was that it was an elitist campaign. He decided to create a troupe of more than 100 average citizen volunteers from every walk of life and train them in public speaking. They were briefed on the campaign statistics, which Weiner wanted them to use in their talks to ensure every audience got the same message. Engagements were made for these people throughout the state to speak to groups of their peers: construction workers spoke to construction workers; teachers to teachers; doctors to doctors; accountants to accountants, and so on. In addition to getting out the message by ordinary people on common terms, Weiner had regional campaign headquarters established with primary emphasis on the populace in urban areas of northern New Jersey. Paid campaign workers, assisted by busloads of Atlantic City residents, hit the streets giving out literature and recruiting supporters. In many instances they had the help of the local political organizations who made casino gambling part of their campaigns. Weiner's troops were on the move.

As Election Day approached, Weiner launched a media blitz that surpassed anything ever done in support of a referendum in New Jersey. From mid-October to November 2, C.R.A.C. bought more than $750,000 worth of advertising. High-powered commercials were placed on the area television networks, and airtime was bought on nearly every local radio station. During the last two weeks of the campaign, Weiner prepared 14 different television commercials and scheduled more than 1,200 spots on the Philadelphia and New York stations that covered New Jersey. As for radio, during the final 14 days there were nearly 4,500 ads on 70 different stations. In a typical radio spot a sincere voice described the plight of a 72-year-old woman. "Although old and alone, she can still be helped if only you vote YES for casino gambling in Atlantic City." The announcer explained how the money raised by casinos would help this poor old woman with her rent and utility bills. Everyone had an aging mother, grandmother, aunt, or neighbor. It would cost the voter nothing to lend her a hand with her utility bills and prescriptions. It was Atlantic City marketing at its best.

In addition to the electronic media there were thousands of billboards, posters, and bumper stickers saturating the state's highways and shopping centers. The main pitch was to the voters' pocket-book—what casinos in Atlantic City will do for people all over New Jersey. The campaign slogan was "Help Yourself—Casinos Yes." The telephone polling continued in order to gauge the campaign's impact. Where the results showed a large percentage of undecided voters, television and radio spots were increased to saturation levels and campaign workers were sent door-to-door to distribute C.R.A.C. propaganda.

As a final measure of insurance, $170,000 in "street money"—the amount reported—was paid out on Election Day. Street money is a tradition in New Jersey politics; without it, voters in some areas don't get to the polls. In many neighborhoods it takes paid Election Day workers to knock on doors, drag people out of their homes, drive them to the polls and, when necessary, buy them lunch, give them a bottle, or slip them a few dollars. C.R.A.C. saw to it that there was enough money on the streets of every major city in the state to guarantee that when these voters finally did get to the polls, they pulled the right lever.

Sanford Weiner left nothing to chance. By the end of the campaign, New Jersey's electorate had been massaged to vote for the casinos. The election was a mere formality. The referendum was approved by more than 350,000 votes. Several days later Weiner returned to San Francisco. In less than four months he had played a major role in reversing Atlantic City's fortunes.

In the years to follow there would be many winners in casino gambling. In the short term, the biggest winner was the one that had gambled the most to finance Weiner's efforts—Resorts International.

There's a lot to be said for being first. From the start of the referendum campaign there was never a doubt Resorts International would own the first casino to open its doors for business. What no one could foresee was the dominant role this newcomer would play in the early years of casino gambling. Not since Jonathan Pitney and his Camden-Atlantic Land Company had there been anyone with the opportunity to reap the type of profits realized by Resorts International. Ironically, Resort International's beginnings were as foreign to casino gambling as Pitney's were to the founding of a beach village.

The story of Resorts International begins with a family named Crosby and a company known as Mary Carter Paint. John F. Crosby was a businessman-lawyer who had served as Connecticut's attorney general and as a deputy attorney general in the administration of President Woodrow Wilson. Crosby had four sons: One was a real estate developer, another a plastic surgeon, the third a convicted felon, and the last one a stockbroker. The Crosbys got involved in the business world through the Schaefer Manufacturing Company, a foundry business in Wisconsin. In 1955 the Crosbys purchased Schaefer and changed the name to Crosby-Miller. Several years later, Crosby-Miller, with the assistance of financing from an investment group headed by former New York Governor Thomas E. Dewey, purchased the Mary Carter Paint Company. The Crosby son behind this move was James Crosby, the stockbroker.

James Crosby was born in Long Island, New York, in 1928. Educated in prep schools and a graduate of Georgetown University, Jim Crosby's first position was a brief stint with the management of a paint company. From there he moved to a New York City brokerage firm, buying and selling securities. Eight years later, Crosby went to work with Gustave Ring, a Washington, D.C. financier. It was while working with Ring that Crosby became interested in a New Jersey-based firm, Mary Carter Paint.

The thing most noteworthy about Mary Carter wasn't its paint—it was mediocre—but rather its advertising techniques. The company engaged in a merchandising program in which it offered a second can of paint for every can purchased, advertising, "Buy one—get one free." From the start, the company's sales pitch was criticized by consumer groups as deliberately misleading. The Federal Trade Commission agreed and in 1955 filed a complaint, which eventually forced Mary Carter Paint to halt its novel approach to selling. Despite the notoriety, Crosby viewed Mary Carter as a good investment and urged his family to buy control of the company.

By 1960 the character of the corporation that would eventually become Resorts International was taking shape. Crosby recruited Harvard Business School graduate Irving "Jack" Davis to help manage things. Together, they headed a tightly knit group of family and friends who ran the business. Crosby's determination to keep things a family affair was shown by the structure of the stock offered when they decided to go public. Two classes of stock were created: "A" and "B" shares. There were many more A than B; however, a B share had 100 times the voting power of an A share.

Nearly all of the B shares were in the hands of Crosby's inner circle. While outside investors were welcomed, real power in the corporation was kept beyond their reach. Because of this arrangement, which they continued as Resorts International, the stock was barred from trading on the prestigious New York Stock Exchange and was sold only on the American Stock Exchange.

With the resources obtained from their new shareholders, Mary Carter Paint reached out for more customers. By the early 1960s, it owned more than 70 stores and had franchised nearly 200 outlets. Despite the success in expanding Mary Carter's operation, its share of the paint market was eroding. There were too many established competitors and the profit margin was slim. Crosby knew he'd have to diversify Mary Carter's operation if his family's business interests were to survive. Crosby and Davis found an opportunity in a world far removed from the American paint industry—the Caribbean.

When Fidel Castro deposed Cuban dictator Fulgencio Batista, he put an end to capitalism in every form. With his revolution, Castro drove Batista's friend, Meyer Lansky, from the island. Under Lansky's direction, organized crime had been making a fortune through operating gambling casinos in Cuba, catering to American and European tourists. With Batista gone, Meyer Lansky and company needed a new island to do business. They looked to the Bahamas.

Lansky's people found an ally in Sir Stafford Sands, the most powerful man in the Bahamas. In short order, several licenses for casinos were issued in the early 1960s to persons linked to Meyer Lansky. One of those people was convicted stock swindler Wallace Groves. When Groves opened his casino in 1964 the key positions were filled by people who had worked in Lansky's casinos in Cuba. At about the same time Lansky's henchmen were setting up shop, there was a legitimate investor trying, without success, to obtain a casino license. He was A&P heir Huntington Hartford. Groves, Hartford, and Mary Carter—you couldn't find a more unlikely combination.

Crosby was introduced to the Bahamas as a place for real estate speculation in 1962 by a Miami attorney, Richard Olsen. That year, Mary Carter Paint made several purchases on Grand Bahama Island. Three years later, Olsen approached Crosby again. This time it was with Huntington Hartford's failed resort development, Paradise Island.

Beginning in the late 1950s, Huntington Hartford had poured nearly $30 million of his personal wealth into what had previously been known as Hog Island. Hartford had done more than change the name; he had built a luxurious hotel, restaurant, golf course, tennis courts, swimming pools, and exotic terraced gardens. But without a gambling license, Hartford's investment was doomed. After several rejected applications, he got word from the Bahamian government that in order to obtain a license he needed a suitable partner. Hartford was friendly with Richard Olsen and told him of his troubles with Sands. Olsen recalled Crosby's interest in the Bahamas and made the contact on behalf of Hartford.

In February 1965, Crosby and company lawyer Charles Murphy met with Hartford in New York City. Hartford's personality made the negotiations difficult, but they eventually came to an understanding. Before Crosby would put any money into Paradise Island, he needed assurances he'd receive a gambling license. Crosby went directly to Stafford Sands, who gave him the same routine he had given Hartford, namely, that a license could be obtained but that Crosby needed a suitable partner. This time Sands was more direct and told Crosby his partner would have to be Wallace Groves. Crosby agreed and after several months of negotiations in early 1966, the Mary Carter-Groves-Hartford partnership was formed.

It was necessary to create several new companies, and Stafford Sands was retained as the partnership's lawyer. For his services, Sands was paid $250,000 by Mary Carter Paint. The arrangement engineered by Stafford Sands called for Mary Carter Paint to purchase a 75 percent interest in Paradise Island for the sum of $12.5 million. The remaining 25 percent would be retained by Hartford. As for the all-important casino, it would be operated by Groves who would own four-ninths of the business, with Crosby's company controlling the rest. Mary Carter Paint was in the gambling business.

The machinations with Mary Carter, Groves, and Hartford didn't go unnoticed by the United States Department of Justice. The federal government had dispatched a team of investigators to the Bahamas looking for investments in casino gambling by American organized crime families. Justice Department attorney Robert Peloquin — who later joined forces with Intertel, a security firm owned by Resorts International — reported to the government on the casino operation in which Mary Carter Paint was involved. In a memorandum that would later prove embarrassing, Peloquin detailed the arrangements made between the parties and concluded, "The atmosphere seems ripe for a Lansky skim."

The Mary Carter Paint-Wallace Groves partnership didn't last long. In early 1967 articles published in the *Saturday Evening Post* and *Life Magazine* exposed the corruption in the Bahamas casino licensing procedures. The articles focused on the criminal associations of people involved in the Bahamian casino industry, in particular Wallace Groves. Crosby was worried by the publicity and immediately obtained approval from the Bahamian government to purchase Grove's interest. While Groves was gone, the casino staff he had hired, several with links to Meyer Lansky, remained in place running things.

As the paint business continued to dwindle and the gambling casino on Paradise Island prospered, Crosby finally left Mary Carter Paint behind. In 1968 the entire paint operation was sold and Resorts International was born. It wasn't long before Crosby began looking elsewhere to establish new resort hotels and to expand his gambling operation. Inquiries were made around the world without success, and for the next several years Resorts International was confined to the Bahamas. But when the second gambling referendum allowing private investors surfaced in New Jersey, Crosby took a look at Atlantic City.

The city that Jim Crosby found waiting for him in the winter of 1976 was a bleak place, but the locals still knew how to roll out the carpet. When Crosby and his key associates toured Atlantic City for the first time, they were welcomed like conquering heroes. Arrangements were made for the contingent from the Bahamas to ride in a caravan of limousines escorted by local police. No one was sure why the locals were making such a fuss. What mattered was that the resort had an out-of-towner with money.

The squalor and desolation that greeted Crosby was a sobering experience. Within sight of the famed Boardwalk, there were entire city blocks that had been leveled with no signs of rebuilding—acres and acres of trash and rubble. There were hundreds of burned-out buildings and scores of rundown boardinghouses, occupied by poor, frightened old people. The Boardwalk hotels, which were of prime interest to Crosby, resembled huge abandoned caverns. None of them had turned a profit in years. For most of them, there wasn't even enough money to knock them down. A person had to be either a visionary or a fool to see an investment prospect in Atlantic City. Crosby may have been a little of each. He decided Atlantic City would be the place for Resorts' first expansion. Mary Carter Paint was coming back to New Jersey.

Characteristic of moves he made in the past, Crosby didn't dabble when it came to sinking down roots in Atlantic City. He jumped in feet first. Within a short time, Resorts International signed a contract to purchase the Chalfonte-Haddon Hall, an aging, but still salvageable, 1,000-room hotel on the Boardwalk. Crosby's company took title to the property prior to the gambling referendum and paid a purchase price of approximately $7 million. They also took an option on a 55-acre Boardwalk-front tract that had been condemned by the city. More important than its investments was Resorts International's role in the 1976 campaign; C.R.A.C. would never have gotten off the ground but for upfront money contributed by Crosby's firm.

Immediately following the referendum victory, Resorts International moved to secure its position in Trenton. Crosby hired the right people to guarantee he would be plugged into the state house as it began working on the legislation to regulate gambling. Three of the attorneys representing his interests in Trenton were Patrick McGahn, brother of State Senator Joseph McGahn; Marvin Perskie, uncle of Assemblyman Steven Perskie; and Joel Sterns, chief legal counsel to former Governor Richard Hughes and counsel to "Democrats for Byrne" in Brendan Byrne's successful gubernatorial campaign.

By the time the legislature had finished its work, Crosby had little to complain about. Worries over tight controls on casino credit, complimentary liquor, hours, and minimum bets never became a reality. Each of these points was important to casino operators. They understood the psychology of gambling and feared tight controls would hurt the house's take. When the Casino Control Act became law in June 1977, credit for gamblers was easy, drinks for players were permitted free of charge, casinos could operate 18 hours per day on weekdays and 20 hours on weekends, and minimum bets would be dealt with by the newly created Casino Control Commission through regulations that would benefit the casino industry.

There were also proposals talked about in the legislature, which Resorts International fought from becoming law. One early suggestion was that no casino should be permitted to open until a minimum of three casinos were ready for operation. Crosby's lobbyists made sure this never saw the light of day. However short-lived its monopoly might be, Resorts International wanted to reap the profits from being the first casino to open in Atlantic City. Another provision originally discussed, but left out of the Casino Control Act, was language intended to prevent an Atlantic City casino from maintaining another operation outside of New Jersey. Resorts was permitted to continue with its Paradise Island casino, despite its questionable associations in the Bahamas.

A final issue vital to Resorts International was permission to use an existing hotel, the Chalfonte-Haddon Hall, as the site for a casino, rather than being required to construct a new facility. There were still those who believed the purpose of legalizing gambling was to spur the construction of new hotel facilities, not the renovation of old ones. But in the end, no one, not the legislature, the governor, nor the critics of casino gambling could overlook Resorts' willingness to gamble on Atlantic City prior to the '76 referendum. Resorts International would be open long before anyone else. But what Jim Crosby hadn't bargained for was New Jersey's bureaucracy.

The investigative agency, the Division of Gaming Enforcement, was created to screen casino applicants and report to the regulatory agency, the Casino Control Commission. From its inception, the Division was handicapped by internal disputes, questions about the competence of its staff, and friction between the Division and the Commission. Most of the investigators hired by the Division were former state troopers who didn't have the background needed to pursue the questions raised by Crosby and Resorts' financial practices. The skills needed weren't those of a police officer, but rather the experience of an FBI or IRS agent. Working with these police officers was a collection of accountants, lawyers, and administrative personnel all equally inexperienced in the intricacies of a gambling operation. As the months wore on and the Division's bureaucrats sank their teeth into the application process, it seemed their review would go on forever.

By early 1978, some 16 months after the voters had said YES, Resorts was still being investigated. Jim Crosby was upset. The length of the investigation began to draw criticism from the politicians and the media. To the average person, the delay in getting casinos going was bureaucratic foot-dragging. The fact that Resorts International was a complicated financial entity with a long history, various subsidiaries, and some shady relationships in the past meant nothing. The pressure mounted and Resorts' lawyers persuaded the legislature that it had to act. The plan, for which Joel Sterns is given credit, was to give Resorts a temporary license to operate a casino.

Crosby's company was given a six-month permit, renewable for 90 days, while the investigation continued. Having succeeded in making an end-run on the review process, Resorts opened its doors on May 28, 1978, to thousands of customers, literally waiting in line. Within several months time, Resorts International emerged as the most profitable casino in the world. In 220 days of business in 1978, Resorts had gross winnings exceeding $134 million. In 1979, its first full year of operation, Resorts grossed an incredible $232 million.

During the time Resorts was the only game in town, customer demand was phenomenal. Hordes of eager patrons waited in line for hours, in all kinds of weather, for the privilege of gambling. It was a sight to see. Resorts had no marketing problems. Its only concerns were logistical: crowd control, security, staffing, clean up, and counting money.

Resorts International had pulled off one of the biggest business coups ever. It was beyond anything Crosby had imagined.

While the temporary license proved to be a boon to Resorts, it was a nightmare to the Division. Under the Casino Control Act, the Anglo-Saxon tradition of presuming a person innocent until proven guilty is reversed. In order for Resorts' application to be approved, it was supposed to show it was worthy of a license, namely, that it was free from any wrongful conduct or associations that might lessen the public's confidence in its ability to run a casino honestly. However, once the temporary license was granted, the burden of proof was effectively reversed. It was thrown back on the Division to show Resorts was unfit.

The Division's report was submitted to the Commission in December 1978, more than six months after the public had begun gambling in Atlantic City's first casino. To the dismay of the pro-casino forces and the outrage of Jim Crosby, the Division recommended denial of a permanent license. In its report, the Division cited 17 "exceptions"—investigative findings—comprising the basis for its decision to oppose the granting of a license to Resorts International. A majority of the 17 exceptions dealt with Mary Carter Paint's and Resorts International's activities in the Bahamas. The report detailed Resorts dealings with Wallace Groves and the payments to Bahamian government strong man, Sir Stafford Sands. The Division charged that in establishing the Paradise Island Casino, Crosby's firm had secured financing through persons of unsuitable character, including several whose licenses as stockbrokers had been revoked for manipulating the stock of Mary Carter Paint. There were others who had been disciplined for violating criminal banking laws.

The Division claimed that in operating Paradise Island, Resorts had continued its association with people linked to the underworld after informing the Bahamian government it had ended such relationships. The report accused Resorts of maintaining an unrecorded cash fund from which it made payments to government officials in the Bahamas in exchange for what Resorts described as "goodwill" treatment. Finally, the Division was critical of Resorts's accounting and internal controls for both the Paradise Island and the "temporary" Atlantic City casino.

The report complained that the procedures used prevented an accurate accounting of the amount of cash flowing through the gambling operations. The Division noted that these practices had been criticized by Resorts' own security agency, Intertel, as including procedures that create a "wide open area for theft" in the casino. The Division argued that by continuing these practices, after warnings from Intertel, Resorts' management wasn't fit to be licensed. Crosby and his attorneys responded to the Division's charges by demanding an immediate hearing. They claimed there was nothing new in the report and it could all be explained. Commission Chairman Joseph Lordi set January 8, 1979, as the date on which hearings would begin. When the hearing began, Resorts was represented by Newark attorney Raymond Brown.

At the time, Ray Brown was New Jersey's pre-eminent criminal trial attorney. A tall, thin, light-skinned black man in his mid-60s with a gray mustache, Brown was an unassuming figure. Usually attired in baggy suits and scuffed up shoes, his looks were deceiving. As an attorney he was a tiger and dominated every courtroom he entered. As a tactician, he was unsurpassed. Since the burden of proof lay with Brown's client to show it was worthy of a license, Resorts had the chance to respond to the Division's report prior to the state putting on its case. Rather than tackling the 17 exceptions head-on from the start, Ray Brown began his case by calling a list of witnesses whose testimony had nothing to do with the Division's charges. Brown asked his witnesses questions about such things as banquet facilities, meeting rooms, parking spaces, and specifics on the hotel's wiring, plumbing, ventilation, and numerous details on the renovation work at Resorts' hotel.

Brown's strategy was calculated to lull the Commission and bore the media away from the hearings. It worked. At one point, G. Michael Brown, the deputy attorney general handling the state's case, offered to dispense with the witnesses and formally agree that the hotel met the Commission's requirements, but Ray Brown refused and proceeded with his case as planned. As the hearing wore on, Ray Brown eventually produced Jim Crosby and the other key corporate officers. They explained away Resorts' past associations by testifying that once a person's unseemly background was brought to management's attention, the relationship was severed. As for the dealings with the Bahamian government, and the payment of $250,000 to Stafford Sands, that was just the way things were done in the Bahamas.

Ray Brown's presentation to the Commission consumed nearly six weeks. The Division's case, presented by Michael Brown, was completed in three days. It was hardly what was expected from reading the Division's report. Michael Brown called several staff investigators who recounted interviews with individuals who had given them damning information about Resorts. Their statements were a poor substitute for direct testimony from the informants themselves. The Division's presentation to the Commission never measured up to the advance billing of the 17 exceptions reported by the media prior to the hearing. In the end, the Commission voted unanimously to reject the Division's recommendation and granted Resorts International a permanent casino license.

CBS News editorialized on the Commission's decision by giving a mock lecture to future casino applicants:

> You should know it's okay to have employees who gained their experience in illegal gambling operations … to have kept employees on the payroll even after you had good reason to suspect they had connections with organized crime … to have given payments to officials of a foreign country where you had a casino, and to have improperly recorded these payments on your company's

books ... the trick is to admit these things and say sure,
you did them, but that you don't do them anymore.

Regardless of what the media had to say about Resorts International's corporate ethics, it was right at home in Atlantic City. Nucky Johnson and Jim Crosby would have gotten along just fine.

# 11

## It's a New Ballgame

Not even Don Rickles's raunchiest jokes could get their attention. The dinner honoring casino executive Tony Torcasio had drawn more than 700 people, but hardly anyone was listening to the comedian's monologue. Atlantic City's Mayor Michael Matthews was the main topic of conversation at every table, and Rickles' jokes were lost on the crowd.

During the cocktail hour, word spread that earlier in the evening several FBI agents appeared at city hall with a warrant demanding entry to search the mayor's office. Long-time Matthews enemy Patrick McGahn repeated gleefully to everyone with whom he spoke, "The little jerk is finally going to get what he deserves." The people on hand knew immediately this was more than gossip. Many guests left the dinner early to catch the local television coverage on the mayor's problems. Matthews' reputation being what it was, everyone assumed the worst and many couldn't wait to hear the news reports.

Each table had at least one person with a Mike Matthews story—whether philandering with showgirls (Joey Heatherton was a favorite), the betrayal of a supporter, or his drunken foolishness—there were more than enough stories to fill the evening. The only people who didn't chime in were heavy contributors to Matthews' campaign. Those who remained sat silent, barely touching their food, numb at the thought that Mayor Mike wouldn't be around to deliver on their investment. One mumbled softly, in disgust, "Oh shit, now I gotta do business with the nigger," referring to Matthews's likely successor, James Usry.

Mike Matthews was like two people, and you could never be sure which one you'd find. Of medium height and slight build, he was a stylish dresser who wore his 52 years well. His looks favored his Italian mother, and many women found him boyishly handsome, his graying hair enhancing his appearance. Matthews liked to party, and his mornings after could be rough. On his better days he could pass for a maitre d' at a fancy restaurant or the manager of a hotel, but after a long night on the town, he often looked like someone you'd expect to find scrubbing cars at a car wash or frying cheese steaks over a grill in a hoagie shop. Matthews was educated as an accountant, and as an officeholder he used his accounting skills to root out waste in government. He had the potential to be a serious reformer and while serving in county government fought corruption and forced badly needed changes. But he could also be coarse and crude, engaging in a shoving and spitting contest in public with a political opponent. Afterward, he saw nothing wrong with his conduct and wasn't the least bit embarrassed.

Matthews's political climb had been quick. In 12 years he moved from city council in the neighboring town of Linwood, to the Atlantic County Board of Freeholders, to the New Jersey Assembly, and then Atlantic City Commissioner, holding both positions at once. His election to the city commission followed several bitter court battles concerning his residency. Although a native of the resort, Matthews had moved out with thousands of others when Atlantic City's fortunes were on the decline. Following the legalization of gambling, he gained a renewed interest in his town. His political enemies fought his return, but Matthews emerged from the courts as an eligible candidate. Finally in June 1982 after the adoption of a new form of government, which was likewise contested in the courts, Mike Matthews was chosen mayor by less than 200 votes in a run-off election.

Within a short time after his election, Matthews' political ego burst its seams. He behaved as if there were no limits to his power. Never known for being gracious, Matthews rejected an offer from his opponent, James Usry, to pledge his cooperation publicly by participating in the mayoral inaugural. Matthews refused to share the limelight. The result was another bitter legal contest charging election fraud. Matthews won again, but the lengthy trial divided the community further. It generated daily headlines, but the trial made it impossible for him to work with city council, a majority of whom were Black.

Matthews relished the headlines generated by political infighting and cultivated his image as the maverick—a self-styled champion of the underdog. But beneath this veneer was a person too immature to compromise and so paranoid he was incapable of making a lasting alliance. There was no "inner circle" or continuum of personalities whom he relied on from one campaign to another. He remained aloof from the people who supported him. By the time he was elected mayor, Matthews had used up and discarded several valuable advisors who could have kept him out of trouble. Once in office, he followed his instincts, which led to his ruin.

As a former ally observed, "Mike Matthews was a creep. His *independence* was really paranoia. He never trusted anyone in politics and nearly everyone who trusted him got screwed sooner or later." A supporter of social programs for senior citizens, Matthews had charmed thousands of aging voters. They were the mainstay in one election after another, with many of them showing up to work at his campaign headquarters. While the senior citizens licked stamps and made phone calls, he might be found in a back room receiving oral sex from a political groupie young enough to be his daughter.

As mayor, Matthews featured himself as a type of social lion in casino land. He identified with the celebrities who appeared at the casinos and sought them out to pose with him for photos he displayed in his office, and when they were willing, which wasn't often, for a dinner date or a golf outing. He wanted to be the person everyone invited to the party. Had he been honest and kept to the duties of his job, Matthews had the ability to be a capable mayor. Instead, the number one thing on his agenda was his yearning to become a celebrity. People who knew him think that's half the reason he fought so hard to become mayor. "Michael loved the glitter of the casinos and once gambling was legalized, he wanted to be top dog in casino city. He was like the firefly who couldn't resist the flame."

The affair honoring Tony Torcasio was just the type of gathering Matthews was sure to attend. Seated at the head table with the likes of Joe DiMaggio, Mickey Mantle, and Joe Theisman, throwing barbs back at Don Rickles, it was the sort of evening Matthews lived for. But the FBI disrupted the mayor's plans that night. Before the Torcasio dinner was over, Mike Matthews was finished as a politician, having been written off by everyone in attendance. In the weeks that followed, the mayor gained notoriety on a scale to match his ego.

An FBI agent, who didn't even look Italian, came to town posing as a Mafioso and wearing a wire. Within a few short weeks he worked his way into Matthews' confidence and taped hours of incriminating testimony. The transcript reads like something out of a pulp fiction crime story. Never one for understatement, the mayor ran off at the mouth over dinner at a local Chinese restaurant, The Peking Duck, and gave the Feds all they needed. He buried himself when he accepted a $10,000 bribe in marked bills from the undercover agent. At the time of his indictment a full-length photo of the mayor with handcuffs and shackled ankles appeared in newspapers across the country. Mike Matthews had finally received the celebrity status he craved.

The record presented to the Court revealed an unscrupulous politician who all but put a "For Sale" sign on his office door. As Judge Harold Ackerman stated at the time of sentencing Matthews in December 1984, "You were on the take. Anyone with an eighth grade education could reach that conclusion." Rather than gracefully resign as mayor, he was removed from office by a recall election. In little more than two years after taking office, Michael Matthews was on his way to federal prison. By Atlantic City's standards, Michael Matthews' biggest sin wasn't that he stole, but that he was so clumsy at doing it. Matthews was worse than corrupt—he was inept.

Not everyone was as inept as Mike Matthews. After the adoption of gambling, the real Mafioso came to town, not just cops posing as them. Given the town's history with gambling and the way things were in the past, there's little wonder Atlantic City's new casino industry attracted the mob and its friends. This time around the reception wasn't so friendly. Brendan Byrne and leaders of the state legislature had meant what they said during the 1976 campaign. The mob wasn't welcomed. Resorts International got a break, but would-be casino operators who followed them were scrutinized much closer. An example is the Perlmans.

Clifford and Stuart Perlman were no strangers to Atlantic City. Natives of Philadelphia, they knew the resort wasn't the "World's Playground," but rather the place where Philadelphians went to let it all hang out. The Perlmans got their first taste of business on the Boardwalk selling junk to visitors. A couple of decades later, they returned, lured by casino gambling. During the intervening years they had made a fortune in Las Vegas. Upon their return to Atlantic City they were hailed as marketing geniuses. They set the standard for a first-class casino resort, with Caesar's Palace the best-known casino in the world. They were leaders in the casino industry and viewed as natural players in the new Atlantic City.

Shortly after the adoption of the '76 referendum the Perlmans began looking seriously at Atlantic City. Before Resorts International opened its doors, Caesar's signed a deal to lease the Howard Johnson's Regency, a leading local hotel. That a glitzed-up chain motor lodge was one of the city's better hotels was proof of how badly the resort needed casino gambling. The Perlmans let the world know the Boardwalk Regency was just the beginning—a project that would allow them to open as quickly as possible. After the Boardwalk Regency started raking in cash, the Perlmans planned to reproduce their Las Vegas magic and build a Caesar's Palace in Atlantic City. Caesar's and the Perlmans were the type of casino operators Atlantic City wanted. But they had another side, one that had snuggled up to the mob for years. It began with hot dogs.

In 1966, Clifford convinced Stuart to invest nearly every penny they had in a Las Vegas restaurant called Lum's. Stuart hoped it would be a fancy place but found it was a small storefront. Unlike the nearby Forge Restaurant, which was one of Meyer Lansky's favorite spots, Lum's was a tiny place that specialized in hot dogs. These weren't your average wieners though. They were boiled in beer and served with sherry-flavored sauerkraut. But Stuart didn't share his brother's taste. "We went and bought a couple of hot dogs and then we went outside because I didn't want to eat in there." The Perlmans would later claim they knew nothing of the Forge Restaurant's infamous reputation and its notorious patron who held court there, but events convinced people otherwise.

In 1969, Clifford led his brother into another deal, more grand than hot dogs. It was a major turning point in their careers together. The Perlmans, through Lum's, made an offer to buy Caesar's Palace, one of the swankiest casinos in Las Vegas, but widely known to have been built and owned by the mob. When the Perlmans took over, all they changed was the locks, leaving most of the management team in place. Caesar's managers had a strong reputation around town, and the Perlmans saw no need to check into their backgrounds. The Caesar's team included Jerome Zarowitz as director of casino operations. The Perlmans knew Zarowitz had a criminal record and at some point learned he had participated in the so-called Little Appalachia meeting of mob figures in Palm Springs in 1965. While the Nevada gaming regulators were concerned about Zarowitz's suitability to run a casino, they never required him to be licensed. The Perlmans kept Zarowitz on the payroll from September 1969 through the following April. Zarowitz's name didn't appear as an owner, but when the Perlmans bought Caesar's Palace, $3.5 million of the $60 million purchase price went to him.

Shortly after the purchase of Caesar's Palace, Alvin Malnik, who had ties to the mob, approached Melvin Chasens—then president of the new Caesar's World, Inc., nee Lum's—with an offer to sell Sky Lake North, a country club and condominium development in Dade County, Florida. The offer was rejected, but Malnik returned less than a year later. This time he made the deal too good to pass up: no money down, pay for the purchase from the sale of the condominiums, no payments on a second mortgage for three years, and interest only on a first mortgage for two years. During negotiations, Clifford Perlman and other Caesar's officials learned more about Malnik and his partner, Samuel Cohen. A book about mob financier Meyer Lansky identified Malnik as a close associate. As for Cohen, he had a criminal record for violation of the Commodity Exchange Act. But that didn't prevent Caesar's from dealing with Malnik. The Perlmans wanted Sky Lake and were willing to go ahead despite Malnik's and Cohen's reputations.

At the Perlmans' prompting, Caesar's directors approved the Sky Lake deal in July 1971 without being told that Cohen had been indicted four months earlier in a massive skimming operation at the Flamingo Casino. The Flamingo was directly across the street from Caesar's Palace and the case drew intense publicity. The Perlmans knew Cohen was under indictment but never told Caesar's directors, nor did they tell them that a co-defendant with Cohen was none other than Meyer Lansky. "Had this fact been disclosed at the meeting, it might well have brought the Lansky connection into sharper focus. The media allegations about Mr. Malnik and Mr. Cohen, then thought to be baseless, might not have been so readily dismissed." Suggestions by Caesar's legal counsel to seek advice from the U.S. Justice Department before dealing with Malnik and Cohen were also rejected. With the purchase of Sky Lake, Clifford and Stuart became increasingly involved with the mob. They already were in debt to the Teamsters Pension Fund—notoriously corrupt and controlled by the mob—from Lum's purchase of Caesar's. When they bought Sky Lake, they went further into debt with the same pension fund that had held the underlying mortgage for Malnik and Cohen.

The Perlmans were warned by Nevada regulators about dealing with Malnik and Cohen following a 1972 deal with Malnik and two of Cohen's sons for a Florida condominium project. A second warning came in 1975, prior to a deal with sons of the two men. This time, in order to raise cash, the Perlmans sold their honeymoon resorts in Pennsylvania's Pocono Mountains to Malnik and Samuel Cohen's sons and then leased the property back from the pair. In addition to warnings from Nevada gaming regulators, the company's security chief told the Perlmans that Malnik was tied to the mob. He also expressed concern that a number of Teamsters Union officials with ties to the mob had received free memberships at the Sky Lake Country Club.

This was the résumé the Perlmans brought with them when they came to Atlantic City. It proved to be fatal. At the time Caesar's received its temporary license, the Division of Gaming forced the Perlmans to take a leave of absence pending a hearing before the Casino Control Commission. In a report to the commission, the Division concluded, "As long as it maintains a relationship with Alvin Malnik and Samuel Cohen, we do not consider Caesar's World suitable for licensure." When the Boardwalk Regency opened its doors in June 1979, Caesar's agreed to "make its best efforts to terminate all of its existing relationships with Alvin I. Malnik, Samuel E. Cohen, or members of their existing families." But it wasn't until 16 months later, October 1980, after the commission had completed its hearing on the firm's application, that Caesar's finally distanced itself from Malnik and Cohen.

Unable to buy out Malnik and Cohen, Caesar's agreed to establish trusts to take over the firm's leases in the Pocono Mountains honeymoon resorts and its Florida country club. The trusts purchased bonds to generate cash to make the lease payments. Then there would be no direct dealings between Caesar's and Malnik and the Cohens. The company also agreed to prepay the balance of a $4.8 million mortgage it owed to Malnik and Cohen. But it was too little, too late. Less than a week later, the commission ruled the Perlman brothers were unfit to be licensed. The commissioners said their repeated dealings with Malnik and Cohen made them fear "these dealings may not have been isolated transactions." The commission found that "while it may be true that Mr. Malnik and Mr. Cohen were not literally in control of the casino, their financial arrangements provided them with an obvious opportunity to exercise economic leverage against Caesar's World … Thus, Mr. (Clifford) Perlman in a very real sense delivered his company into the hands of Mr. Malnik, Samuel Cohen, and Mr. Cohen's sons."

Both Perlmans were denied licenses and forced to leave the company. Their appeal to the State Supreme Court was unsuccessful despite representation by Irving Younger, one of America's finest legal minds. While they were relicensed in Nevada and obtained a federal license to run an airline, Clifford and Stuart regretted their return to Atlantic City. After all the publicity surrounding their license denial, they could never escape the stigma attached from their dealings with the mob. And they weren't alone. The same fate befell William T. O'Donnell, president and chairman of Bally Manufacturing Corporation.

The Division of Gaming believed O'Donnell, like the Perlmans, had too many ties to the mob. But this time, the ties led to New Jersey. Bally Manufacturing Corporation was a giant in the slot machine, pinball, and jukebox business. It dominated the slot market, having a stranglehold on a number of Nevada casinos. While the slot machine business was profitable, O'Donnell tired of making machines for others. He wanted slot machines of his own and decided Atlantic City was the place to be. He entered the market by acquiring a long-term lease for an aging hotel on the Boardwalk.

The Marlborough-Blenheim was one of the few remaining palatial Boardwalk hotels. The marriage of two grand old buildings—the quaint Marlborough, a wood frame hotel with deep red shingles and a slate roof, built in the Queen Anne style, and the Moorish-style Blenheim, a poured-concrete sand castle—the Marlborough-Blenheim was an architectural gem. Unfortunately, the aging hotel wasn't adaptable for use as a casino and had to be demolished. O'Donnell and Bally's then bought the neighboring Dennis Hotel and combined the two sites. The Dennis was gutted and renovated to provide the required 500 hotel rooms, while new construction on the site of the Marlborough-Blenheim housed the casino, restaurants, and convention space. Upon completion it became Bally's Park Place Casino Hotel.

While Bally's main base of operations was Chicago, O'Donnell was no stranger to New Jersey. The company's biggest distributor of pinball machines and amusement games was based in New Jersey. And that distributor was owned, in part, by one of the state's most notorious mobsters, Gerardo Catena. A well-known racketeer and underboss in the Genovese crime family, it was Catena who ran the family business when Genovese went to prison on federal drug charges. The Division of Gaming received evidence suggesting that during the 1960s some of the funds skimmed from Las Vegas casinos "were ultimately funneled from Las Vegas to New Jersey, where they were shared by, among others, Gerardo Catena."

Runyon Sales, a vending machine company in Springfield, New Jersey, was Catena's front. Runyon was Bally's largest distributor, with the exclusive for New York, New Jersey, and Connecticut. Through Runyon, Bill O'Donnell had regular contact with Catena's people, especially Abe Green. O'Donnell had met Catena during a visit to Runyon Sales and had heard rumors about his mob ties. When he asked Green about the roles of both Catena and Joseph "Doc" Stacher in Runyon, he was told they were still partners. At the time of the O'Donnell-Green conversation, Catena was in prison for contempt of court. He had been called to testify before a New Jersey grand jury hearing testimony on organized crime. Despite a grant of immunity, Catena refused to answer the grand jury's questions and spent five years in prison.

While Catena's interest in Runyon linked Bally's to the mob, there were even stronger ties. Bally's corporate predecessor was Lion Manufacturing Corporation. When Lion's founder died, the bank managing the estate decided to liquidate the company, creating an opportunity for O'Donnell to buy the company. His efforts to raise money failed, and he turned to Green for help. Together with five other investors, they put together a corporation known as K.O.S. Enterprises, which bought Lion for $1.2 million. Gerardo Catena acquired an interest in the company through Abe Green and Barnet Sugarman. When Sugarman died in 1964, Green and Catena acquired his interest. While Catena's name was never listed officially as a stockholder, he owned 12.5 percent of the company. In July 1965, O'Donnell bought out Catena for $175,000, in a transaction filtered through Green. In April 1968 K.O.S. became Bally Manufacturing Corporation. O'Donnell and Green each owned 22.2 percent of the company. Sam Klein and Irving Kaye controlled the balance of the stock. Both Klein and Kaye had links with Catena through a Brooklyn-based billiard table company. These acquaintances were heavy baggage for Bill O'Donnell.

Before Bally's could be licensed to sell slot machines in Las Vegas, Nevada's regulators demanded O'Donnell and Bally sever ties from Catena, Green, and Kaye. Nevada later forced Sam Klein to leave the company after he had been seen playing golf with Catena in Florida. Even though Bally's wasn't supposed to use Klein in any capacity, he was the one who approached Caesar's Palace President William Weinberger to see if he'd be interested in running Bally's new casino in Atlantic City. Klein also tried to put together a deal for Bally's to buy the Howard Johnson's Regency Hotel. While the deal never went through—the property was bought by the Perlmans—O'Donnell had promised Klein a "finder's fee" if it had. Abe Green also kept doing business with Bally's despite the Nevada Gaming Commission's ruling.

Green's son, Irving, formed a company called Coin-Op, which was separate from Runyon and in which his father owned no interest. New Jersey regulators claimed that the younger Green told O'Donnell that the new company was just another name for Runyon. That was true. Bally's kept receiving purchase orders from Runyon and listed it on service orders, even though the bills went to Coin-Op, whose offices were next to Runyon's. In late 1977 to '78, at the time Bally's was beginning construction of its new casino, Coin-Op physically separated itself from Runyon, but Runyon remained its only customer. And if Coin-Op/Runyon weren't enough, there was Dino Cellini. O'Donnell had hired him as a slot salesman despite the fact that Cellini had run a casino in Cuba for Meyer Lansky—even more baggage. O'Donnell had to know he'd have big problems being licensed.

Despite his many ties with unsavory people, Bill O'Donnell refused to go quietly. At the hearing on his application, he offered an impressive parade of character witnesses to convince the commission he should be licensed. The witnesses included the former head of the Chicago Strike Force; a retired agent in charge of the FBI's Chicago office; and a former U.S. Attorney with a record of prosecuting organized crime. Touching every base he called a federal judge, two Jesuit priests, and a half dozen bankers who tried to convince the regulators O'Donnell should be licensed. The commission members were impressed. They found, "He is obviously a man with many fine attributes, including those of kindness, generosity, loyalty, intelligence, and leadership ability." But it wasn't enough. The taint of dealing with the mob was too much. Like the Perlmans, O'Donnell was forced to leave Bally's before the casino could be permanently licensed.

Setbacks with the Perlmans and O'Donnell didn't discourage the mob. They tried to infiltrate casinos that had already been licensed. Golden Nugget, Inc. was an example.

Golden Nugget Chairman Stephen Wynn represented the new, mob-free Las Vegas, and when he decided to branch out to Atlantic City he was licensed without a hitch. Wynn had visited the resort shortly after the 1976 referendum. He was one of a large number of out-of-town investors who came to town to size things up, but most of them couldn't see past the burned out buildings and squalor. They went away—Wynn included—believing it was a big joke, satisfied that Atlantic City could never compete with Las Vegas.

Shortly after Crosby and friends opened Resorts International, Wynn made a return visit. He was dumbfounded by the thousands of people waiting in line for hours to get onto the casino floor. The line went through the hotel lobby and out the door, spilling onto the Boardwalk where police were needed to control the crowd. Once inside, there was pushing and shoving for seats at the blackjack tables. Wynn was in awe of Resorts' success. "I had never seen anything like it. It made Caesar's Palace on New Year's Eve look like it was closed for lunch."

The unexpected success of Atlantic City's first casino was like an explosion. It sent out shock waves that stirred interest across the nation. Not since the coming of the railroad had Absecon Island been such hot property. Within no time, there were dozens of firms beating a path to the resort, investing fortunes and gobbling up real estate.

Steve Wynn is typical of the "moneymen" lured to Atlantic City by the news of Resorts International's profits. Handsome, charming, articulate, and polished, Wynn is a gambling prodigy. His entire life has been involved with gambling. "Since the day I took my first breath I have been a kid who has never had a meal, a dollar for tuition, or a piece of clothing on my back that didn't come from gambling." The son of a bingo parlor manager who grew up in suburban Maryland watching his father gamble away his earnings, Wynn learned an important lesson while still a child. "One thing my father's gambling did was that it showed me at a very early age that if you wanted to make money in a casino the answer was to own one."

After graduating from the University of Pennsylvania in 1963 where he was an English major, Wynn went home to Maryland to run his family's bingo games. Things went well but Wynn was frustrated;

bingo was small time and merely whetted his appetite for the real thing—he headed for Las Vegas. Wynn wasn't there long before he came into contact with a banker named Parry Thomas, who at the time was a major figure in Las Vegas. Thanks to Thomas, when Howard Hughes bought the Frontier Hotel in 1967, Wynn got his first break. At the age of 25 he was named vice-president and put in charge of the slot machine operation. The following year he bought a liquor distributorship, which he owned until 1972 when he parlayed everything for his first big gamble. The $1 million he had raised was used to purchase a casino site from the Hughes organization next to Caesar's Palace. Wynn knew that Caesar's didn't want a competitor right next-door and waited for Caesars to make him an offer; eventually they did—the sale price was $2.5 million.

With the profits from Caesar's, Wynn bought more than 100,000 shares of stock in the Golden Nugget. Parry Thomas felt the stock was undervalued and told Wynn that if he wanted control of a casino, this was his chance. While the Nugget had a prime location and a popular name, it was poorly managed and had no hotel rooms. Wynn's stock purchase was enough to gain a seat on the Board of Directors and appointment as executive vice-president. But he wasn't satisfied; he wanted to be boss, and at the age of 31, made a bold power play. He confronted Golden Nugget President Buck Blaine with proof of mismanagement and stealing by casino employees. Wynn threatened Blaine with a stockholder's suit, exposing his incompetence, unless he stepped down immediately. Blaine couldn't take the heat and agreed to exit with a contract as a consultant.

By August 1973, less than a year after his initial stock purchase, Steve Wynn was in charge of the casino. Within a year casino profits skyrocketed from $1.1 million to $4.2 million. By 1977 he completed construction of a 579-room hotel tower, with the casino's profits soaring to $12 million. Steve Wynn had come a long way from running bingo games.

When Wynn learned of the money being raked in by Resorts International, he decided to fly east again. One look at the lines of people was enough to convince him. He wasted no time looking for a casino site. By the time he left Atlantic City to return to Las Vegas, Wynn had an agreement for a choice piece of real estate. The property chosen was the Strand Motel on the Boardwalk. The Strand was one of the motels built during the '50s when Atlantic City was trying to capture part of the tourist market traveling in cars. There were a few good seasons but as its novelty wore off, most of the Strand's rooms were empty. Had Wynn wanted to purchase the site prior to the '76 referendum, he probably could have acquired it by simply assuming the mortgages against the property; however, by summer 1978, the Atlantic City real estate market was on fire and the sale price was now $8.5 million.

Within months Wynn demolished the Strand and began construction of a tinsel palace that soon became a magnet. Golden Nugget invested nearly $200 million in creating a glittering Victorian hotel casino. With huge murals depicting early 1900s beach scenes, mirrored ceilings and walls, crystal chandeliers, stained glass, marble columns, and gold-colored slot machines, the Golden Nugget was a dazzling, and purposely overstated, piece of architecture (later sold to Bally's and now the Atlantic City Hilton). It was designed to appeal to the middle-class's craving for nostalgia and established Wynn's name in Atlantic City.

Steve Wynn thought he had found a new marketing executive in Mel Harris. He was the person Wynn needed in Atlantic City. They had met during college and Wynn's wife Elaine had known Harris since high school. The three rekindled their relationship in the early 1980s, and Wynn was so impressed he hired Harris in the summer of 1984 to be vice-president of marketing at a salary of $400,000. Wynn admitted that he thought so highly of Mel Harris he believed Harris might move quickly into the position of chief operating officer, a step below Wynn.

The decision to hire Harris was made with the knowledge that there were some skeletons in his closet. Harris admitted to a "social" relationship with some mob figures. After all, his father "Big Allie" Harris had been one of the biggest bookmakers in the Miami area. In addition, Harris' first wife was the daughter of Louis Chessler, another Lansky associate who had worked to bring the mob to the casinos in the Bahamas. His security staff was aware of these links, but Wynn concluded that Harris' social relationships weren't enough to prevent hiring him. What Wynn didn't know was that a few months before he was hired, Harris had met with Anthony "Fat Tony" Salerno. Fat Tony was head of the Genovese crime family in New York. In December 1984, a month after Mel Harris was elected to Golden Nugget's Board of Directors, the Division of Gaming learned of the meetings with Salerno. Harris, who insisted he had nothing to do with the mob, was captured on videotape during an FBI stakeout of Salerno. On at least two occasions, he was seen entering the Palma Boys Social Club in Manhattan where Salerno held court. Harris claimed he only stopped to talk to Salerno about the death of his father. The FBI was skeptical of his explanation because there had been two meetings with Fat Tony, one of which lasted an hour. Learning of Harris' meetings with Salerno, the Division of Gaming called him in for questioning. When it was over, he reported back to Golden Nugget officials and said the Division's staff had asked a lot of questions about his contacts with Salerno. That was enough for Steve Wynn. Within days, Harris was gone.

The Harris episode caused Wynn some uncomfortable moments, but he survived it. At the time of its license renewal, Golden Nugget was criticized by the commission Chairman:

> I must note that the prospect of a person having uncontested access to Anthony Salerno sitting as an officer and director of a casino enterprise is, to say the least, frightening ... It is simply unacceptable for a company functioning in this most highly regulated of all industries to place a person of Harris's known background in its highest operational and policy making echelons based on hit-or-miss investigations and haphazard and conclusory oral reporting to the chairman.

Wynn publicly conceded his company had blundered and admitted that hiring Harris had been an embarrassment to Golden Nugget. Several years later, after Fat Tony's trial was over, the government revealed how close the mob had come to infiltrating the Golden Nugget. The FBI had managed to bug the Palma Boys Social Club and recorded a number of conversations involving Salerno and his cronies. Those discussions made it clear the mob intended to use Harris to make inroads into the Atlantic City casino industry.

Harris, O'Donnell, and the Perlmans—their stories only begin to tell the tale of a long cast of unscrupulous characters who thought they could cash in on legalized gambling. There were many lesser lights of organized crime that tried to infiltrate the casino industry as vendors in everything from junkets for high rollers to sales of food and beverage supplies. Given Atlantic City's past and New Jersey's reputation for corruption, many criminal types assumed the only thing needed for admission was money. They never had a chance. What they hadn't bargained for was a licensing process akin to a proctology exam. That process was established by the Casino Control Act and the scope it created amplified the tiniest warts.

There's nothing quite like the Casino Control Act anywhere. As a threshold, every applicant has the burden of proving a negative, namely, that he or she isn't corrupt and has no ties to corrupt individuals. As William O'Donnell and the Perlmans learned, a person can be guilty by association. An applicant can be so tainted by his ties and acquaintances that he will never be licensed, even if he's never been charged with a crime and is an asset to his community. Every applicant, whether an individual or corporation, must consent to a background examination that an ordinary, thinking person would find very disturbing. For starters, an applicant waives his rights under the 4th Amendment to the U.S. Constitution, which prohibits unwarranted searches. When you apply for a license in the Atlantic City casino industry, you authorize investigators to inspect, demand production of, and, if necessary, seize any documents or records of any kind, pertaining to any aspect of your past. It's heavy-handed stuff but has been upheld by the courts. The reason is because a license is a *privilege*, not a *right*. If you want the privilege to own or work in a casino, you must agree to subject yourself to scrutiny, which the courts have described as "extraordinary, pervasive, and intensive."

The architect of the Casino Control Act was Steven Perskie. Perskie was elected to the state assembly on the ticket with Senator Joe McGahn, which unseated Hap Farley in 1971. The adoption of the '76 Referendum had raised the political ante in Atlantic City. By 1977, Perskie was tired of following Joe McGahn's lead. He particularly bristled at having to contend with Joe's brother, Pat, who was the Senator's alter ego. Farley's long tenure in the position of state senator had made it the most coveted position in city and county politics. His career still cast a shadow over local politics and was the standard for leadership. In the perception of politicians and the public alike, state senator was where the power was. Perskie wanted it for himself.

Some observers believe Perskie's clash with McGahn was unnecessary. With his ally Brendan Byrne in the governor's office, Perskie had all the clout he needed in Trenton to make his mark on any casino legislation. But Steve Perskie wanted to do it as senator, not as an assemblyman, and the McGahns were in his way. With the help of Democrats who feared that Pat McGahn wanted to become another boss, Perskie denied Joe McGahn the party's nomination. Perskie went on to win an intensely bitter three-way general election (McGahn ran as an Independent) in a campaign, which, at the time, was the most expensive ever waged for a New Jersey legislative seat. Fortunately for Atlantic City and its new casino industry, Perskie's legislative talents equaled his political ambitions. Working with the governor's office, Steve Perskie crafted a statute that ensured the mob could never control a casino.

While criminal types would make occasional inroads into related businesses and unions, they never had a prayer at dominating Atlantic City as they had under Kuehnle, Johnson, and Farley. The rigorous standards for admission to Atlantic City's casino industry greatly reduced the number of eligible applicants and, in the process, spawned a new type of casino management. Additionally, the requirements that applicants for a casino license must post a $200,000 application fee *and* fund the investigative and licensing process (often resulting in total costs exceeding $1 million), plus guarantee construction of a 500-room hotel, created a situation in which only corporate America would operate casinos in Atlantic City. The demands of the Casino Control Act made it extremely difficult for anyone but a publicly traded corporation to own and operate a casino.

Steven Perskie had raised the bar for admission beyond the reach of the mob. The standards he created ensured that the leaders of Atlantic City's new industry would be educated, experienced businesspersons. They would have degrees from distinguished universities and hotel management schools. Many would have a masters in Business Administration or degrees in the Law, Hotel Management, or Accounting. The training grounds to be an executive in Atlantic City were now places like the Cornell University Hotel Management School and the University of Pennsylvania Wharton Business School. One graduate of the prestigious Wharton School soon became a major player in the new Atlantic City.

# 12

## The Donald Comes to Town

Donald Trump stood on the bridge of his $30 million yacht, the *Trump Princess*. Despite gray skies and showers, hundreds of people— politicians, reporters, the paparazzi, and devoted Trump watchers— huddled out of the rain in the waiting area of the Frank Farley Marina. They had come to see the New York City real estate tycoon, turned casino mogul, sail proudly into Absecon Island with his latest toy.

"The Donald" and trophy wife number one, Ivana, beamed their biggest smiles and waived triumphantly as the 282-foot yacht maneuvered slowly into its custom-made slip. Television and news photos later made it appear they were waiving to cheering throngs, but in truth, the rain, together with Trump's security people, had kept most onlookers far from the vessel. Trump's people had loaded another ship with reporters and camera crews to record the arrival. The animated gestures were merely photo opportunities. Heavy rains left the pier empty and the planned reception was hastily moved indoors to the Donald's casino hotel, Trump Castle (now Trump Marina).

The *Princess* was Trump's new plaything. It reeked of wretched excess. A floating pleasure palace, it would have made Nucky Johnson green with envy. The six-deck ship had every convenience imaginable, whether sailing the ocean or at anchor in a Mediterranean port. It boasted eight staterooms, six suites, and two master suites. Bathroom vanities were hand-carved from single pieces of onyx and the basins for the sinks were plated in gold. During an $8.5 million renovation, every screw in the public areas was removed, gold plated, and replaced. There were dozens of telephones throughout the ship, supplemented by a satellite link to keep Trump in touch with his empire anywhere on the globe. A pair of high-speed cigarette boats was kept in davits at the stern of the ship to quickly ferry people to shore at ports where the harbor wasn't deep enough for the *Princess*. And if the Donald needed to get to shore quickly, the *Princess* had her own helicopter on the upper deck.

The *Princess* was conspicuous proof its owner was world-class wealth. Christened *Nabila* in honor of its original owner's daughter, the ship had been built for Saudi Arabian arms dealer Adnan Khashoggi, a middleman used by Oliver North in the Iran-Contra scandal. When asked about the rumored secret passageway, crew members would smile silently, feigning ignorance of such things. Times got tough for the gunrunner. Over his head in debt, he used the *Nabila* as collateral for a loan from the Sultan of Brunei. Khashoggi defaulted, and the Sultan took the ship. The yacht was estimated to cost as much as $85 million to build and was heralded as one of the most luxurious vessels in the world. But the Sultan didn't need another yacht. He had one of his own, which he hardly used. He wanted to unload the *Nabila*; Trump took it off his hands for $30 million.

Shortly after purchasing his new yacht, Trump was contacted by Khashoggi, who had been a guest at a number of Atlantic City casinos. The arms dealer wanted Trump to remove his daughter's name from the yacht. Khashoggi didn't understand the Donald's ego, which may be the biggest since the Pharaohs of ancient Egypt. For a man who put his name on nearly everything he owned, there was never a doubt he would rename his new toy. Had Khashoggi waited awhile, it wouldn't have cost him the $1 million Trump demanded to change the yacht's name. By the time she sailed into Atlantic City, the yacht had become the *Trump Princess*.

The event was Trump's coronation as the self-anointed prince of the local casino industry. Inside the ballroom of the Trump Castle, hundreds of locals joined the Donald and his people to mark the occasion. The guest list read like a "Who's Who" of Atlantic City. Area business leaders, the mayor, members of city council, state legislators, and even a U.S. Congressman were on hand. The crowd was a tribute to Trump's success at cultivating his image as the billionaire developer whose touch turned everything to gold. He was bringing Atlantic City more than a glitzy yacht, he was increasing the resort's visibility to a national audience. At the time the Donald came to town, the name Trump was on its way to becoming a legend in the real estate world and an icon in popular American culture. But the Donald is only part of the Trump legend and in truth, the lesser part. His father, Fred Trump, was the stuff of genuine legends. He's where

Donald got his start—standing on Fred's shoulders. To appreciate the Donald, it's important to know his roots.

Frederick Christ Trump was born October 11, 1905, in New York City. At the time, the family home was a cold-water flat at 539 East 177th Street in Manhattan. The son of German-born parents, Fred's father, Frederich, wandered from place to place in search of his fortune. He even went back to Germany to find a wife before returning to America and settling permanently in New York. Unsuccessful as a hotelier and restaurateur, he began a real estate business in the Queens section of New York City. Time proved it to be the beginning of an empire. Frederich died when Fred was 11 and his wife, Elizabeth, struggled to provide for Fred and his brother and sister.

Elizabeth Trump was a seamstress, and Fred went to work shortly after his father's death. Early in his teens, Fred supplemented the family income working in the booming New York housing industry as a "horse's helper." In winter months it was often impossible for horse- and mule-drawn wagons to make it up hilly streets with construction materials to a job site. In an age when there were no child labor laws, contractors hired strong young boys to substitute for horses. Fred carted many heavy loads of building materials up icy slopes to busy carpenters. "I replaced a mule," he said later. While still a teenager, Fred became a carpenter himself. Studying at Pratt Institute in Brooklyn, he immersed himself in the building trades, learning how to read blueprints and prepare mechanical drawings. He would later say, "I learned how to frame walls more efficiently than other people, how to read a blueprint more accurately and faster. They weren't huge skills, but they gave me an edge." He had the edge on his competition his entire career.

Fred was self-employed by age 18. Too young to enter into a contract or even sign checks, Fred's first company was "Elizabeth Trump and Son." His initial project was a single-family home in the Woodhaven neighborhood in Queens. From the profits on the sale of that home, he built two more in Queens Village, followed by 19 in Hollis. No need to wander from where his father had begun, the Borough of Queens was where he established himself, building everything from mansions in Jamaica Estates to homes for teachers, firefighters, and merchants in Woodhaven and Queens Village.

As he branched out into Brooklyn and Staten Island, Fred built thousands of units for sale and rental. In July 1938 the *Brooklyn*

*Eagle* praised Fred Trump as "the Henry Ford of the home-building industry." By exploiting government financing and tax incentives available after World War II with a skill unequaled by anyone in New York City's history, Fred amassed a fortune. Throughout the '50s and '60s he was dogged by controversy and government inquiries from one development to the next. While there were allegations of bribes and kickbacks, Fred remained unscathed and became the city's largest landlord. By the time his son, Donald, had completed prep school at the New York Military Academy in Cornwall-on-Hudson and graduated from the Wharton Business School at the University of Pennsylvania in Philadelphia, Fred's empire comprised nearly 25,000 units, with rental income of more than $50 million annually. And it was his alone—he had no partners.

The enormous equity Fred had built up in his rental properties was irresistible to his son. Donald convinced his father to use that untapped cash to venture where Fred had never gone, across the East River to the island of Manhattan.

The Manhattan real estate market is no place for amateurs. Smart players with equity and good timing can make fortunes in Manhattan but it's also a graveyard for many would-be real estate barons. Donald Trump had not only his father's money but also his instincts. From the time he was a child, he had watched and worked with his father whenever he wasn't in school. He learned much. While still in his 20s, Trump had developed maturity for the real estate game far beyond his years.

Trump's first opportunity to test his talent in Manhattan came on property owned by the ailing Penn Central Railroad. In 1974, Trump Enterprises secured options to buy several large waterfront parcels along the Hudson River. The timing was critical. Not only was Penn Central in trouble, but New York City was having serious financial and image problems of its own, and there were no other buyers. The purchase price for Penn Central's land was $62 million, but Trump paid nothing for the option. Better still, the railroad agreed to pay all of Trump's soft costs for the approvals needed to build a housing project that would contain thousands of units. Tax abatements from the city and long-term, low-interest financing (Fred had close ties to Mayor Abe Beame) assured success of his plans. Another deal where Trump put up little of his own money was the Grand Hyatt. Again, Penn Central was the seller, and this time Trump had a partner in the

Hyatt Hotel chain. He agreed to buy the aging Commodore Hotel for $10 million and convinced the city to give him an unprecedented 40-year tax abatement, valued at a minimum of $160 million. When terms of the deal became known to other developers, the city was widely criticized. But Trump was probably the only buyer for the Commodore and, at the time, the only developer willing to gamble on building a new hotel in New York City.

Trump had seized the opportunity created by a city desperate for development. He continued his roll going on to acquire the Bonwit Teller building and the air rights above the adjacent Tiffany's on Fifth Avenue. There, he built the centerpiece of his Manhattan empire, Trump Tower, a glittering palace housing hundreds of seven-figure condominiums—only in New York. Shortly after that transaction Trump expressed interest in becoming a player in Atlantic City.

Despite the initial success of casino gambling, a mind-set similar to New York's prevailed in Atlantic City at the time Trump began looking for property—namely, development of any kind was welcomed. It had been so many years since anyone was willing to invest in Atlantic City that for the first 10 to 15 years after the legalization of gambling, any new developer, especially a high-profile real estate tycoon like Trump, was received with open arms. There was so much rebuilding to be done that Donald Trump was embraced immediately. While he was eager to cash in on the Atlantic City boom, Trump had waited too long to get in on the really easy, big money raked in by Resorts, Bally's, and Caesar's. During their early years, the first three casinos were virtual money factories. Trump didn't begin looking seriously for a casino hotel project until early 1980. By that time, there were at least six other casinos under construction and a dozen more on the drawing boards. The lure of a quick return on investments had attracted all types, ranging from established firms like Hilton Hotels and Holiday Inns to stock swindlers and the mob.

Before he became involved, Donald Trump's first casino hotel, the Trump Plaza, had started life as a con game. Plans for the casino were first developed by Robert Maheu, an associate of reclusive billionaire Howard Hughes. It had been eight years since he was forced out of Hughes' Summa Corporation, where he was involved in the company's extensive Las Vegas casino operations. In 1978 when Resorts International opened, he was president of Houston Complex, Inc., a Las Vegas company that claimed to be in the computer software business. His partner in the venture was Grady Sanders, president of Network One, Inc. Like Steve Wynn, Maheu and Sanders saw gamblers waiting in line to lose their money at Resorts International and they wanted a casino of their own. With a bravado bested only by the likes of Donald Trump, Maheu and Sanders announced they would build a 1,000-room hotel on an undersized Boardwalk lot next to Convention Hall. It would cost more than $100 million.

Maheu's press release attracted the attention of the Securities and Exchange Commission (SEC). Comments by Maheu and Sanders about their plans had generated intense speculation on Wall Street, and the price of the stock of the two companies shot up. In late August 1978, just days after they signed a lease for the property, the SEC halted trading in the stock for 10 days while it took a closer look. About two weeks after the SEC first intervened, Maheu and Sanders unveiled plans for another project, a $60 million, 600-room casino hotel. "The marching orders have been given and everyone is gung-ho," Maheu said at a press conference. The announcements continued. Partners were added, leases and financing packages were developed, and construction plans were revised. There were other projects, too. Network One told stockholders earlier in the year that it was developing a "tamper proof" videotaping system that would be sold through 90 distributors and generate $2 million in sales in the first year. A year later, there were no distributors and no sales. The firms also made announcements about a planned satellite cable television network and a two-mile-long roller coaster project in Las Vegas—neither of which ever got off the ground. Then the SEC returned. It charged the two companies had issued "false and misleading statements about the firms which were designed to create the illusion that they were well established, highly regarded Las Vegas firms engaged in diverse activities." Instead, the two were nothing but "defunct publicly traded shell corporations."

With financing next to impossible, Maheu and Sanders recruited partners Midland Resources and developers Robert Lifton and Howard Weingrow to help salvage the project. But Maheu and Sanders didn't have the resources to continue and control of the venture was turned over to the new partners. Plans again were revised, but they were unable to secure funding for what they dubbed the "Atlantic Plaza Hotel Casino." That's when Trump arrived. The

Donald reached a deal to lease the land from the partnership and took over the project, permitting him to enter Atlantic City cheaply.

At the time of Trump's arrival, Atlantic City's casino industry was having growing pains. The industry had expanded faster than the market could grow, and that led to some difficult moments. There were nine casinos in place—several losing money—and none under construction. With the resort far from rebuilt, state and local officials were desperate for someone to put construction workers back to work and bring additional tax ratables and employment to the city. Trump sensed the anxiety and seized the moment. He moved in with grand plans, which officials praised as the start of the "second wave." Then he held his plans hostage until he received concessions from city and state government that would insure his investment.

Trump brashly insisted he wouldn't go forward unless he was first licensed as a casino operator. "I didn't want to be in a weak negotiating position with the Casino Control Commission. … My strongest card was the fact that construction of new casinos in Atlantic City had come to a complete standstill. State and city officials, I knew, were hungry for new evidence that Atlantic City was a good investment." He told the state he wasn't willing to "sit around twiddling my thumbs waiting for answers" if the license investigation took a year or more. The result was an informal agreement to complete the process within six months.

Technically such a request was impossible to fulfill. Regulators license a building and find that its owners are qualified to run and operate it. The distinction had not been a problem before Trump because every other operator opened its gaming hall under a temporary license—a convenience that allowed regulators to open a casino complex as soon as it was physically ready even though investigation of the owners wasn't complete. By this time, temporary licenses had been abolished and Trump wouldn't risk building a casino without first knowing he could run it. The move accomplished two goals simultaneously. It gave Trump the excuse he needed to go out and find others to risk their money on the project and also put pressure on regulators to move quickly with their investigation. The commission couldn't issue a license to him, but it did the next best thing—it held a hearing and determined Trump met all the qualifications to hold a license, once his building was complete.

One of the first design problems faced by Trump was that the hotel was to be built on a narrow sliver of land. The location next to the Boardwalk Convention Hall was fine, but a hotel less than 200 feet wide would be difficult to build and operate. Trump needed more width for his project. To handle this problem, he reached out to local attorney Pat McGahn. Resorts International had used McGahn effectively for years to get matters through local government, and Trump recognized the value of a local player. Quietly, McGahn arranged several private meetings with his friends in city hall to discuss a radical new plan for the project. A proposal was developed to allow Trump to buy the air rights over Mississippi Avenue, the street separating the hotel site from Convention Hall. The street is the only access to the Hall's underground parking garage and was used heavily by traffic visiting the Hall. Being able to build above it permitted Trump to develop a much wider casino, more attractive to gamblers. In a period of just one month—lightning speed by Atlantic City standards—the new plan was approved by the city, and the air rights over Mississippi Avenue were sold for $100. McGahn's ability to secure the air rights for a token is in stark contrast to a similar situation at Caesar's Boardwalk Regency. When Caesar's requested the air rights over a narrow alley, rarely used by the public, city hall demanded $500,000.

Shortly after work started, Trump reached a deal with Holiday Corporation, the Memphis-based firm that owned Harrah's Casino Hotels in Nevada and the Harrah's Marina Hotel Casino in Atlantic City. It was July 1982, and Holiday agreed to provide the financing and manage the casino hotel. All Trump had to do was build it and turn over the keys. In exchange, he would receive one-half the profits. Trump had found someone else to assume the risks while he shared in the rewards, but he wasn't happy. Within months of the Plaza's opening, Trump grew restless with Harrah's control of *his* casino. He wasn't content to sit on the sidelines and let someone else get all the glory. There was constant bickering between the partners over how the facility should be run. Trump was convinced that Harrah's was doing a lousy job.

To the Donald, one of Harrah's biggest mistakes was the failure to take advantage of *his* name. Trump felt his name had drawing power and he wanted it shouted to the world. The official name of "Harrah's Boardwalk Hotel Casino at Trump Plaza" had to be changed. He demanded that his name be moved up. So it became

"Harrah's at Trump Plaza." While the name change fed his ego, it didn't solve the underlying differences between the partners, nor did it quench his thirst to run a place of his own. Trump got the opportunity in 1985 by a means no one could have predicted.

The Casino Control Commission, in what will likely be remembered as that agency's biggest blunder ever, denied a license to the Hilton Hotels Corporation. Unlike Trump, Hilton had started construction of its $325 million casino hotel prior to being cleared by the regulators. After all, who could anticipate the denial of a license for an international hotel chain that hosted presidents and kings at its luxurious hotels? Under intense pressure, the commission agreed to reopen the Hilton hearing and reconsider additional evidence. But the initial denial left the Hilton organization so angry it refused to risk further damage to its reputation and gave up on being licensed. To make things worse, Hilton was facing several other problems at the time. Steve Wynn of Golden Nugget, Inc. was threatening a takeover of the company, and the estate of the company's founder, Conrad Hilton, was contesting a claim by his son Barron to the estate's controlling block of company stock. To add to the problems, an order of nuns who were the principal beneficiaries of the estate believed the estate would receive more for the stock in a sale to someone other than Barron Hilton—a sale that could help them in their mission to care for orphans and the poor. Unable or unwilling to fight major battles on both coasts, Hilton put the casino up for sale and the Donald was ready to buy.

Trump obtained a $325 million loan from Manufacturers Hanover Trust Corporation to purchase the Atlantic City Hilton—a large risk for a single bank, but revealing of how strong Trump's standing was then at only age 39. Uncomfortable, perhaps because he was on the hook for the money, Trump quickly sold $350 million in mortgage bonds in the junk bond market to finance the property, removing his personal guarantee. He didn't have to worry about finding someone to run "Trump's Castle Hotel Casino," since part of the deal with Hilton required its management team to stay in place, at least until the end of the year.

Upon opening his second casino in June 1985, Trump was a prince, and not just of his Castle. By owning more than one casino, Trump had positioned himself to become a major player in Atlantic City—more influential than politicians or casino regulators. There was only one annoyance. As he basked in the glory of the casino's opening, Trump was hit with a lawsuit by his partner on the Boardwalk, who was also his competitor across the street at the Marina. After fighting with him over the name of Harrah's at Trump Plaza, Holiday Corporation didn't want Trump to use his name on his new property, which was across from Harrah's Marina. Having a taste of what it was like to run his own casino, Trump went back to the junk bond market and raised the funds needed to buy out Holiday's interest in the Plaza. A short time later, he successfully fought, and bought, his way out of costly road improvements, which Hilton had agreed to as part of the approvals for the casino hotel. Trump then made some quick money in the stock market, employing "green mail" to weaken several competitors, by threatening takeovers of Holiday Corporation, Caesars World, Inc., and Bally Manufacturing Corporation.

Trump's next big move came shortly after the death of Resorts International's Jim Crosby in 1986. He convinced Crosby's heirs he was the one to complete Crosby's dream hotel, the "Taj Mahal." They sold their stock in a deal resulting in Trump having control of three casinos—the maximum allowed by law at that time. To comply with the three-casino limit, Trump proposed to close the casino at Resorts when the Taj Mahal was completed. While casino regulators are supposed to encourage competition and prevent "economic concentration," they accepted his plan to shut down a gaming hall rather than force him to sell it. Resorts never did close because entertainer/game show producer/investor Merv Griffin acquired it.

There was a brief struggle between Trump and Griffin for control of the corporation, but in the end they both acquired what they wanted. Griffin had purchased large amounts of Resorts' stock while Trump was dealing with the Crosby heirs. He was someone Trump had to reckon with. In an arrangement between the two, Griffin took control of all of Resorts assets except the partially constructed Taj Mahal, which was the only asset Trump wanted anyway. A few months later, after the Casino Control Commission refused to renew a license for Elsinore Atlantis Casino Hotel, formerly Playboy, Trump exploited Elsinore's fears that the state might appoint a conservator to run its casino hotel. Shortly before the company's license expired, Trump bought the property. Since he couldn't have another casino, he bought the Atlantis as a non-casino hotel to provide rooms for his Trump Plaza on the opposite side of the Boardwalk Convention Hall. With a Plaza and a Castle in hand, Donald Trump turned his attention to the Taj Mahal.

Construction of the Taj Mahal was floundering badly when Trump stepped in. Crosby's fantasy had become a money pit and spelled financial disaster for his company. The project was too costly for Resorts International and had drained the company's cash. Most casino industry analysts believed it was simply too expensive to finish and was better off abandoned. Trump was unfazed. He promised that not only would the Taj Mahal be completed, it would be "an incredible place—the eighth wonder of the world." He set a completion date of spring 1990 and met that deadline, opening in April.

The grand opening was befitting of both Trump and his new casino hotel. Standing on a large platform erected for the occasion in front of the hotel, Trump rubbed an over-sized magic lantern, which spewed smoke and shot a laser beam hundreds of feet into the air, cutting an enormous red ribbon and bow draped from the top of the 42-story hotel tower. The laser show and speeches were followed by a thunderous fireworks display along the Boardwalk. Thousands were on hand both indoors—the gambling had already begun—and out. Despite the usual dignitaries and celebrities on hand, it was the people inside at the slot machines and gaming tables who were most important to Trump. The Taj Mahal would need many thousands of gamblers to be successful.

"Success," namely *survival* for the Taj Mahal, required truckloads of cash. Prior to its opening, it was widely speculated by serious observers that Trump had to generate revenues in excess of $1 million per day in order to meet his debt service and operating expenses. Trump had leveraged himself so completely that as the grand opening of the Taj approached he didn't have enough cash on hand to operate his three casinos. In order to comply with Casino Control Commission regulations on the cash reserves required for a casino, Trump secured an interest-free loan from his father. That spring, Fred Trump came to town in one of the Donald's limousines and brought a suitcase full of cash. Fred exchanged the cash for $3.5 million in Trump Castle Casino gambling chips and provided his son with badly needed cash. The incident led to the adoption of a new regulation by the Commission and enabled Trump to bridge a gap in his financing.

The size of Trump's financial obligations were exceeded only by the Taj Mahal itself. At the time of its construction, it was the biggest and most expensive building ever erected in New Jersey. Trump's Taj bears no resemblance to the elegant mausoleum of an Indian Princess for whom the original one is named. Its eclectic architecture incorporates bits and pieces of several extravagant buildings, including the Regency Pavilion in England's Brighton Beach, the Alhambra Palace in Spain, and Moscow's candy-cane striped St. Basil's Cathedral. There's also some early Miami Beach thrown in together with touches of Las Vegas. Captain John Young would have loved it.

From a distance, Trump's Taj looks like a gigantic, thickly frosted, multilayered wedding cake, custom-baked for someone with more money than taste. What Trump calls "quality," others might consider gaudy. Regardless, the numbers on this behemoth of a building are staggering. While only a visit to the property can give one a sense of the place, a recitation of some of the parts that make up the building is helpful in appreciating the commitment Donald Trump has made to Atlantic City. It's a marriage that won't end anytime soon.

Trump's Taj Mahal stands nearly 500 feet tall, making it one of the highest buildings in New Jersey. It covers 17 Boardwalk acres and includes 1,250 guest rooms (400 luxury suites), 175,000 square feet of meeting and exhibit space, an 80,000-square-foot arena, a 1,500-seat theatre, a 30,000-square-foot ballroom, and a 6,000-space parking garage. There are a dozen places to eat and when all the restaurant and banquet facilities operate at capacity, 13,000 people can be served at a time. Construction of the Taj consumed enough steel girders to make nearly five full-scale replicas of the Eiffel Tower. There are acres and acres of marble used lavishly throughout the hotel's lobby, guest rooms, casino hallways, and public areas—the quantity consumed nearly two years' output for Italy's famed Carrara quarries. Austrian-made chandeliers hang over the gaming tables, escalators, and throughout public spaces of the building—the total chandelier bill came to $15 million. Another $4 million was spent on uniforms for the staff of more than 6,500 employees. At the time of the grand opening, mercifully scaled back since, *everyone* was outfitted in outlandish costumes, a mixture of Arabian Nights fantasy and traditional Indian garments.

The core of Trump's Taj—and from which all blessings flow—is a 120,000-plus-square-foot gambling casino, the world's largest at the time of its opening. On the day this mirror-lined cavern opened, it increased Atlantic City's gaming floor space by more than 20 percent. The casino contains more than 3,000 slot machines and nearly 200 gaming tables. To accelerate the pace at which money is fed to the house, there are 1,300 compact change machines scattered over the casino floor along with dozens of ATM machines. The roaring and ringing of the slot machines, and shouting and groaning from the blackjack and craps tables, are endless.

Visually, the casino is dazzling. The lighting is the type you get when you decorate a room in crimson, violet, purple, orchid, fuchsia, salmon, and scarlet—the type of light that makes everyone's hair look as if it's been dyed. Toss in big-breasted cocktail waitresses, statues of elephants decked out in jewels, and men on stilts with turbins, and the effect is dizzying. As the *New Baedeker* said of Atlantic City nearly a century ago, so may be said of Trump's Taj, "It is overwhelming in its crudeness—barbaric, hideous, and magnificent. There is something colossal about its vulgarity."

The only vulgar thing to Donald Trump about his Taj Mahal was the debt incurred in constructing it. Despite early receipts averaging in excess of $1 million per day, Trump still couldn't handle both the construction debt (nearly $1 billion) and daily operating expenses. Within less than a year after opening the Taj, Trump made a prepackaged bankruptcy filing, which reorganized the debt with his banks and bondholders. However, the reorganization plan approved by the Bankruptcy Court clobbered many contractors who had worked on the job. To this day there are local contractors and suppliers who cringe at the mention of Donald Trump's name. It wasn't a proud day for the Donald, but he survived it and his Taj Mahal is a winner, earning slim but consistent profits. In the Taj and his other holdings, Donald Trump's presence will be felt in Atlantic City for many years to come.

Another person who helped transform Atlantic City was Arthur Goldberg of Park Place Entertainment, who died at age 58 in October 2000. Smart and tough, yet ethical and courteous, almost courtly, Goldberg was a leader in the true sense of the word. In the brief period he was active in the gaming industry he earned an enviable reputation with casino moguls and Wall Street investors alike. In August 1999, *Barron's,* the Dow Jones business and financial weekly, declared him "King of Craps" in a feature article.

Arthur Goldberg's empire began with his family's Newark-based trucking company, Transco Group, a hauler of goods for such national accounts as Tropicana, Safeway, and Pepsi-Cola. A graduate of Villanova Law School, he gave up the law after only two years to run the family business for his father, who had suffered a serious heart attack. In 1979, with earnings from Transco, Goldberg acquired a major position in Triangle Industries, a wire and cable maker. He quickly became CEO of Triangle and realized a $7 million profit on his investment when Triangle was bought by other investors a year later. In 1983, Goldberg made another large investment into International Controls, a conglomerate producing everything from bomb casings and electric utility towers to tractor-trailers. Again, Goldberg became CEO and several years later, after improving the value of the company, sold his stock for another large profit. His reputation as an investor willing to get his hands dirty by involving himself in the management of the companies he bought added to Goldberg's aura.

As the decade of the '80s came to a close, Goldberg had been so successful that he found himself with little to do. In 1989, he acquired controlling position of a food distributor, DiGiorgio Corporation, which sold Italian food items. It was profitable, but not enough of a challenge. A year later he paid $14 million, or $8 a share, for a 5.6 percent interest in Bally Entertainment, Inc., the owner of Bally's Park Place Casino Hotel. At the time, Bally's was in serious trouble and was in danger of being forced into a Chapter 11 bankruptcy filing.

Goldberg had bought into a headache. Consistent with past ventures, he dove into the casino business feet first, never contemplating failure. He went to Bally's Board of Directors with a turnaround plan, conditioned on his being named Chairman and CEO. The Board accepted his proposal and Goldberg never looked back. His performance in turning Bally's around was extraordinary by anyone's yardstick. Investors who stayed with Goldberg from the day he joined the company in November 1990, to the Hilton Hotel's purchase of Bally's nearly six years later, saw their shares increase in value from $3.50 to $28. At Goldberg's encouragement, despite the earlier debacle, Hilton reapplied for licensing and this time was successful.

The Hilton merger moved Arthur Goldberg and the Hilton organization—and with them, Atlantic City as well—to the first tier of the gaming industry, worldwide. Goldberg became President of Hilton

Gaming and brought 11 Hilton properties, including the Flamingo and Las Vegas Hilton, under his control with the four he had. That total increased to 18 gaming properties with the purchase of three major Mississippi casinos when newly formed Park Place Entertainment was spun off from Hilton. The final addition to his empire before his early demise was Paris-Las Vegas, a lavish $800 million casino hotel that opened in September 1999. Arthur Goldberg set the standard for the new gaming entrepreneur in Atlantic City and the nation. He is sorely missed.

Several political leaders whose efforts in the public arena throughout the 1980s and '90s complimented the dynamism of people like Goldberg, Trump, and Wynn are James Usry, William Gormley, and James Whelan. Despite differences in politics and styles, each, in their own way, worked to keep Atlantic City moving forward.

James Usry was part of the last wave of Blacks drawn from the South to Atlantic City's hotel industry. Born in Athens, Georgia, in 1922, Usry's family came north shortly after his birth. He was a soldier in World War II, serving in a famous segregated unit, the "Black Buffaloes." An outstanding athlete, he played for a short time with the "Harlem Globetrotters." A graduate of Atlantic City High School and Lincoln University, Jim Usry devoted most of his career to education. As a teacher and school administrator, he touched the lives of thousands of local children.

Usry had been a community leader for years prior to making his first run for political office in 1982. He lost to Michael Matthews in a bitterly contested election. Following Matthews' indictment, Usry was elected Atlantic City's first African-American mayor in the recall election of 1984. Re-elected to a full term in 1986, Jim Usry's agenda was Atlantic City's residents. As stated by the *Press of Atlantic City* at the time of his death:

> His legacy is found in the daycare facilities, the youth centers, and the new housing complexes that dot the city—even though many of those improvements were built after he left office. He was the one who sent the message: Atlantic City's residents cannot be passed by.

Jim Usry's tenure as mayor was scarred by bribery charges arising out of the "COMSERV" investigation in 1989. COMSERV was a seriously flawed state "sting operation," long on press releases and short on hard evidence. Usry eventually pled guilty to a minor campaign finance violation and was defeated in his re-election bid in 1990 by James Whelan.

Jim Whelan, a genuine Democrat (not an Atlantic City "Republicrat"), came to city politics by a different route. A native of Philadelphia, he vacationed in Atlantic City during the summer and as a teen became a lifeguard on resort beaches. After completing college at Temple University, where he was an All-American swimmer, Whelan relocated to Atlantic City and was hired as a teacher and swimming instructor in the local school system. Through his involvement with both students and parents, he built a strong network of supporters. In the '80s he was elected twice to City Council, where he was often a lone voice of reason. During his several terms as mayor beginning in 1990, Jim Whelan displayed uncommon political courage in leading a city divided by race and petty factions. He is the first post-Farley era mayor to govern effectively. During Whelan's three terms in office, whole portions of the city were transformed. His integrity and maturity place him in a class apart from political types. Atlantic City's debt to Jim Whelan is a large one.

The third player who has had a key role in beginning the rebuilding of Atlantic City over the past 20 years is State Senator William Gormley. Bill Gormley is steeped in city and county Republican politics. He is the son of the late Atlantic County Sheriff Gerald Gormley, a loyal lieutenant in the Republican organization under both Nucky Johnson and Hap Farley. Gormley is a graduate of Notre Dame and Villanova Law School. Despite the makings of an attorney, politics and government are his profession. As a legislator, conciously or not, he emulates Hap Farley. Regardless of his aspirations for higher office, he's been successful at exploiting his relationships in the state capitol to Atlantic City's benefit. In the 20 years he has been in Trenton, Bill Gormley has earned the respect of every key player in the State House. In the time he has served as Chairman of the Senate Judiciary Committee, he has grown into one of the most powerful public officials in New Jersey. He should continue to be a force in both Trenton and Atlantic City.

Working together throughout the '90s, Gormley and Whelan provided not only the leadership but the vision and political will to get things done. Whelan was the mayor Gormley needed as an ally and the city needed as a leader in order to begin rebuilding the resort. And the rebuilding has begun.

The numbers speak for themselves—casino gambling is a success. The annual gross win by Atlantic City's 12 casinos compares well with that of the more than 50 casinos in Las Vegas, with the Atlantic City take exceeding $4.3 billion annually. Since the coming of casinos, nearly 50,000 new jobs have been created in a county with a total workforce of just over 80,000 in 1977. The casinos have spurred nearly $7 billion in new construction, increasing the property tax base from $295 million in 1976 to nearly $8 billion in 2002. More than 11,000 new first-class hotel rooms have been constructed. The property taxes paid by the casinos to Atlantic City's government now total approximately $165 million per year, representing nearly 80 percent of local tax revenues. Additionally, the casinos provide funding of approximately $340 million annually for seniors and, to date, more than $700 million has been paid into a fund for public improvement loans administered by the Casino Reinvestment Development Authority. Finally, more than 30 million people will visit Atlantic City this year. Not even Sanford Weiner would have dared to predict those kinds of numbers.

What does the future hold? In one critical way, today mirrors the past. Atlantic City remains a town with a singular purpose for its existence—to provide leisure time activities for tourists. As ever, the economy is totally dependent on money spent by out-of-towners. Visitors must leave happy. If they don't, they won't return. And getting them to return frequently requires a lot of effort and imagination.

The attractions available to lure leisure-time dollars generally, and gambling in particular, have increased dramatically during the past 25 years. From Native American Reservations (Foxwoods Resort Casino in Connecticut is now the largest casino in the world) to riverboat operations, casino gambling has swept across the country. When state-run lotteries are thrown into the mix, competition for the gambling dollar is everywhere. But, the public is fickle, and the history of gambling reveals an ebb and flow in its popularity. There's good reason to believe that Atlantic City and Las Vegas will have the greatest staying power as gambling resorts. Nevertheless, if Atlantic City's growth is to continue and the local economy remain vital, it must become more than a gambling resort.

Atlantic City must transform itself into a destination for more than day-trippers by bus and car. And that is a large task. Surveys show that few people consider Atlantic City as a place to "vacation" but, rather, merely a place to gamble, have dinner, see a show, and return home. If they stay overnight, it's usually a single evening. Major changes are needed to shatter that image. The new Convention Center is an important building block in broadening the resort's economic base, but many more hotel rooms are needed to attract the large national conventions and trade shows. Equally important to the convention trade and new hotel rooms is air transportation.

The resort will never be more than Philadelphia's Playground, dependent on the northeast region, until it is able to support an airline providing regularly scheduled national air service. To date, the most striking failure of Atlantic City's casino operators has been their inability to cooperate with one another in either attracting a major airline or sewing the seed money and financial guarantees for a start-up to provide service to the major metropolitan regions of the country. The casino operators seem more intent on competing with one another for day-trippers and bus patrons than joining together to expand their base nationally. It's difficult to understand why, after 20-plus years of success, the major casino players have been unable to work together to establish air transportation service. If they continue to wait for a solution to come from government, the resort will never have dependable airline service and this town's horizons will remain limited.

Admittedly, the airline industry is no place for amateurs, especially since the events of September 11, 2001. The costs and perils are enormous, but they aren't insurmountable. Their success on other issues demonstrates that if Atlantic City's 12 casinos join together and make a concerted effort, the resort would, in short order, have an airline providing service nationwide. Whether by means of the formation of a financial consortium to underwrite an air carrier's initial losses or pledges to purchase a given number of seats, filled or not, regularly scheduled air service is within the resort's grasp. The only ingredient missing is the collective will of the gaming industry to make it happen.

The political will needed to propel Atlantic City forward can only come by means of a consensus among casino executives, political leaders, and the community, generally. But achieving a broad consensus to provide continuing direction and an enlightened plan for the future is difficult in this town because of its past.

Atlantic City has yet to adjust fully to life without political corruption. Hap Farley's defeat was more than the collapse of a political machine—it was the end of an era. Under Farley and his predecessors, the political ward system was Atlantic City's dominant institution. For nearly a century, it was the prime means for distributing constituent services and political power and operated more by consensus than bossism. Ward politics was akin to a social compact, and its actions were respected by the entire community. It was the thread that united the city. The passing of the political ward system marked the end of effective government in Atlantic City. The Republican machine was corrupt, ruthless, and greedy, but it got the job done. At its worst, it extorted money from anyone who came into contact with city hall and obstructed needed reforms. At its best, the Kuehnle-Johnson-Farley regimes were responsive to individual needs of their constituents and, surprisingly, more often than not, provided able leadership on issues important to the city.

If constructed properly, Atlantic City would be served well by a new partnership comparable to the one forged at the beginning of the 20th century by Louis Kuehnle with the hoteliers and the local vice industry. This time around, it could be a structured dialogue between city, county, and state officials with representatives of the gaming industry. If it is to work, the initiative must come from the casinos. The reality is that the casino industry is the dominant institution in the new Atlantic City. It is obliged to assume a greater leadership role and must make the affairs of government, and the community generally, a priority. There are many bright, informed, and energetic people employed by the casinos. Because upward of three-fourths of them reside outside of Atlantic City, they believe they have no real say in the city's affairs. But that doesn't mean they can't or shouldn't.

The casinos must work together not only to further their own agendas but that of the greater Atlantic City community as well. They must make their voices heard in Atlantic City's neighborhoods and the region's schools, as well as city hall and the State House. Each casino could select representatives who would educate themselves on city, county, and state government and, correspondingly, begin educating public officials on the peculiarities and needs of their business. These delegates can't be upper echelon executives— they change too often—rather, they should be chosen from among mid-level managers and ordinary employees whose positions aren't subject to corporate takeovers and palace coups.

These casino delegates could meet regularly among themselves and designate agencies of government and local organizations to whom they would serve as liaisons. By becoming informed on the full range of government and community issues and meeting regularly with local decision makers, the casino delegates could, with much effort, but in a short time, begin the dialogue and create the partnership that Atlantic City needs if it is to flourish.

There's no reason Atlantic City can't flourish as a *community* as well as a tourist destination. The two aren't incompatible. While there were those who predicted Atlantic City would become an adult theme park with no room for families, the past decade has proven otherwise. Through the cooperation of the Casino Reinvestment Development Authority, city hall, and the casinos, many blighted areas of the city have been demolished and thousands of affordable units have been built to house local residents and casino employees. Despite the many high-paying jobs in the casino industry, the average worker earns barely $30,000 per year. If affordable housing and public transportation are available, many of those workers would choose to live in Atlantic City and their quality of life and, with them, that of the entire community and the region would be improved. Small but important steps in the right direction have already occurred. While Atlantic City as a *community* is a long way from being restored to the vitality it once had, tangible progress is being made. The pace may not be to everyone's liking, but given the fact that Atlantic City had been deteriorating for nearly 40 years prior to casino gambling, it's unrealistic to think redevelopment should be occurring more quickly.

In the past 25 years casino gambling has transformed a squalid little city on the verge of oblivion into one of the largest tourist attractions in the world. The profits, jobs, total investment, and tax revenues generated from gambling to date far exceed the early estimates of even the most optimistic proponents in 1976. While there are some original supporters who are disappointed, they should know—given the resort's past—that nothing but the legalization of gambling would have revived this town's fortunes. Had the '76 Referendum been defeated, Atlantic City would have continued to deteriorate and sink further into despair. Critics of the casino industry can drive up the Garden State Parkway to Asbury Park to see what would have become of Atlantic City without gambling. It would have been a grim existence for anyone left behind. Absecon Island would have become desolate in a way its early developers could never have envisioned.

Jonathan Pitney's beach village remains an experiment in social planning grounded in tourism. The new Atlantic City is in partnership with corporate America's hotel and recreation investors, a fact that the residents have yet to grasp fully. Once the community and the casino industry appreciate their relationship and understand their respective roles, Atlantic City will be positioned to reach full bloom. Working together, the experiment will succeed.

# AFTERWORD

Wesley Hanna had been anticipating the implosion of the Sands Casino Hotel for weeks. Eccentric but brilliant in a mix that is disarming, Wes is the type of guy to get excited contemplating the demolition of a 21-story, 500-room hotel. A recent graduate of Rutgers Law School, Wes was spending most of his waking hours serving as a law clerk to a Superior Court Judge. That brought him to Atlantic City daily, and he became mesmerized by the town's quirkiness. Wes was taken by the contrast of the competing realities and quickly sized things up. "The city has a culture of naked reality, while the casinos are a place where reality exists under many layers of lipstick and rouge." His instincts told him that watching the destruction of a casino hotel would be much fun. Upon learning the date for the Sands' implosion—October 18, 2007—Wes calendared it as if he and his fiancée Patty were going to a party.

When Wes arrived at the Boardwalk that Thursday night, he was tickled by the festive atmosphere. Throngs of local residents, hotel workers, peddlers, and escapists (in other words vacationers) crowded onto the Boardwalk, all hoping to be part of a history-making event. Wes took it all in. "It was an escapist crowd but VIPs were being ushered around and street performers were out in force. A guy impersonating Frank Sinatra won the contest for eyes and tips. You could tell people were there solely for the spectacle of seeing the building come down." It was a hodgepodge of humanity: young, old, black, white, brown, yellow, executive, and blue collar. People were dressed in everything from formal business attire to cut-off jeans. Some spectators wore face masks hawked by vendors to counter the expected dust. Everyone was enjoying themselves except Sands' employees and loyal gamblers, who were sad to see the building go.

Pre-demolition fireworks paid for by Pinnacle Entertainment, which was to build a new *mega*-casino, washed the area in bright flashes of light, while a public address system blared Sinatra crooning "Bye Bye, Baby." Shortly after 9:30 PM, Governor Jon Corzine and Pinnacle chairman Daniel Lee—who was celebrating his 51st birthday—pushed a wooden-handled plunger attached to a wire leading to the building, igniting strategically placed explosives. Seventeen deafening booms, seconds apart, followed the first explosion. Less than ten seconds after the final detonation, the massive structure groaned and began collapsing on itself. The falling concrete, steel, and glass emitted a roar, with dust floating out in all directions.

Wes' trip to Atlantic City met his expectations in ways he hadn't figured on. "The event had the *vibe* of any other casino spectacle—until it happened. When it did, there was no denying it was real. The explosions were real. The building really went down. The skyline really was different. The Sands really was no more. And a crowd accustomed to phony spectacles was genuinely stunned. Then, the people and the dust scattered—and Atlantic City went back to business."

Business, for Pinnacle's people, meant carting away the debris and clearing several adjoining properties. When they were done, Dan Lee and company had a total of 19 acres of oceanfront property between Indiana and Kentucky Avenues. A huge open expanse in the heart of the Boardwalk was ready for new construction. The plan was to erect a $1.5 billion Las Vegas-style, world-class hotel resort to compete with the new Borgata Hotel Casino and Spa, which had opened in Atlantic City's marina section in 2003. Joe Weinert of the trade publication *Gaming Industry Observer* termed Pinnacle's venture the "talk of the town." He predicted that within four years the site would be transformed into "a master-planned masterpiece stretching from the Boardwalk to Pacific Avenue." With gaming analysts pronouncing the arrival of a "building renaissance," Atlantic City was on the march—or so everyone wanted to believe.

Not accounted for were two obstacles capable of causing the town to stumble on its grand march into the future: one looming, the second ever-present.

Within months following the Sands implosion, "Wall Street laid an egg"—so said economic historian Niall Ferguson. Much has been written, and more will be, by scholars such as Ferguson, Paul Krugman, Robert Reich, and Michael Lewis. Nothing said here can add to their insights. Suffice it to say that Atlantic City's gaming industry—along with many others—didn't see the burst of the credit bubble coming. The turmoil in the financial markets will hinder growth locally and may push several casino properties into bankruptcy. Many observers believe that the over-leveraging of our nation's economy, which was many years in the making, will take as long to resolve. Welcome to the new normal. Farewell to the Pinnacle.

Ever-present, but often ignored, is the "naked reality" of just how much work remains to be done to rebuild Atlantic City. Thirty-four years after the 1976 gambling referendum much of the town looks as drab and dismal as it did before the casinos came in. For portions of the population and segments of the city, it's as if gambling never happened.

While the Casino Reinvestment Development Authority has funded important housing and commercial projects re-invigorating sections of the city, only one development—The Walk/Atlantic City Outlets—has been a game changer. In many parts of town the deterioration that started in the 1960s continues undeterred. There has yet to materialize a sustained effort to rebuild the entire city into a clean, safe, first-rate resort. For the past thirty-plus years, it's been a hit-or-miss, piecemeal effort.

Numerous buildings that had fallen into disuse pre-casino gambling still haven't found a purpose, and no one seems to know whether to permit them to continue standing or demolish them and create yet another empty lot. A threshold question to begin valuing any city's real estate is to ask, "If the building occupying a site were to burn down, would the owner rebuild?" By that standard, large portions of Atlantic City have a meager value. A recent editorial in *The Press of Atlantic City,* commenting on real estate eyesores, suggested to local readers, "Drive through the city with a fresh set of eyes, see it for the first time as visitors do, and these buildings cast a bleak and ugly pall over the city trying to market itself as a glitzy, vibrant, *always turned on* resort."

Two knowledgeable observers whose profession is to investigate and report on events in Atlantic City cast their cold eye in this direction to help assess where the resort stands today. If newspapers are the "first draft of history," then investigative reporters Donald Wittkowski and Michael Clark are first-rate historians of the casino and political worlds that dominate today's Atlantic City. Wittkowski spends his days scrutinizing every aspect of the casino industry. Clark's beat is City Hall, and he probes for answers to the puzzle of local government.

Wittkowski finds no virtue in subtlety. "Atlantic City blew it. It enjoyed a monopoly as the only casino city east of the Mississippi for 14 years, yet squandered that time by failing to develop the jaw-dropping, Vegas-like attractions that would ensure gambling customers would keep coming back for more. Only one new casino was built from 1990 to 2003, an astonishingly long lull. Profits rolled in like waves from the ocean, so casino operators felt no pressure or need then to invest in rebuilding the city."

With profits down, Wittkowski fears that more properties may go the way of the Sands. "Atlantic City gaming revenue has plummeted 25 percent, from a peak of $5.2 billion in 2006 to $3.9 billion in 2009. No one knows when it will finally hit bottom. Inevitably, there will be a shake-up. Vanishing profits, competition, and a still-fragile economy will force weak casinos to close." Wittkowski believes a turnaround is possible but it will take many years and require committed leadership from both the casino-hotel industry and City Hall.

Clark's take on City Hall is every bit as unsettling. "City Hall has been a place where potential goes to die. Whether newly elected officials with promises of change or a project to revitalize a neighborhood, the promises broken here reverberate throughout the city. And in all the discussions about combating the city's challenges from growing gambling competition, local government's problems are no longer part of the conversation. They're accepted as an unavoidable fact, the *That's-City-Hall-for-you* excuse."

As Clark notes, "City Hall's failings have a major affect on Atlantic City's hopes to be a premier resort. The city has one of the highest ratios of employees to population in the country—a direct product of the endless cronyism that has dominated City Hall since the early 20th century. The mantra continues like a drum beat, 'How do I get my piece?' With so much money tied up in salaries, there's little left for infrastructure, which continues to slip into disrepair."

Wittkowski's and Clark's assessments may be grim but they aren't surprising.

From this observer's perspective, the challenges facing the resort are just history playing out. Atlantic City remains an experiment in social planning. Today, as was true when Jonathan Pitney founded his resort more than 160 years ago, the only reason for the town's existence is to provide leisure-time activities for visitors. Today as then, repeat business by vacationers and conventioneers is critical, but the heady days of the 1990s when the casino industry was like a money factory are gone. One needs look no further than the empty Pinnacle site—19 acres sitting idle—to see that things have changed.

Also true today, as it was in the era of Nucky Johnson, is that this city has yet to embrace the customs and practices of most local governments for the exercise and transfer of power. Nucky's legacy of machine politics has been replaced by an endless free-for-all among politicians hoping to be the next boss, who use the city's payroll to swell the ranks of their supporters. Despite its corruption, the "Boardwalk Empire" of the Kuehnle/Johnson/Farley machine delivered essential municipal services in a competent manner. That can't be said today.

Complacency is fatal for a town like Atlantic City. Keeping the experiment prospering and re-imagining an empire (this time a partnership of community leaders and casino-hotel interests) requires each generation of leaders to develop a vision for accomplishing the town's singular mission.

All the pieces for a "renaissance" are here: the mighty Atlantic Ocean, beautiful beaches, the world famous Boardwalk, easy access by more than one-fourth of the nation's population, a modern convention center, a first-rate entertainment venue in Boardwalk Hall (part of Nucky's complex legacy), institutions of higher learning eager to share their knowledge, the building trades required to finish reconstructing the town, and most important, a skilled hotel workforce capable of making a hotel-resort economy operate with grace and efficiency. The only pieces missing from a formula for success is enlightened leadership and a sense of urgency, the likes of which propelled the adoption of the 1976 gambling referendum. When those two pieces emerge, Atlantic City will be on its way to once again becoming a premier resort destination.

# SOURCE NOTES

To avoid cumbersome footnotes interspersed throughout the text and still provide the reader with my sources, I have utilized the practice of reference to particular passages by page number, here at the end, rather than with breaks in my narrative. Hopefully, it will be easier on the reader's eye. These Source Notes list the personal interviews, newspapers, magazines, books, public records, studies, journal articles, and treatises that were the most influential in shaping my perspective on Atlantic City's history.

Due to personal and professional commitments, my research spanned two decades. Within a short time of beginning my interviews I quickly realized that I was in a race against death. So many of the key players were along in years that I feared I might never get to the most knowledgeable persons. I was fortunate to speak with as many as I did. More often than not, repeat visits were necessary. Sometimes these additional visits were to confirm what other persons had said, other times to test the accuracy of my perspectives as they evolved. Interestingly, some key people opened up to me only after several visits. The more some people knew of what I had learned, the more willing they were to talk to me. A few, like Dick Jackson and Murray Fredericks, initially spent most of the time asking questions and didn't answer many of mine. They were testing me. As Dick Jackson said at the beginning of our third meeting, "Now that I know you've done your homework and are serious about this, we can talk."

## Prologue

The vignette of the housewife/summer laundress and her visit with Nucky in his suite at the Ritz is based upon an interview with Mary Ill, long-time Atlantic City resident, active in local politics and charity groups, before the Great Depression and the social welfare programs that it spawned. Mrs. Ill's story was confirmed and recounted by several other persons with tales of similar incidents.

## Chapter 1: Jonathan Pitney's Beach Village

The "early" history of Atlantic City was fun to research. There are surprisingly good sources available at the Heston Room of the Atlantic City Library and at the Atlantic County Historical Museum in Somers Point.

1　**enjoy civil and religious liberty ...** taken from a biographical sketch written by Allen Brown entitled, *Jonathan Pitney, M.D.: Fifty Years of Progress on the Coast of New Jersey* (Daily Advertiser Printing Company, 1848).

2　The description of "**Further Island**" found at pp. 2–3 relies, in large part, on the work of Sarah W.R. Ewing and Robert McMullin, *Along Absecon Creek: A History of Early Absecon, New Jersey* (C.O.W.A.N. Printing, 1965) and William McMahon's work in *So Young ... So Gay!*, (South Jersey Publishing Company, 1970).

5　**"Railroad to Nowhere"** was a term used many times contemporaneously with Pitney's efforts and by several historians. See S.W.R. Ewing and R. McMullin, Ibid., and Arthur D. Pierce's work on the Richards Family, which was a powerhouse in South Jersey for several generations, *Family Empire in Jersey Iron: The Richards' Enterprises in the Pine Barrens* (Rutgers University Press, 1964). The chapter entitled "Railroad to Nowhere" pp. 225–240 is an excellent recount of Samuel Richards's efforts in making Jonathan Pitney's dream a reality.

7　**... looked like a bank president ...** A.D. Pierce, *Family Empire*, p. 226.

8　The initial investors in the Camden and Atlantic Railroad are discussed by A.D. Pierce, Ibid., p. 228.

9　**... a weird, wild look, a veritable desert ...** These first-hand observations are of Richard Osborne, the civil engineer who laid out the Camden and Atlantic Railroad, speaking at its 25th anniversary dinner in June 1879. S.W.R. Ewing  and R. McMullin, Ibid., p. 135.

10　The profits made on early land sales are detailed by John F. Hall in *The Daily Union History of Atlantic City and County, New Jersey* (Daily Union Printing Company, 1900) p. 187.

11　**A terrible Northeast storm ...** S.W.R. Ewing and R. McMullin, Ibid., p. 142.

11  **manifest destiny …** W. McMahon, Ibid., p. 38.

11  **… Finally, a bit after 9 A.M. …** A.D. Pierce, Ibid., p. 230.

12  **desolate succession of pine trees …** S.W.R. Ewing and R. McMullin, Ibid.,  p. 145.

13  **When I wanted to stop the train …** S.W.R. Ewing and R. McMullin, Ibid., p. 145.

13  **greenhead flies …** A.L. English, *History of Atlantic City, New Jersey*, (Dickson & Gilling, 1884) pp. 70–72.

14  **Prior to 1864…** A.L. English, Ibid., p.75.

15  **Unpropitious times…** S.W.R. Ewing and R. McMullin, Ibid., p. 179.

16  **… brought in by ships from Baltimore …** A.D. Pierce, Ibid., p. 236.

## Chapter 2: The Grand Illusion

20  **The fare was …** A.L. English, Ibid., p. 154.

22  **… swiftness in constructing new hotels …** W. McMahon, Ibid., Chapter V, "Hotels of the Boardwalk" pp. 117–152.

23  **… many establishments used the term "cottage" …** An analysis of boardinghouses versus hotels is found in the work of Charles E. Funnell, *By the Beautiful Sea, The Rise and High Times of That Great American Resort, Atlantic City* (Alfred A. Knopf, Inc. 1975) pp. 34–35. Despite its limited focus, Funnell's book is an excellent work. I recommend it to anyone interested in early Atlantic City. Notwithstanding the fact that it was originally a doctoral dissertation, it is more accessible to the reader (and more accurate) than some of the earlier histories. Funnell's work is one of the first serious histories of the resort, written without rose-colored glasses. Mr. Funnell died while still a young man. It would have been interesting to learn his thoughts on Atlantic City today.

24  **… Perfect health …** W. McMahon, Ibid., p. 57.

25  **… endless panorama …** Alfred M. Heston was Atlantic City's all-time cheerleader. He wrote a series of "hand-books" spanning

1887 to past the beginning of the 20th century and beyond. The handbooks were entitled, *Illustrated Hand-Book of Atlantic City, New Jersey*, published by A.M. Heston and Company. Heston's handbooks were widely circulated by the railroads throughout the entire country.

25 **... absence of art!** Quote from letter written by Walt Whitman in 1879.

25 **... *No snow on the Boardwalk* ...** W. McMahon, Ibid., p. 80.

26 **Boardman opened the meeting ...** W. McMahon, Ibid., pp. 70–74.

28 **... something colossal about its vulgarity.** *The New Baedeker*: "Casual Notes of an Irresponsible Traveler," September 1909.

30 **... envy of his customers ...** The career of Captain John Lake Young is discussed at length by W. McMahon, Ibid., pp. 159–166.

31 **President Ulysses S. Grant.** Grant's visit to the resort was recalled by Mary Ill in an interview conducted by the author. She quoted her father's friend, Al.

## Chapter 3: A Plantation by the Sea

Pulling together the pieces for a coherent history of Atlantic City's African-American community was a challenge. In my opinion, it was a story that cried out for proper treatment. I hope I succeeded. I realize that there may be some who will be offended by the title of this chapter. I consider it an apt description of the way things were.

Understanding the African-American experience in Atlantic City is critical if one is to have a true picture of the resort. Without the Black community, Atlantic City, as we know it, would never have come to be. The resort was founded at a point in time when Philadelphia was emerging as a major industrial power. For a decade and more before the American Civil War, and for two to three generations thereafter, Philadelphia boomed as an industrial employment center. It may be hard to grasp today, but at the time, Philadelphia's factories gobbled up nearly every available able-bodied White worker who wasn't a farmer in the region.

Late 19th-century hoteliers within the orbit of Philadelphia's economy had no choice but to recruit Black workers from the South. Without newly freed slaves from the Upper South, there would have been no one to service hotel patrons. Remove the affordable labor of African-Americans from early Atlantic City and it would have remained a *beach village*.

I have high regard for the excellent work and thorough research of Professor Herbert James Foster and relied heavily on his work. I believe the African-American experience in Atlantic City warrants a book unto itself. Hopefully, that will occur.

35 **... cooly told them ...** Herbert James Foster, *The Urban Experience of Blacks in Atlantic City, New Jersey*: 1850–1915. (Written in partial fulfillment of the requirements for doctor of philosophy, graduate program in History, Rutgers University, 1981). See p. 38, citing U.S. Department of Commerce and Labor, Federal Writers Project.

36 **Negroes are servants ...** W. E. B. Du Bois, *Dark Water* (Schocken Books, New York, 1920); reprint ed., 169, p. 115.

37 **... artisans dwindled to only a handful.** E. Franklin Frazier, *The Negro in the United States* (Macmillan, 1957), p. 165.

37 **... 4 percent of that city's population.** E. Franklin Frazier, Ibid., p. 596.

37 **By 1915, 50 years after the Civil War ...** H. J. Foster, Ibid., p. 60.

39 **... highest paid at the time ...** H. J. Foster, Ibid., p. 101.

40 **... "by the dump," or "back of the hill" ...** *The Negro in New Jersey*, report of a survey by the Interracial Committee of the New Jersey Conference of Social Work in Cooperation with the NJ State Department of Institutions and Agencies, December 1932.

41 **Unlike many other cities ...** H. J. Foster, Ibid., p. 141, note 12.

41 **Time, time is the great cure-all ...** Samuel Lubbell, *White and Black, Test of a Nation*, (Harper & Row, 1964) p. 15.

43 "Down by the Sea Shore – Atlantic City," *Philadelphia Inquirer*, July 23, 1900, p. 1.

45  **The Negro Church ... survived slavery.** W. E. B. Du Bois, *Some Efforts of American Negroes for Their Own Betterment* (Schocken Books, 1898) p. 4.

45  **... Du Bois argued ... resentment of the stolen people.** W. E. B. Du Bois, *The Negro Church* (Schocken Books, 1898) p. 5.

45  **invisible institution ...** George F. Bragg, *History of the Afro-American Group of the Episcopal Church* (Schocken Books, 1922).

47  **... shouting ...** E. Franklin Frazier, Ibid., p. 355.

48  **A cornerstone of their church doctrine ...** H. J. Foster, Ibid., p. 198.

49  **Among them were the Northside Board of Trade ...** H. J. Foster, Ibid., p. 202, citing U.S. Department of Commerce and Labor, Federal Writers Project.

50  **Engine Company #9 ... held the city record for efficiency six years in a row.** Interview with Richard Jackson.

51  **This young man is right.** H. J. Foster, Ibid., p. 219.

52  **... separate play yards ...** H. J. Foster, Ibid., p. 221.

52  **The employment of colored teachers ...** Annual Report of the N. J. Board of Education, 1903, p. 93.

53  **The few local Black physicians there were ...** H. J. Foster, Ibid., p. 201.

## Chapter 4: Philadelphia's Playground

Despite Atlantic City's promotion of itself as the "World's Playground," Atlantic City was and is a creature of Philadelphia. Throughout its history, the Philadelphia Metropolitan Region has looked to Atlantic City as a place to go for a no-holds-barred good time. And in turn, Atlantic City has looked to Philadelphia not only as a prime source of patrons, but as the "big city," where one would go to handle important matters, whether they be medical, financial, legal, or educational.

In some ways, Atlantic City was to Philadelphia what Coney Island was to New York. However, the relationship was and is more complex, and unlike Coney Island, Atlantic City was more remote geographically and had a very strong identity of its own. Coney Island was a resort within a city. Despite its dependence on Philadelphia, Atlantic City was a bustling little city all to itself.

55  **What community would hail …** *Philadelphia Bulletin*, August 2, 1890.

56  **Do you gentlemen realize …** *Philadelphia Bulletin*, August 10, 1890. Atlantic City was a favorite target of the *Philadelphia Bulletin*. The newspaper frequently published scolding editorials that began each summer season and trailed off with the coming of fall.

56  Excellent material on 19th-century Philadelphia and its emergence as a major industrial power and urban center is found in *Philadelphia: A 300 Year History* edited by Russell F. Weigley, (W.W. Norton & Company, 1981).

59  **If the people who came to town had wanted Bible readings …** Interview with Murray Fredericks, Esquire. Murray Fredericks's family moved to the resort from New York City in 1905. As long-time associate in the practice of law (they were not "partners") and adviser to Hap Farley, Murray knew where "the bones are buried." It was a privilege to know him. I'm honored that he was so candid with me.

60  **As to gambling houses …** *Philadelphia Bulletin*, August 7, 1890.

61  **"Newspaper is what you wrap fish in."** Interview with Richard Jackson.

61  **It has been impossible to get indictments …** *Philadelphia Bulletin*, August 13, 1908, pp. 1, 4.

61  Governor Fort's "Proclamation" was published by the *Philadelphia Bulletin* on page 1, August 27, 1908.

62  The "Atlantic City Manifesto," in reply to Governor Fort's proclamation was printed by the *Bulletin* on September 8, 1908, p. 11.

65  **The source of Kuehnle's power …** See "The Rise and Fall of Kuehnle," *Literary Digest*, December 27, 1913, pp. 1285–93.

68 **"the rawest ever known in the country"** See *Literary Digest*, Ibid.

70 **"The domination of politics by corporation-machine alliances had reached its full flower."** David W. Hirst, *Woodrow Wilson, Reform Governor*, (D. Van Nostrand Company, 1965) p. 33.

71 **Harvey took it upon himself ...** D.W. Hirst, Ibid. p. 5.

72 The report of the Macksey Committee is discussed in the *Literary Digest*, Ibid.

75 **entrapment** by "Mr. Franklin." See *Literary Digest*, June 29, 1912.

77 **The Commodore served his time without complaint.** Interview with Mary Ill.

## Chapter 5: The Golden Age of Nucky

79 **There I am driving along ...** Interview with Joseph Hamilton, bus driver and backup chauffeur. I owe my chance opportunity of meeting him to my dear friend, Lou Testa, who provided physical therapy treatments to Mr. Hamilton prior to his death.

80 The personal sketches of Smith and Virginia Johnson are based on interviews with Mary Ill and Richard Jackson. By all accounts, Smith and Virginia were quite a force in early Atlantic City.

81 **"Mabel Jeffries ... Nucky just adored her."** Interview with Mary Ill.

82 **"My father said ... he was a changed man."** Interview with Mary Ill. Mary was the only person who possessed any reliable knowledge of Nucky's relationship with Mabel. She claims Mabel was his one true love and that he would likely have been a very different man had she lived.

82 **"Running for election was beneath a real boss."** Interview with Richard Jackson.

83 **Nucky Johnson "owned" the Black vote ...** Interviews with Richard Jackson and Murray Fredericks.

83  **"With Nucky … You paid or he shut you down."** Interview with Murray Fredericks, Esquire.

84  **"Edge was a stuffed shirt, but he knew where to go … Nucky Johnson."** Interview with Joseph Messick, Professor of South Jersey History at Atlantic Community College. Joe was a wealth of information on the history of southern New Jersey. I had the privilege of serving with him on the Atlantic County Board of Chosen Freeholders.

85  **"Can you imagine that …"** Interview with Richard Jackson.

86  **"I make my money by supplying a public demand."** John Kobler, *The Life and World of Al Capone,* (G. P. Putnam's Sons 1971). See p. 157.

86  **"Prohibition didn't happen in Atlantic City."** Interview with Murray Fredericks, Esquire.

87  **"Everybody helped out. If you worked for the city …"** Interview with Richard Jackson.

87  **"You gotta understand, nobody did it the way we did here."** Interview with Murray Fredericks, Esquire.

89  **"There never really was a second political party in Atlantic City … everyone was on the same team."** Interview with Richard Jackson, confirmed by many, including Patrick McGahn Esq., Lori Mooney, Mildred Fox, and Harold Finkle Esq.

93  **"I went to my first World Series with Nucky … He sure knew how to have a good time."** Interview with Murray Fredericks, Esquire.

94  The quote by the **retired detective** was made to me by a friend of Richard Jackson who requested anonymity.

96  **"Remember, there aren't any cemeteries in Atlantic City— it's an island."** Interview with Richard Jackson.

97  The futile efforts of the Committee of One Hundred were reported on by Jack Alexander in "Boss on the Spot" in *The Saturday Evening Post*, August 26, 1939.

99  The "Seven Group" and Nucky Johnson's involvement with Lucky Luciano is discussed in "Boss on the Spot," Ibid.

100 **A hurried call to Nucky Johnson ...** Martin A. Gosch and Richard Hammer, *The Last Testament of Lucky Luciano,* (Little, Brown and Company, 1974).

101 **I told them there was business enough ...** Kobler, Ibid., p.265.

102 The story of Nucky's kidnapping by Tony "the Stinger" Cugino was reported on seven years later by Alexander Kendrick in the *Philadelphia Inquirer* on May 19, 1939. Despite the span of time between the incident and Kendrick's news article, it is a credible story, especially given the company that Nucky kept.

## Chapter 6: Hard Times for Nucky and His Town

The story of the investigation into Nucky Johnson's empire, his indictment, and conviction are an epic. This chapter attempts to capture that story and relies on the formal report prepared by William E. Frank, the Special Agent assigned to lead the investigation. The report is entitled, "The Case of Enoch L. Johnson, a Complete Report of the Atlantic City Investigation." Prepared by William E. Frank, Special Agent, Intelligence Unit, Treasury Department, and Joseph W. Burns, Special Assistant to the U.S. Attorney for the District of New Jersey. Notwithstanding the title, and the fact that it was written by FBI Agents, it's an entertaining read.

Securing hard evidence on Nucky was a difficult task for the FBI. The agents faced many obstacles. The resistance was broad-based and represented most of the community. They received virtually no cooperation from anyone with knowledge of how Nucky's empire was organized. As you read the report, you can feel the growing anxiety and near paranoia as they move closer to Nucky and are frustrated by rampant perjury and jury tampering. But for Joseph Corio's carelessness it's likely the FBI would never have had the evidence needed to obtain a conviction. The report is exciting stuff. I recommend Agent Frank's report to anyone interested in the "nuts and bolts" of what it took to convict Nucky Johnson. The Report was completed in 1943. It is referred to hereinafter as *Report of W. E. Frank.*

103 The confrontation between Nucky Johnson and Ralph Weloff was recounted to the author by Richard Jackson's friend, a retired Atlantic City detective. He also told me that it was in the lobby of the Ritz that Nucky first made acquaintance with

James Boyd. Boyd was Nucky's protégé on administering the operations of the Republican organization. He got his start as a bellhop at the Ritz. This fact was confirmed by several persons.

104 **"Losin' Prohibition really hurt ..."** Interview with Patrick McGahn, Esquire, relating events told to him by his father.

104 **"A bartender I knew ... all that trouble over a broad."** Interview with Richard Jackson, confirmed by Patrick McGahn, Esquire. Rumors, and the myth that grew out of them, that "Two Gun Tommy Taggart" was somehow behind the charges against Nucky are without basis. Taggart was a loyal player in the Republican organization and despite his ambition, he would not have done anything to undermine Nucky's power.

105 **"Hearst was tight with FDR ..."** Interview with Richard Jackson, confirmed by Patrick McGahn, Esquire. Hearst's newspapers had been critical of Nucky for years. And it's true that they had more than one confrontation during the times Hearst was in town. With Nucky's and Hearst's fondness for the ladies what it was, the story of Hearst's involvement is credible.

105 The wide-open nature of Atlantic City's gambling operations is discussed in the *Report of W. E. Frank,* pp. 24–30.

105 The discussion of the details of the investigation into Nucky's organization is derived from the *Report of W. E. Frank.*

110 **"Joe Corio surprised everybody ..."** Interview with Murray Fredericks, Esquire.

111 The discussion of the details of the investigation into Nucky's organization is derived from the *Report of W. E. Frank.*

113 **The whores hung in there—they were tough old girls."** Interview with Richard Jackson.

113 **Nucky was Boss because he delivered ...** Interview with Murray Fredericks, Esquire.

114 **Only the very best people went to Babette's ...** Interview with Mary Ill.

115 **"If you went to the corner store ... a business wrote numbers."** Interview with Richard Jackson.

116 The quote from Special Agent Frank at *Report of W. E. Frank,* p. 60.

121 **"We admit that we received money … we did not report for taxes."** Walter Winne as quoted in *Report of W. E. Frank*, p. 136.

122 **"Nucky sure knew how to throw a party."** Interview with Mary Ill.

## Chapter 7: Hap

When I began my research, I perceived Hap Farley as a corrupt political boss who had contributed to the fall of Atlantic City. I quickly learned that my uninformed assessment of Farley's career was naïve and that he could not be dismissed so easily. Frank Farley was a complicated person. There is no doubt he was deeply involved in the workings of a corrupt organization. He couldn't have become and remained the boss any other way. But Hap was also a skillful legislator, tireless public servant always looking to improve his community, and a loyal friend. In many ways, he was a role model for an aspiring politician. Any attempt to measure him outside of the system in which he worked yields an incomplete portrait.

The transfer of power from Nucky Johnson to Frank Farley is a complex story involving many players. It required many interviews and follow-up discussions, after learning another piece to the puzzle, in order to confirm important details and pull together the entire story. In writing this portion of Chapter 7, I relied on the differing perspectives of both players and observers as told to me by Richard Jackson, Murray Fredericks, Frank Ferry, Robert Gasko, Bill Ross, Skinny D'Amato, Mary Ill, Florence Miller, Lori Mooney, Harold Finkle, and Patrick McGahn. I believe I've told the complete story.

126 **"What can I say? He liked boys, young boys."** Interview with Paul "Skinny" D'Amato. Skinny D'Amato was an Atlantic City original. He was proud to have been a protégé of Nucky's and had fond recollections of him. My interview of Skinny took place in his bedroom, in late afternoon, with him still in pajamas. He was in poor health at the time, and I have his nephew Paul D'Amato to thank for arranging the meeting.

126 **"What you had was a solid organization man."** Interview with Murray Fredericks, Esquire.

127 **"If your uncle got locked up for being drunk ... the ward leader would make sure he wasn't convicted."** Interview with Richard Jackson.

127 **"Here, take care of these."** Interview with Richard Jackson.

127 **Taggart thought "everything was up for grabs ... "** Interview with Paul "Skinny" D'Amato.

130 **"... Despite his politics, Hap thought that Nixon crowd were fools."** Interview with the Honorable John Sirica. During my research, I learned that Farley and Judge Sirica had graduated from Georgetown Law School the same year. I wrote to him and asked if he recalled Hap. Much to my pleasant surprise I learned they had maintained their relationship over the years via telephone.

I interviewed Judge Sirica by phone. He loved talking about Farley and recalled what a great athlete Hap was. The judge laughed frequently, reminiscing about their many conversations over the years. Judge Sirica was the classic raconteur. He had an idiosyncratic figure of speech that he used frequently and which you wouldn't expect to hear from such a learned person, "don't cha see?" that was both disarming and endearing. Talking to him over the telephone was a treat. I can only imagine what it would have been like to have him over for dinner.

130 **"Whatever you do, do it thoroughly or don't touch it."** This quote is from "A Conversation with a Politician," an interview of Hap Farley by Robert Hughey and Chick Yaeger. The interview was conducted several years before Farley's death and is an excellent piece of oral history. It's on videotape and is on file at the Library of Stockton State College. Anyone interested in Farley's career should view it.

130 **"Hap was one of those kind, when you're gonna do something, you're gonna do that and nothing else."** Interview with Murray Fredericks, Esquire. Dick Jackson and many others confirmed that from the moment you encountered Hap there was no mistaking his seriousness of purpose when it came to Atlantic City politics. There was nothing *casual* about a political alliance with Hap Farley. He wasn't forgiving. If you

betrayed him ever, or disappointed him one time too many, the alliance was over *permanently*.

131 **"Hap's people were poor, and the Feyls always thought their daughter was too good for him."** Interview with Mary Ill. I have Bill Ross to thank for introducing me to Mrs. Ill. She was a delightful person and a wealth of information, not just about Farley but about Johnson and Kuehnle as well. Mary grew up with Hap and taught him how to dance. She met him in Philadelphia on weekends while he was a student at the University of Pennsylvania. They went to dance halls that charged a "dime a dance" to be on the floor. When they were teenagers, at his prompting, she passed love letters between Hap and Honey during their early courtship.

131 **"Honey was an alcoholic for as long as I knew her … It was like that most nights."** Interview with Joseph Hamilton, confirmed by Mary Ill and others.

133 **"He was as smooth a glad-hander as ever lived … "** Interview with Richard Jackson.

135 **"Ripper Resolutions."** *Atlantic City Press,* May 22, 1942.

135 Farley's representation of **George Goodman** was a skillful move in his efforts to succeed Nucky. I learned about it from Patrick McGahn, Esquire, and it was confirmed by Murray Fredericks, Esquire.

136 The discussion of Farley's career as a legislator in Trenton is in substantial part the product of an interview with his colleague, Senator Wayne Dumont of Phillipsburg, Warren County. Senator Dumont was a gentleman from the old school. His bond with Farley was strong one, forged over many years of working together as legislators. He credited Farley with arranging to have Richard Nixon appear in New Jersey when the Senator ran, unsuccessfully, for governor. I met with Senator Dumont in his law office, and we had lunch together. He took his dog with him everywhere, including lunch. At one point in the interview he became tearful when reminiscing about his personal fondness for Hap Farley.

140 **"Hap's agenda was always first."** Interview with Senator Wayne Dumont.

145 **Kefauver's Committee produced ...** Final Report of the Special Committee to Investigate Organized Crime in Interstate Commerce, pursuant to S. Res. 202 (81st Congress) August 31, 1951.

147 **"Farley could never cultivate the Blacks the way Johnson had."** Interview with Richard Jackson.

148 The several quotes concerning Jimmy Boyd's role in Farley's organization are based on an interview with Richard Jackson, confirmed by Bill Ross and Murray Fredericks, Esquire.

151 **"It was a strict system ... you'd have to wait until there was."** Interview with Richard Jackson.

151 The system guaranteed that **"if you were going to move up ..."** Interview with Richard Jackson.

151 The story of Richard Jackson's career is based on interviews with him. In hindsight, I now realize he should have been interviewed on videotape, as Hughey and Yaeger did with Farley. It would have been a valuable piece of oral history. I consider it a privilege and an honor to have known him.

## Chapter 8: The Painful Ride Down

155 The incident regarding the photo of the dog—without Farley— was told to me by Frank Ferry, Esquire. Hap and Ferry were very close, comparable to father and son. He smiled sardonically as he told the story. There was no mistaking that Frank Ferry felt Hap had been treated badly in his final years.

157 **Today, aside from the conventioneers ...** *Time* magazine. August 31, 1964.

160 **Hotel services broke down ...** Theodore H. White, *The Making of the President, 1964,* (Antheneum Publishers, 1965) at p. 290. As noted by White, more than 5,000 newspersons descended on Atlantic City in August 1964 for the Democratic National Convention. Instead of a *marker on the road back,* the

Convention was a public relations disaster. The reports published and broadcast throughout the nation destroyed what was left of Atlantic City's aura and revealed it for the beat town it was.

160 **Never had a town …** T. H. White, Ibid., p. 291.

161 **Of Atlantic City it may be written: Better it shouldn't have happened …** T. H. White, Ibid., p. 289.

163 *Baker vs. Carr*, 369 U.S. 186, (1962) was followed by a second U.S. Supreme decision, *Reynolds vs. Sims*, 377 U.S. 533, (1964). These two decisions dictated the ruling that Haneman and his colleagues on the New Jersey Supreme Court had to make on legislative districting in New Jersey.

163 **"There comes a time in the career of practically every judge** … Justice Vincent Haneman in his separate opinion in the decision of *Jackman vs. Bodine*, 43 N.J. 453, 205, A. 2d. 713 (1964). Justice Haneman's opinion is a lesson in the history of New Jersey's bicameral legislature. Haneman eloquently traced New Jersey's history from colonial days when the province was divided into East and West Jersey. He explains that New Jersey had always had an upper and lower house in its legislature with representation in the senate being "based upon territory as distinguished from population." Each time the State Constitution was revised, this practice was preserved. Justice Haneman's concurring opinion is really an "unanswerable dissent." Despite the persuasiveness of Haneman's opinion, my hunch is his real audience wasn't his brethren on the Court or the legal community but rather his old friend, Hap Farley. The opinion is a tribute from one old warrior to another.

165 **"Farley was scared to death of Marvin."** Interview with Patrick McGahn, Esquire.

167 **"If they want to pay … "** *Atlantic City Press*, August 9, 1968.

170 **"… in need of more enlightened leadership …"** *Atlantic City Press*, November 13, 1970.

171 **Hap Farley was "very pleasant" …** Interview with Patrick McGahn, Esquire.

172 The story of Farley's defeat in the '71 election is based upon interviews and conversations with Richard Jackson, William Ross, Robert Gasko, Murray Fredericks, Esquire, Frank Ferry, Esquire, Patrick McGahn, Esquire, Lori Mooney, Harold Finkle, Esquire, and others.

## Chapter 9: Turn Out the Lights

175 The vignette of the prostitute is based upon an interview with Paul "Skinny" D'Amato.

177 **"How could you get anyone ... to share a bathroom?"** Interview with Richard Jackson.

178 **"It was our only hope ... becoming a ghost town."** Interview with Mildred Fox.

180 **"Governor Brendan Byrne has said he is receptive to a referendum ... Public approval is regarded as certain."** *Atlantic City Press*, January 6, 1974.

181 **"The state can expect to profit very little ..."** *Atlantic City Press*, December 19, 1973.

182 **The governor suggested that gambling should be limited to Atlantic City.** Interview with Steven Perskie.

183 **"I am concerned that the very same interest ..."** *Atlantic City Press*, October 17, 1974.

184 **"I am concerned with the future of Atlantic City ..."** *Atlantic City Press*, October 16, 1974.

184 The quote of the *Vineland Times Journal* is from "Another Public Conning" by Ben Leuchter, reprinted by the *Atlantic City Press* on May 23, 1974.

## Chapter 10: A Second Bite at the Apple

187 I was personally acquainted with Lea Finkler. This was one of many incidents she related to him in her inimitable anger and disgust.

191 **The challenge, when Weiner took it on …** Jeffrey Douglas, "The Selling of Casino Gambling," *New Jersey Monthly*, June, 1977.

193 **"She said she's made her last speech …"** *Atlantic City Press*, July 13, 1976.

197 **… real power in the corporation …** Gigi Mahon, *The Company That Bought the Boardwalk* (Random House, 1980) p. 57.

198 **Mary Carter Paint was in the gambling business.** Gigi Mahon, Ibid., pp. 65–83.

204 The CBS-TV news editorial was broadcast on February 28, 1979.

## Chapter 11: It's a New Ballgame

207 **"The little jerk is finally going to get what he deserves."** Patrick McGahn, Esquire. Pat McGahn nearly chortled whenever he spoke of "Mayor Mike" and his troubles with the law.

209 **"Mike Matthews was a creep …"** Interview with Ralph Palmieri.

209 **"Michael loved the glitter …"** Interview with Harold Finkle, Esquire.

211 The comments concerning Jerome Zarowitz and Alvin Malnik are taken from the *Opening Statement* of the Division of Gaming Enforcement (DGE) made at Caesar's Licensing Hearing on September 9, 1980.

211 The statements regarding Clifford and Stuart Perlman were contained in the DGE's *Opening Statement* of September 9, 1980, and were reported in a page 1 news article in the *Atlantic City Press*, September 19, 1980.

213 The findings of the Casino Control Commission were memorialized in its formal opinion denying licensure, NJCCC Docket #80-CL-1 *In the Matter of the Application of Boardwalk Regency Corp. and the Jemm Company for Casino Licenses*, opinion, p. 35, ("Accordingly, Clifford Perlman is not qualified.").

214 The discussion of Bally's licensure is contained in the DGE's report to the CCC entitled, "Report to the Casino Control Commission with regard to the Application of Bally's Park Place, Inc., a New Jersey corporation, for a Casino License and the Application of Bally Manufacturing Corporation, a Delaware corporation, for a Casino Service Industry License," dated 8/4/80.

214 The comments regarding Gerardo Catena were taken from the DGE's report of 8/4/80.

220 **I must note ... reporting to the chairman.** Walter "Bud" Reed, Chairman of the CCC, quoted by the *Press of Atlantic City*, September 20, 1986.

## Chapter 12: The Donald Comes to Town

225 Fred Trump was a master builder and genuine real estate mogul. While he had his critics, he was a critical player and positive force in meeting the housing needs of a growing New York City. Without Fred's fortune, the Donald would have played in a different league. There's been much written on both Trumps. My thumbnail sketch of Fred's career is based on news accounts and Gwenda Blair's book, *The Trumps: Three Generations That Built an Empire* (Simon and Schuster, New York, 2000), pp. 118–122,154.

226 Trump's arrival in Atlantic City and his early moves as a local player were carefully observed and reported on by Daniel Heneghan, while a staff reporter with the *Press of Atlantic City,* prior to assuming his position of director of information for the Casino Control Commission. Dan is a wealth of information. I relied heavily on his knowledge and expertise.

235 The profile of Arthur Goldberg is based on my personal knowledge and a feature article, "King of Craps" in *Barron's*, August 1999.

239 The statistics on Atlantic City's success to date were confirmed by Daniel Heneghan relying on numbers compiled by the Casino Control Commission.

# ABOUT THE AUTHOR

Nelson Johnson, whose family's presence in Atlantic County predates the founding of Atlantic City, is a lifelong resident of Hammonton, New Jersey. He practiced law for 30 years and was active in Atlantic City and Atlantic County politics through much of that period.

As attorney for the Atlantic City Planning Board at the time of the approvals for many of the casinos, Johnson was inspired first to make sense of Atlantic City and later to write an objective political history. The interviews, research, and writing involved in preparing *Boardwalk Empire* span nearly two decades.

# INDEX